Charles MacLean

Whiskypedia

A Compendium of Scottish Whisky

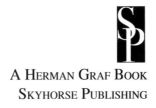

A HERMAN GRAF BOOK
SKYHORSE PUBLISHING

For Sheila MacLean

'At first I found my descriptive task beset
with difficulties far exceeding what I had
contemplated; but ... my interest grew with
the work, making it easier for me; until,
after a time, I acquired quite a zest for
these distillery studies.'

ALFRED BARNARD, THE WHISKY
DISTILLERIES OF THE UNITED KINGDOM,
1887

Skyhorse Publishing books may be purchased
in bulk at special discounts for sales promotion, corporate gifts, fund-raising, or educational
purposes. Special editions can also be created
to specifications. For details, contact the Special
Sales Department, Skyhorse Publishing, 555 Eighth
Avenue, Suite 903, New York, NY 10018 or
info@skyhorsepublishing.com.

www.skyhorsepublishing.com

10 9 8 7 6 5 4 3 2 1

Library of Congress Cataloging-in-Publication Data
is available on file.

ISBN: 978-1-61608-076-1

Printed in China

Contents

Foreword

This is a book about Scotch whisky distilleries, but it is also a book about why Scotch whisky tastes as it does, and how flavour might have subtly changed over the years.

It embraces both malt and grain distilleries, including those which have closed since 1945, but whose product is still available. Each entry provides a brief account of the distillery's history, highlighting anything that I find especially interesting, and lists the 'expressions' (i.e. bottlings and variations) currently offered by the distillery owner. A secondary text also supplies details of how the whisky is made there, for those who are interested in such minutiae! With the help of the introductory 'Notes', I hope this will provide enthusiasts with some idea of what the make from each distillery tastes like, and why, by explaining how raw materials, plant, process and wood contribute to flavour.

My hope is that the book will provide a succinct and reliable account of each distillery and its products. I am aware that this has been done before – not least by myself! – but it is surprising how quickly things change in the whisky industry, especially over the past twelve months, and how soon whisky books become dated.

I began writing about Scotch whisky in 1981 – a brochure for Bell's. Only in retrospect have I learned how the industry has changed since then. During the 1980s I was fortunate to be asked by several whisky companies to research and write materials for them – summary company histories, such as those for Highland Distilleries Centenary and Glenmorangie's Sesqui-Centenary; brand histories, such as that for the nascent United Distillers. By training and temperament I am an historian (during the same period I wrote five books on Scottish-historical subjects) and working for Scotch whisky companies brought together my passion for Scotland, its social history and our national drink.

By 1988 I had written enough about whisky to make a credible approach to a publisher for a book on the subject. This appeared five years later as *The Pocket Guide to Scotch*, in Mitchell Beazley's series of the same name. Following its success, a further three books were commissioned by other publishers, then Mitchell Beazley asked me to write a larger illustrated book. *Malt Whisky* was published in 1997 and won a Glenfiddich Award for its photography and design, and has since been reprinted four times and translated into seven languages.

My editor moved to Cassell and commissioned *Scotch Whisky: A Liquid History*. This took four years to research and write, but won Best Wine & Spirits Book in the James Beard Awards (the first time in the history of these prestigious American Awards that a spirits book has won!) and Best Drinks Book in the World Media Awards. It was also runner up in the U.K.'s André Simon Awards.

As will be apparent, it takes a long time to write a book! One of the reasons is that one has to make money from other sources than book royalties. In my case this came from whisky companies which employed me to write or talk about my pet subject, to present tastings and host events around the world. I am eternally grateful to them. Without such support I would not have been able to continue my researches.

This *Whiskypedia* has taken a mere four years to complete! I hope it will be a cheerful companion for those of you who are starting out on the journey of discovery into the world of Scotch whisky, as much as for those who are already familiar with the subject, experienced in the nuances of flavour which distinguish the product of one distillery from another, even one bottling from another. The purpose of Scotch whisky is to give pleasure, and such pleasure can be as sophisticated as you like. This is the glory of the drink, and it is what distinguishes Scotch from less noble liquors!

Charles MacLean
Edinburgh

Historical Overview

2007 was the best year for Scotch whisky exports in the entire 500-year history of the trade, measured both by volume (1.13 billion bottles) and value (£2.82 billion), and 2008 promises to be even better.

Scotch whisky is enjoying a period of unprecedented popularity in every market in the world – except in the land of its birth, but I have been told that the, as yet unreleased, 2008 figures for the U.K. are 'promising' . . .

Not since the 1960s has the whisky industry invested so much in expanding production. Four brand new distilleries have opened in the past two years (Glenburgie, Kilchoman, Daftmill and Ailsa Bay) and I know of a further seven that are on the stocks, in varying degrees of development – not least a gigantic operation at Roseisle, on Speyside, which is being built by Diageo, and which will open in January 2009. Others are being substantially expanded to meet the anticipated demand (especially from China and India), including famous names like The Macallan, The Glenlivet and Glenmorangie.

In May 2007, United Spirits, led by the charismatic Dr Vijay Mallya and a subsidiary of his massive United Breweries Group, acquired Whyte & Mackay for £595 million – one of the largest ever overseas acquisitions by an Indian company. Negotiations had been going on for many months, and the high price may have something to do with the fact that the Indian government had at last been persuaded by the World Trade Organisation to reduce its punitive tariffs on imported spirits.

India is the largest consumer of whisky in the world, but 99% of it is locally made, mainly from molasses alcohol (so it is not, strictly speaking 'whisky'). If the Scotch industry can win only a tiny amount of this market ... Exports to India rose by 75.6% in 2007.

Then there's China, which has rocketed into tenth place in the league of 'World's Largest Consumers of Scotch' from 75th position five years ago. In 2002 the People's Republic was importing only £500,000 worth of Scotch; last year the figure had risen to over £25 million (an increase of 86% on 2005).

Two years ago, many distilleries were operating part-time, since their owners reckoned they had enough maturing stock to satisfy anticipated demand, but the phenomenal growth in the Chinese economy, the situation in India and fast-growing markets in Russia and Brazil has changed all that.

Let's hope the marketers have their projections right. The history of Scotch whisky is a story of booms and busts. The expansion of the 1780s terminated suddenly in 1788. Of the dozens of new distilleries that opened after 1823, only a small percentage survived 'the hungry '40s'. The great Whisky Boom of the 1890s turned dramatically to bust in 1900. The post-1945 expansion led to over-production and closures by the mid 1980s. And just as we go to press we have the Credit Crunch and pending Global Recession. Historically, Scotch whisky has continued to prosper under such conditions, but we shall see ...

THE ORIGINAL SCOTCH

This book is principally about Scotch malt whisky. Let me briefly look at the 'renaissance' of malt whisky during the past 20 years.

Whisky made in Scotland from malted barley is the original Scotch, although by the late eighteenth century, with the arrival of large-scale commercial distilling in the Lowlands, mixed grains (wheat and rye, as well as barley) were being used. With the invention of the continuous still in the late 1820s (perfected and patented by Aeneas Coffey, former Inspector of Excise in Dublin, in 1830), Lowland distillers gradually came to devote themselves to grain whisky production in such stills, producing very pure, very high-strength, somewhat bland spirit, with which they inundated the new industrial towns in the Central Belt of Scotland, as well as sending quantities to England for rectification into gin.

Pot still malt whisky was extremely variable in flavour. Like Longfellow's little girl, 'when she was good, she was very, very good and when she was bad she was horrid'!

It was drunk straight and young in the Highlands, and mixed into a punch in the Lowlands, with water, sugar, lemons and sometimes spices. The first reference to the benefits of maturation that I know of is in Elizabeth Grant of Rothiemurchus's *Memoirs of a Highland Lady*, where she recalls sending 'pure Glenlivet whisky ... long in the wood, long in uncorked bottles [this is mysterious!], mild as milk and with the real contraband *goût* [i.e. taste] in it' for the delectation of King George IV in Edinburgh in August 1822.

THE ECLIPSE OF MALT WHISKY

It is safe to suppose that wine and spirits merchants would have mixed the light grain whisky with variable and pungent malts to create a drink with broader appeal, from at least the 1820s. Many were familiar with blending teas, wines and cordials, which were often also part of their stock in trade. But the first branded blend appeared in 1853, Usher's Old Vatted Glenlivet, and only after Gladstone's Spirits Act of 1860, which allowed the mixing of malt and grain whiskies under bond (i.e. before duty had to be paid), that blended Scotch took off.

And take off it did – in a very big way – helped by a variety of factors, not least of which was the devastation of European vineyards by the louse *Phylloxera vastetrix*. By the late 1860s non-vintage cognac was unobtainable, and since 'brandy and soda' was the drink of the English middle classes, this caused considerable dismay. Blended Scotch (and soda) was now so improved as to be in a position to replace it.

Historians refer to the 1890s as the era of 'The Whisky Boom'. Henceforward the fortunes of malt whisky distillers would be inextricably linked to those of the blenders, and the leading blending houses built or bought or took an interest in malt distilleries in order to secure the fillings for their blends. Thirty-three new distilleries were commissioned during the 1890s, 21 of them on Speyside (almost all of which are still in operation).

Alfred Barnard, the indefatigable Victorian traveller

and editor of *Harper's* magazine, visited 118 malt distilleries in the late 1880s while compiling his monumental book *The Whisky Distilleries of The United Kingdom* (1887) – the first and still the most thorough account of distilling in these islands.

 With considerable foresight, he remarked: 'We shall be treading on delicate grounds when we refer to the fact that there are those who hold that the future of the Whisky trade lies with Malt Whisky. Certainly "the present" is not entirely in the hands of that product. Blenders without number can be found who will strenuously affirm that to give the public a moderate priced article with sufficient age, there is no way but to use good old Patent Still Grain Whisky as a basis.' (p.12)

 'Delicate grounds' indeed. Matters came to a head with the 'What is Whisky?' Inquiry, prompted by an English court in 1905 ruling that, to be named 'whisky', the spirit must be made in a pot still. This was followed by a Royal Commission (1908–09), which found that 'The market for blended whiskies is greater than that for individual whiskies; so much so that it would probably be safe to say that the majority of Englishmen who drink whisky seldom drink anything but a blend', and, therefore, that patent still spirit made from grains other than malted barley, and a mix of this with straight malt (i.e. blended whisky) had equal rights to be called 'whisky'.

 In truth, very little malt whisky was released as 'single' – Barnard remarks: 'there are only a few of the Scotch Distillers that turn out spirit for use as single whiskies' (p.94) – and those single malts that did appear were usually bottled for local sale by hotels or spirits merchants, or bought in bulk by the small cask or stoneware jar by private customers.

 In 1930 it was possible for Aeneas Macdonald to lament: 'the notion that we can possibly develop a palate for whisky is guaranteed to produce a smile of derision in any company except that of a few Scottish lairds, farmers, gamekeepers, and bailies, relics of a vanished age of gold when the vintages of the north had their students and lovers'. (*Whisky*, 1930)

Not long after he wrote this, the owner of The Glenlivet Distillery, Bill Smith Grant, began selling his make as a single on Pullman coaches in the United States, but this was the exception to the rule: 99.9% of the malt whisky made went into blends.

As will be apparent from a cursory reading of the individual distillery entries herein, there was a huge growth in production in the two decades following the end of World War II. Scotch was again enjoying a boom period, embraced as 'the drink of the free world' in Europe as well as the U.S.A. and the U.K. Exports rose from 23.15 million proof gallons in 1960 to 107.08 million proof gallons in 1980; in the U.K. consumption tripled from 7.2 to 21.22 million proof gallons.

Four new grain distilleries and 24 new malt distilleries were built between 1962 and 1972, five of them within existing grain distilleries and 11 alongside existing malt distilleries. The latter were built by Scottish Malt Distillers (S.M.D.), the malt distilling division of the Distillers Company Limited (D.C.L.), the largest whisky company, all to a similar design, the so-called 'Waterloo Street' style, named after S.M.D's headquarters in Glasgow (see *Caol Ila*). Many other distilleries were modernised and expanded, most to double capacity.

By the mid 1970s, economic conditions were less stable and the huge U.S. market had begun to contract. Moreover, in both the U.S.A. and the U.K., there was a shift in consumer taste towards blander spirits (white rum and vodka) drunk with mixers, and wine; younger drinkers had been especially targeted and lifestyle advertising was designed to appeal to them. Scotch lost its fashionable cachet, and was now seen as 'Dad's drink'.

Whisky companies responded by exploring other markets, particularly in South America, Japan, Hong Kong and Europe, but production far outstripped demand. By 1980 the amount of whisky being held in bond was more than four times that in 1960. There was talk of a 'whisky loch', comparable to the 'wine lake' in France and the 'butter mountain' in northern Europe.

Furthermore, during 1981 the world economy slipped rapidly into recession. Output of both grain and malt whisky declined sharply (in 1983, it was at its lowest level since 1959). Between 1981 and 1986, no fewer than 29 distilleries were taken out of production; 18 of these have not worked since, and several have been demolished.

THE RENAISSANCE OF MALT WHISKY

Throughout all this period, single malt whisky remained relatively uncommon. Glen Grant and Glenfiddich were the exceptions.

Glen Grant was one of the few single malts widely available in the U.K., but it was in Italy during the 1960s that sales really took off, and this was owing to the efforts of the brand's distributor, Armando Giovinetti. Convinced that malt whisky would appeal to the Italian palate, he approached several distillers during the late 1950s, but was turned down: 'all our make goes for blending'. When he approached Glen Grant, Douglas McKessack, the owner and great-grandson of the founder, referred him to Charles H. Julian, the company's bottler in London. In 1960 he obtained 50 cases of 12YO; as he told me himself, 'My attitude was, if I don't sell it, I'll drink it.'

Within a year, and after visiting the distillery, he had decided that a younger whisky was required and obtained 100 cases from Julian. Through his efforts Italy became the leading export market for Glen Grant by 1970, and the first country in the world to embrace single malt Scotch whisky. By 1977 sales of Glen Grant were around 200,000 cases a year.

In 1964 the directors of William Grant & Sons, all descendants of the founder, decided to bottle their Glenfiddich Pure Malt as an eight-year-old, keep it pale in colour – like the successful Glen Grant – and present it in a dark green version of the characteristic triangular bottle used for their Standfast blend. The company also set about promoting the brand heavily, often with events and clever stunts that attracted editorial coverage and free publicity – the very novelty of 'pure malt' (it was labelled 'Straight Malt' in the U.S.A.) attracted interest. The company even struck on the simple but effective idea of supplying London's theatres and film studios with bottles of Glenfiddich filled with flat ginger ale, which tasted a whole lot better than cold tea! By 1970, the brand was selling 24,000 cases in the home market, and was being heavily marketed through the newly enfranchised airport duty-free shops.

William Grant & Sons effectively achieved a ten-year 'first mover advantage', to use a marketing term, over the other malt distillers, some of whom looked on with interest at their achievement in promoting their product as single malt, notably the independent companies Macallan-Glenlivet and Macdonald & Muir, owners of Glenmorangie distillery.

As early as 1963, the Chairman of Macallan, George Harbinson, reported that 'the sale of Macallan in bottle is gaining momentum with a steadily increasing demand for the over 15-year-old from the south of England', and again in 1965: 'the interest in single malts is undoubtedly increasing and larger sales are expected'. Next year, Messrs Fratelli Rinaldi of Bologna were appointed sole agents for The Macallan in Italy, and, following an advertising campaign, in 1967 they 'ordered more whisky than the total amount which went towards the home market'. Agents in France were appointed three years later.

The 1972 Annual Report noted that 'sales of cased Macallan had doubled during the year', and added, prophetically, that 'a large increase in this type of business was anticipated in light of a fantastic growth in public interest, which would eventually see malt whisky becoming extremely fashionable'. The directors decided to conserve stocks of mature whisky, even at the expense of demands from blenders, and to 'put larger proportions aside for selling in cases'.

In 1978 Macallan appointed its first marketing director, Hugh Mitcalf, who moved across from Glen

Grant, following Seagram's takeover of that company, and who had been instrumental in the tremendous success of the brand in Italy. The year he arrived, the entire promotional budget allocated to The Macallan amounted to £50, but this was about to change. Witty advertising, tasteful repackaging and word of mouth soon made Macallan a household name.

Glenmorangie's story was similar, although unlike Macallan, which relied on outside companies (mostly Robertson & Baxter, its fillings agent) to buy its make, its owners, Macdonald & Muir of Leith, had a raft of blends of their own to supply, notably the popular Highland Queen range. Demand was heavy during the 1970s, and the distillery's capacity was doubled (to four stills) in 1977, but only a small amount was bottled as a single, and it was not supported by advertising until 1981.

That year the company allocated just under £200,000 to a print campaign in broadsheet newspapers. Compared with other whisky advertisements, the style and approach was novel, stressing the 'craft' elements that went into the making of the whisky and focusing on the fact that the distillery has the tallest stills in the industry. The strapline was 'A little nearer heaven than other malt whiskies'. The craft theme would be developed and extended in the 1980s and 1990s, with the long-running but hugely successful 'Sixteen Men of Tain' campaign.

ON THE BANDWAGON

Other companies began to follow suit, either bottling their malts for the first time or repackaging and using limited advertising. Justerini & Brooks launched Knockando in 1978 as a 12-year-old, with stated vintages. Highland Park, Tamdhu and Bunnahabhain were repackaged by Highland Distillers and relaunched in late 1979, and Highland Park rapidly took off. Possibly the most elegant repackaging of all was that for The Balvenie, by William Grant & Sons in 1982. Now named Founder's Reserve, without an age statement, it was filled into a long-necked vintage cognac bottle, unlike any other Scotch. Aberlour began to be heavily promoted in France around 1980 and a lavish booklet was produced in 1983 by Long John International to promote Tormore in the U.S.A. Glen Garioch was repackaged by Stanley P. Morrison around the same time, as was Auchentoshan. Bell's made Blair Athol, Inchgower, Bladnoch and Dufftown available for the first time. Whyte & Mackay promoted Jura and Tamnavulin. And so on.

Cardhu, owned by the mighty Distillers Company, had been available as a single since the 1960s. Now D.C.L. began to promote it with print advertising, stressing its rarity ('There are approximately 10,000 cases of Cardhu offered for sale each year. This is not a lot, and the whisky is, therefore, quite scarce.'); they even took the novel step of allowing press and V.I.P. visitors to the distillery. In 1982 Distillers launched 'The Ascot Malt Cellar' – Ascot was the company's home trade base – a collection of four singles and two vatted malts. By all accounts this was done reluctantly and was not widely promoted. It made no impact on the marketplace, but the seeds of exploring different styles and regional differences were already there, and this would be widely exploited in years to come.

Significantly, in 1988, D.C.L.'s successor, United Distillers, launched a range of six malts on the market that stressed 'regional differences' and opened up the whole sector. From their huge inventory of available whiskies, they selected six and named them 'The Classic Malts'. They were Lagavulin, Talisker (to represent the heavily peated style of Islay, and the slightly less smoky style of the Isles), Oban (maritime in character, representing the West Highlands), Dalwhinnie (a typical Highland malt), Cragganmore (a complex Speyside) and Glenkinchie (standing for the lighter Lowland style).

It was a move whose time had come, and was hugely successful. Other distillers attempted to follow suit. Allied introduced its 'Caledonian Malts' in 1991, featuring Tormore (a Speyside), Miltonduff (also a Speyside), Glendronach (from Aberdeenshire) and Laphroaig (from Islay), but it was not a success. Later Scapa (from Orkney) replaced Tormore, but the exercise was abandoned in 1994. That year Seagram tried the same idea with its 'Heritage Selection' – Longmorn, Glen Keith, Strathisla and Benriach – all good malts, but all from Speyside, and having a broadly similar flavour profile. The project did not last.

Some distillers who did not have a portfolio of regional malts to offer sought to extend their product range by offering their malts at different ages, or matured in different woods. Pioneers of this were Teacher's, who offered two 12-year-old versions of Glendronach in the late 1980s, one matured in sherry-wood, the other, described as the 'Original', in a mix of sherry and bourbon casks. About the same time, Macdonald & Muir produced an 18-year-old expression of Glenmorangie, which also included some sherry casks in its mix.

In 1994 the latter went a step further, launching an expression of Glenmorangie which had been reracked into port casks for the final months of its maturation, a process known as 'finishing'. This was followed by Madeira and sherry-finishes (1996), and subsequently by many other versions, mostly in limited editions. At exactly the same time as the Glenmorangie Port-wood appeared, William Grant & Sons issued an expression of Balvenie 12-year-old, finished in Oloroso casks and named 'Doublewood'. Since the mid 1990s several brand owners have followed Glenmorangie's and Balvenie's lead.

Further variations could be introduced by bottling only a single cask, usually straight from the wood, at 'cask strength' and without chill-filtration. The latter is a technique to remove compounds that precipitate when water or ice is added, causing the whisky to go slightly hazy. Chill-filtration 'polishes' the spirit and prevents haze, but the compounds it removes make a big contribution to flavour and texture, so connoisseurs prefer them left in!

Single cask bottlings are often done by independent bottlers, the number of which increased dramatically in the 1990s. (See 'Leading Independent Bottlers'.)

Never in history have so many varieties of malt whisky been available to the consumer. Never in history have there been so many enthusiasts for the drink! Demand has led to shortages of certain makes in certain markets, and to various ways of solving the problem. At its simplest, the price goes up. Or, the brand is pulled from specific markets to supply others. This happened to The Macallan in Taiwan in the early 21st century, where demand for the 'traditional' style of sherried malt was met by moving stocks from other markets and replacing them with a parallel range of ages, matured in ex-bourbon casks, of which the company had plenty.

Famously, Diageo attempted to meet the demand for Cardhu in Spain by introducing 'Cardhu Pure Malt', a mix of Cardhu and Glendullan. The industry was outraged – or at least Diageo's competitors were, principally William Grant & Sons who raised a storm of protest, maintaining that consumers were being conned, and that the reputation of single malt Scotch would be tarnished. 'Pure Malt' was withdrawn, and the S.W.A. set up a committee to look into definitions (see 'Understanding the Label').

What is certain is that stocks of old mature whisky are in big demand, especially for deluxe and super deluxe blends, which are leading the way in the emergent markets. I have been assured by the larger distillery owners that supplies of malt for single bottling have been 'ring fenced' and guaranteed, but we will see. Already, and in spite of what the independent bottlers were saying to me a year ago (see 'Leading Independent Bottlers'), good casks of mature whisky are becoming difficult to find. So it may be that our choice of malts will narrow, as independents leave the trade – or become distillers, as an increasing number are doing.

These are exciting times for Scotch!

Understanding the Label

Scotch whisky is the most tightly defined spirit in the world – for good reason: its popularity and high reputation make it an obvious target for counterfeiters. The Scotch Whisky Association (S.W.A.), the industry's governing body, is engaged in around 70 counterfeit actions around the world at any one time!

After two years of consultation, S.W.A. recommended to the U.K. Government and the European Commission that the definition be tightened, so as 'to ensure that consumers have clear information about what they are buying'. It is anticipated that these recommendations will become law early in 2009.

① *Brand Name* is almost always the name of the distillery in which the whisky was made. The new rules will prohibit the use of a distillery name other than the distillery in which it was made (e.g. a defunct distillery), with certain exceptions.

② *Single Malt* is the product of an individual distillery. There is no such thing as a 'double malt', except in the glass!

③ *Scotch Whisky* must be made and matured in oak casks in Scotland for at least three years. New-make spirit is not Scotch.

④ *Isle of Skye*, etc. indicates the region in which the distillery is located (see 'Regional Differences' below).

⑤ *Age Statement.* If the bottle has this, it is the age of the youngest whisky in the bottle. It is permissible to add older whiskies.

⑥ *Date Bottled or Date Distilled.* Not all whiskies carry this, but it is useful if read against the age statement. However, whisky does not continue to mature in the bottle.

⑦ *Cask Strength.* The standard bottling strength is 40% or 43% Alcohol By Volume (A.B.V. or simply Vol.). Where the label says 'cask strength' it means it has been bottled without dilution, typically at around 60% A.B.V., although the term is not defined by law.

⑧ *Natural or Non-chill-filtered.* Often associated with 'Cask Strength'. Most whisky undergoes chill-filtration on the bottling line to make sure it remains bright and clear when ice or water is added. This takes out certain compounds, which many connoisseurs prefer left in.

⑨ *Capacity.* 70cl is now the standard bottle-size in the E.U. Until 1990 it was 75cl, and it remains so in certain markets.

⑩ *Bottler.* This may be the distillery owner or an independent bottler. Under the S.W.A.'s new recommendations, Scotch Malt Whisky must be bottled and labelled in Scotland. This was not formerly the case.

● *Single Cask.* Bottled from an individual CASK: a rarity – most single malts are vattings of many casks. (Not shown on this label.)

● *'Wood Finished' or 'Sherry/Port Finished', or 'Double Matured' etc.* tells you that the whisky has been reracked into different casks for the final months or years of its maturation. (Not shown on this label.)

⑩ TALISKER DISTILLERY
T, ISLE OF SKYE, IV47 8SR
④

R™

SKY **③**

⑥ bottled in **2008**

INGLE MALT SCOTCH
M THE ISLE OF SKYE
31030773

A Taxonomy of Scotch

(with apologies to Linnaeus)

KINGDOM: Alcoholic Drinks

ORDER: Distilled Beverages (as Opposed to Fermented Beverages)

FAMILY: WHISKY (Not vodka, brandy, rum etc.)

GENUS: SCOTCH (Not Irish, American, Japanese etc.)

SPECIES: SINGLE MALT SCOTCH WHISKY
the product of an individual malt whisky distillery

BLENDED MALT SCOTCH WHISKY
a mix of malt whiskies from more than one distillery

SINGLE GRAIN SCOTCH WHISKY
the product of an individual grain whisky distillery

BLENDED GRAIN SCOTCH WHISKY
a mix of grain whiskies from more than one distillery

BLENDED SCOTCH WHISKY
a mix of malt and grain whiskies

GEOGRAPHICAL VARIETIES: Under the proposed legislation, only the five 'traditional regional names' – 'Highland', 'Lowland', 'Speyside', 'Campbeltown' and 'Islay' – may be used

MONO-SPECIFIC VARIETIES: 'Cask Strength' and 'Non chill-filtered'

Regional Differences

Over the past 20 years it has become common to approach malt whiskies in terms of their regional differences, on the principle that the malts made in one part of Scotland are different to those made in another for mysterious reasons of *terroir*.

It was a brilliant marketing idea, which effectively communicated the fact that all malts are different in a way which was familiar to wine drinkers, used to the idea of differences within regions such as Bordeaux. The concept also made malts more accessible and encouraged consumers to explore whiskies from different parts of Scotland. What's more, it was justified by history in the ancient division between 'Highland' and 'Lowland' regions (first introduced for tax reasons in the 1780s), and the later identification of different styles from 'Islay', 'Campbeltown' and 'Speyside' (originally called 'Glenlivet') by the end of the nineteenth century.

The first faltering step in the direction of marketing a selection of whiskies which displayed regional differences was made by the Distillers Company Limited when it launched – or, rather, slipped discreetly onto the market – 'The Ascot Malt Cellar' in 1982. This was a collection of six whiskies: Rosebank (a Lowland malt), Linkwood (from Speyside), Talisker (from the Isle of Skye), Lagavulin (from Islay), Strathconnan (a blended malt) and Glenleven (also a blended malt).

The idea was extended by D.C.L.'s successor, United Distillers, in 1988 when the 'Classic Malts' range was launched, specifically to demonstrate the differences between malts made in one region and another. (See p. 17). All come from small, traditional, picturesque distilleries: the company had in mind the fact that consumers would want to visit the places where the malts were made, and soon developed visitor facilities at each.

It was an intelligent and appropriate move, and was hugely successful. Everyone began to talk about malts in terms of region – 'a cheeky little Lowland', 'rather a good example of the North Highland style', 'classic Perthshire whisky, of the sherried kind'. Writers divided and sub-divided the country into smaller and smaller 'regions'. Actually, in my own experience, this was driven by publishers, for whom a 'regional' or even 'sub-regional' breakdown of malt whiskies was more accessible and made for a more attractive book. As we have seen (p. 18), other whisky companies began to imitate the concept, but not having United Distillers' huge inventory of distilleries, their attempts were half-hearted.

THE LIMITS OF REGIONALITY

But, although useful, the concept of regional differences is by no means infallible. If Islay malts are famously smoky – 'the most pungent whiskies made' – why are Bruichladdich and Bunnahabhain so mild, with not a trace of smoke? Lowlands are typically dry and short in the finish, yet Auchentoshan can be sweetly fruity and medium length? Speyside, where two-thirds of today's malt whisky distilleries are located, embraces a wide range of styles, light-, medium- and full-bodied. On top of this there's the influence of the cask during matura-tion, which can supply up to 80% of the flavour of ma-ture whisky.

The truth is that it is not location – *terroir* – that dictates the style of a whisky, it is tradition. For 150 years, the main customers for malt whisky have been the blending houses, and the last thing they want when they buy malt x from Islay or malt y from Speyside is for those malts to have changed in style – if they have done, it messes up the formula for the blend.

The style, character and flavour of any malt whisky come from two principal sources: the way it is made and the way it is matured.

The way it is made embraces the peating levels in the malt, the way the malt is processed, how long the wash is fermented, the size of the stills and how they are operated, the style of the condenser (traditional worm tub or 'shell-and-tube') – above all, the craft of whisky making: how each individual distillery makes its whisky, and has been making it for decades.

The way it is matured encompasses the length of time the whisky has lain to the wood and the nature of the casks used – American or European oak? First-fill or refill? The kind of warehouse in which the whisky is matured (traditional or modern) and the location of the warehouse also play a part – but it's a small part, in relation to all the other factors.

Because of all these elements, I have included an account of plant and wood policy under each of the distillery entries, and an idea of the style of the new make spirit and the mature whisky.

If they choose to, the owner of distillery x (on Islay) can make a 'Highland' style malt (and they do: see *Caol Ila, Ardbeg, Bruichladdich*), while distillery y (on Speyside) can produce a smoky 'Islay' style (and they do: see *BenRiach, Benromach*) – although neither could produce a replica of the make of another distillery, even if that distillery was next door.

But if the main customers for these distilleries are blenders – and remember that around 93% of the malt whisky made goes for blending – Mr X and Mr Y run the risk of losing their key customers. So they tend to stick to the way they have always done it, and to the extent that this way has been the way it has always been done in Islay or Speyside, or wherever, a local style emerges, a 'regional difference'.

A
6677

89   1995
&G.   GRANT
GLENFARCLAS
BALLINDALLOCH

95
NT
AS

Key to Entries

DISTILLERY

The name is that of the distillery, not the brand of single malt/grain whisky.

In most cases the two are the same; however, there are exceptions (Black Barrel from Girvan Grain Distillery, Longrow from Springbank Distillery, Old Pulteney from Pulteney Distillery etc.)

STATUS

All currently in operation, unless indicated:
mothballed can reopen relatively easily
dismantled buildings still stand, but plant gone
demolished buildings gone as well
redeveloped buildings are now used for something else
museum only one – Dallas Dhu

REGION

The regions adopted (per the current Scotch Whisky Association recommendations) are: Lowland, Speyside, Highland (Island in brackets), Campbeltown, Islay.

ADDRESS, PHONE, WEBSITE, VISITORS

All self-explanatory

OWNER

In some cases, the owning company or licensee is a subsidiary of a larger international concern (see 'Who Owns Whom?'). Thus, Chivas Brothers is wholly owned by Pernod Ricard, John Dewar & Sons by Bacardi, Inver House Distillers by ThaiBev, Burn Stewart Distillers by C.L. World Brands of Barbados, The Glenmorangie Company by Louis Vuitton Moët Hennessy, Morrison Bowmore Distillers by Suntory, Whyte & Mackay by United Breweries Group of India, Tomatin Distillery Ltd by Takara & Okura of Japan.

CAPACITY

m L.P.A. = millions of litres of pure alcohol per annum

Since 2007, most Scotch whisky distilleries have been operating at capacity, and several have recently expanded capacity. Prior to this many distilleries only operated for part of the year, and some were mothballed for periods to allow for 'stock adjustments'.

The spirit made in both malt and grain distilleries in Scotland cannot be called 'Scotch whisky' until it has matured for three years. Annual production – usually fixed at the beginning of the year – is geared to the requirements of customers, who are mainly the blending houses. Currently around 93.5% of the malt whisky made, and more or less 100% of grain whisky, goes into blends.

Only a small amount of the make of a malt whisky distillery (typically around 10%) is allocated for single malt bottling. So distilleries gear production to the needs of the blenders, their principal customers.

On their side, the blenders have to anticipate what the demand for their individual brands will be in 5, 8, 10, 12, 18, 25 (etc.) years' time. *In every market in the world, in which their brand has a presence.* A complicated forecast!

In truth, the availability today of single malts of advanced age is largely attributable to blenders 'getting the forecasts wrong', or to 'poor stock management' – epitomised by the Whisky Loch surpluses of the early 1980s.

HISTORICAL NOTES AND CURIOSITIES
Self-explanatory, and should be read in conjunction with 'Historical Overview' (pp. 9–19).

EXPRESSIONS
The whiskies listed are current bottlings released by the distillery owner, sometimes called 'proprietary bottlings'. I have endeavoured to be comprehensive, but this is difficult. Some owners release hoards of expressions each year. Some bottlings are very limited and sell out quickly. Some are only available in specific markets, or in duty-free. I have not attempted to list the many expressions released by independent bottlers. 'CS' = cask strength (i.e. around 60% vol).

WHERE DOES FLAVOUR COME FROM?

Nobody knows for *certain* – which is why Scotch is such a rewarding subject for study! And also why you can't make precisely the same flavour on a different site. Over the last 20 or so years, our knowledge of what influences flavour has increased hugely.

It was long thought that the location of the distillery (particularly a malt whisky distillery) was essential. 'Regional differences' between the styles of malt made in various parts of Scotland were discerned. Thus, many (but not all) Islay malts are smoky; Speyside malts tend to be sweet; Lowland malts are generally lighter in style, etc.

In fact you can make a smoky malt anywhere (see 'Malt' below) – and some Speyside distilleries are doing so; if you start saving spirit earlier, your make will be sweeter; if you run your stills and condensers in such a way as to encourage contact with copper, you will produce a lighter style of spirit (see 'Stills' below) – and so on.

Having said this, broad regional characteristics are discernible, not because distilleries can't change the style of their make, but because they don't want to, and neither do their customers, the blending houses. It is difficult to make a consistent blend if the component malt and grain whiskies are variable. (See 'Regional Differences'.)

Flavour comes from three sources: raw materials, production and maturation. Each entry details aspects of each.

RAW MATERIALS

Water

Copious amounts of water are essential for distilling. It is used for production ('process water'), for cooling the condensers ('cooling water'), for reducing the strength of the spirit prior to filling into cask ('reduction water') and for the boilers that create the steam to heat the pans and coils in indirect-fired stills (see below).

In most cases one source of water supplies all these needs; in others, process and cooling water come from different sources.

It used to be thought that the nature of the water, its mineral content and acidity (i.e. hard or soft, and whether it was peaty or not) made a crucial contribution to the flavour of the whisky. The general view today is that this is not the case, although many distillers still believe it makes a small contribution, so I have indicated 'hard' or 'soft' in the notes.

The temperature of the water in the condensers certainly makes a difference; some distilleries choose to run them 'hot' or 'cold'; in the past, distillery operators could judge whether the spirit was made during summer or winter (the former was lighter in character than the latter).

Some stills are fitted with 'after-coolers' (a second condenser) or 'purifiers' (a pipe from the lyne arm, which allows condensed vapour to return to the still for redistillation, producing a lighter style of spirit).

Malt

Until the 1960s most distilleries malted their own barley on site, and where possible I have indicated when such maltings closed. Increased production at this time made it necessary for distillers to buy in malt from large centralised maltings, mostly owned by independent maltsters (Diageo has its own maltings), and this practice continues today.

Today, only eight distilleries make their own malt: Tamdhu and Glen Ord have large maltings attached; Springbank makes all its requirement; Highland Park, Laphroaig, Bowmore, Kilchoman and Balvenie have old-fashioned floor maltings to supply a proportion of their needs.

The variety of barley used to make the malt is not considered to affect flavour (although some would disagree!), but varieties change every few years, so I have not attempted to specify them.

If peat is burned during the drying stage, this will

impart a smoky flavour to the whisky. Distillers specify the degree of peating they want, measured in 'parts per million phenols' (ppm). Phenols are the chemical compounds that impart smokiness or medicinal characteristics: lightly peated = around 2ppm, medium peated = around 15ppm, heavily peated = 25–35ppm, or in rare cases more than this.

PLANT

Mash tun

The 'mash' is a mix of ground malt (called 'grist') and hot water; the 'mash tun' is the large tub with a perforated base (cast iron, mild steel or stainless steel; usually covered, occasionally open) where this takes place, and where starches in the malt are converted into sugars. The resulting liquid is called 'worts'; it filters through the bed formed by husks in the grist and may be 'clear' or 'cloudy' (i.e. containing small particles of starch). Cloudy worts give rise to a uniform 'maltiness' or 'nuttiness' in the spirit.

Until the 1970s, Scotch distillers used 'traditional' infusion mash tuns, called 'rake-and-plough' or 'rake-and-pinion' tuns. These have a rotating arm, equipped with revolving rakes to disturb the bed of the mash and facilitate draining.

During the expansion of the 1960s and 1970s, many distillers went over to 'Lauter-tuns', invented by German brewers. In these, the rakes are replaced by small fins or 'knives'. In the case of 'semi-Lauter' tuns, the arms merely rotate; in 'full-Lauter' tuns the fins may also be moved up or down, to take account of the depth of the bed.

The relevance of the style of mash tun is that it is difficult to achieve clear worts with a semi-Lauter tun, so I have indicated which kind is used in the individual distillery. I have also indicated its size, by noting the weight of grist used in each mashing.

SPIRIT STILLS, DUNDASHILL DISTILLERY.

STILL-HOUSE, NEVIS DISTILLERY.

Still design has changed little since the nineteenth century, but stillhouses are tidier places since the stills ceased to be fired directly, by coal.

Washbacks

A 'washback' is a fermentation vessel. Traditionally they were made from wood (principally Oregon pine/Douglas fir); many distillers now use stainless steel washbacks. Chemists deny that the material makes any contribution to flavour, although those who use wooden washbacks maintain that bacteria lurking in the wood assist in secondary fermentation (they cannot be cleaned as rigorously as steel vessels), and also that they insulate the wash in cold weather.

Although I have not listed it, the length of fermentation times makes a very important contribution to flavour: short fermentations (around 48 hours) make for a malty spirit; long fermentations (60–70 hours) develop fruity and floral flavours.

Stills

Malt whisky is always distilled twice – sometimes two-and-a-half times, sometimes three times – so in most distilleries the stills are arranged in pairs, called the 'wash still' and the 'low wines' or 'spirit still'.

Stills come in three principal shapes: plain (or 'onion'), boil-pot (or 'boil-ball') and lamp-glass (or 'ogee'). There are many variations in size – indicated in the text by the amount of liquid charging each still – and in height. The still is connected to the condenser by the lyne arm (or lye pipe).

Stills must be made from copper; this metal acts as a purifier, removing unwanted sulphury compounds. The more contact the alcohol vapour has with copper (e.g. if the still is very tall, or if it is fitted with a purifier, or if it is run very slowly), the lighter and purer the spirit will be.

Condensers

The condensers continue the 'purification' theme. They are of two kinds: 'worm tubs' and 'shell-and-tube condensers'.

Worm tubs were the traditional condensers, and were (almost) universal until the 1960s. The 'worm'

Plate 38.

COPPER STEAM-JACKETED STILL, WITH RETORT AND CONDENSING COILS. BLAIR,
CAMPBELL, & M'LEAN, LTD., WOODVILLE STREET, GOVAN, GLASGOW.

Plate 39.

COPPER STILL, FOR DIRECT FIRING, WITH CONDENSING COIL, FOR WHISKY,
RUM, OR BRANDY. BLAIR, CAMPBELL, & M'LEAN, LTD., WOODVILLE
STREET, GOVAN, GLASGOW.

STILL HOUSE, BOWMORE DISTILLERY.

The top illustration is
an 'onion' or 'plain' still
shape, indirect fired
by steam; the middle a
'lamp-glass' style; the
bottom a mix of the two,
with worm tubs beyond
the back wall.

is a serpentine copper pipe, of gradually diminishing diameter. It sits in the 'tub' – an open vat of cold water. Copper contact in a worm tub is limited, so the resulting spirit tends to be heavier and richer than that coming from a condenser.

The 'shell' in a 'shell-and-tube condenser' is a copper or stainless steel column, within which is mounted a hundred or so small-bore copper pipes (the 'tubes'), through which flows cold water. The alcohol vapour enters the top of the column and condenses on the cold tubes, to be drawn off at the bottom. This kind of condenser increases copper contact, so makes for a lighter spirit.

MATURATION

Casks

The cask in which the spirit matures makes a huge contribution to the flavour of the mature whisky – in extreme cases determining over 80% of the flavour.

By law, Scotch whisky must be matured in oak casks. Most of the casks (around 90%) are made from American white oak (*Quercus alba*), the rest from European oak (*Quercus robur*).

The species of oakwood influences colour, aroma and taste (together, the last two are the 'flavour' of the whisky). American oak imparts a golden hue and sweet, vanilla or coconut flavours; European oak, being more tannic, makes for a richer, umbrageous colour, a drier taste and typically introduces dried fruits, nuts and spices to the flavour, and sometimes sulphury notes.

The casks are invariably second-hand: they will have been used previously to mature bourbon (for around three years; always American oak) or will have contained sherry (for one to two years, usually Oloroso sherry; mainly European oak, some American oak). Occasionally ex-wine barrels, or wine-treated casks are used (mainly European oak).

Casks come in a range of sizes. The commonest are 'barrels' (*c*. 200 litres, also called 'American Standard

Barrels' or 'A.S.B.s'), 'hogsheads' (250 litres, also called 'remade hogsheads' – they are made by combining staves from A.S.B.s; four of the latter make three hogsheads), 'butts' (500 litres, usually made from European oak and ex-sherry) and 'puncheons' (also 500 litres, dumpier than butts; made from both European and American oak).

Casks are used three or four times before they are deemed to be 'exhausted'. The first time they are filled with Scotch they are termed 'first-fill casks', thereafter they are 'refill casks'. Once they have become exhausted, they may be 'rejuvenated' by being scraped out and retoasted or charred.

Warehouses

Warehouses are of three kinds: traditional (or dunnage), racked and palletised.

Dunnage warehouses are low, damp and cool. The casks rest on top of each other, three high.

Racked warehouses are higher and drier. They are fitted with metal frames, into which rows of casks may be mechanically slotted, up to around 14 high.

Palletised warehouses are a recent innovation. Here the casks stand upright – not on their sides, as in the other two – six to a wooden pallet, which is then mechanically raised into position, as in a racked warehouse.

As the spirit matures it 'breathes' through the walls of the cask. Harsh alcohols are expelled – 2% by volume per annum is allowed by Customs & Excise, the so-called 'Angel's Share' – and water vapour seeps in.

In a cool, damp warehouse, the volume lost during maturation will be less than in a dry warm warehouse, but the strength will be lower (owing to dilution by incoming water vapour). In a dry, warm warehouse, the opposite will happen.

Most distilleries have warehouses on site, but few have enough space to accommodate all their casks. Accordingly, the spirit is shipped, usually by road tanker, to be filled into cask and matured elsewhere in Scotland. To be called 'Scotch whisky' the spirit must be matured in Scotland, and it does not become 'whisky' until it has matured for three years.

Individual warehouses, their location and micro-climates make a contribution to flavour, but it is a small one in relation to other factors.

Style

The 'style' or 'character' in each entry refers to the new-make spirit, not the mature whisky. The descriptors used here are mainly those used by the distillery owner.

Mature character

My evaluation of this is based upon samples at around 12 years old. Clearly the character will change in older expressions, typically becoming more complex, deeper and often richer.

Aberfeldy

REGION
Highland (South)
ADDRESS
Aberfeldy, Perthshire
PHONE
01887 822010
WEBSITE
www.aberfeldy.com
OWNER
John Dewar & Sons Ltd
VISITORS
Dewar's World of Whisky
visitor centre
CAPACITY
2.6m L.P.A.

HISTORICAL NOTES: Aberfeldy distillery was built a quarter of a mile to the east of Aberfeldy village by the Dewar brothers, Tommy and John (Jnr), to supply fillings for their increasingly successful blends. The site chosen was that of the former Pitilie Brewery, which had also once been a distillery of the same name, operating from 1825 to 1867. The founders' father, John Dewar, had been born on a croft about two miles away. The new distillery opened in 1898 and was built according to 'the most modern principles': barley went in one end of the distillery and whisky came out at the other. There was even a private railway line to Dewar's blending operation in Perth, to bring in grain and coal, and to carry away casks of whisky. An old 'Saddle' shunting locomotive, known as the 'Puggie' (a Scots word for 'monkey'), at the distillery is all that is left of this railway connection, which closed during the 1960s.

The distillery passed to D.C.L., along with the brand, when Dewar's joined in 1925 (the Big Amalgamation), and was subsequently operated by S.M.D. When building regulations were relaxed in 1960 S.M.D. replaced Aberfeldy's two stills with exact copies, converted to mechanical coal-stoking; in 1972/3, the stillhouse and tun room were rebuilt using the original stone, now with four indirect fired stills.

When D.C.L.'s successor U.D. merged with Grand Metropolitan in 1998 to become U.D.V. (and later Diageo) the company was obliged to divest some of its spirits interests. The Dewar brands and four distilleries, including Aberfeldy, were bought by the Bacardi Corporation.

Since then, over £3 million has been spent on the distillery, including the creation of a first-rate visitor centre, Dewar's World of Whisky, which makes good use of the company's extensive archive to tell the story of the remarkable Dewar brothers and of the global success of the brand, which has long been number one in the United States. It opened in 2000 and welcomes around 40,000 visitors a year. There are plans to develop another warehouse for hospitality and training in 2009.

*The company
has only had seven
master blenders
in the past
100 years.*

CURIOSITIES: The ground upon which Aberfeldy stands was feued from the Marquis of Breadalbane, who retained the right to mine gold there. This right was acquired in 2007 by Alba Mineral Resources, who are currently embarked on research into potential gold reserves in a 322.4 sq. km. area around Loch Tay.

Dewar's master blender in 1902 was A.J. Cameron, who pioneered the idea of returning whisky to cask after blending to allow the spirits to marry for three to six months. His successor, Stephanie Macleod, continues this for Aberfeldy single malt, as well as for the blends. (Dewar's Signature blend is married for two years).

In 2007 Bacardi bought land near Motherwell to build new warehouses and marrying facilities, with a planned investment of £120 million.

EXPRESSIONS:
- First bottled 1991 (@ 15YO, Flora & Fauna series)
- In 2000 a 25YO @ 43% was released to mark the opening of the visitor centre.
- Aberfeldy 12YO @ 40%
- Aberfeldy 21YO @ 40%

RAW MATERIALS: Unpeated malt from Simpson's, Berwick-upon-Tweed; water from the Pitilie Burn.

PLANT: Full-Lauter mash tun (6.3 tonnes); eight Siberian larch washbacks; two of stainless steel. Two plain wash stills (charge 16,500 litres); two plain spirit stills (charge 15,000 litres). All indirect fired by steam coils. Shell-and-tube condensers.

MATURATION: Around 90% refill U.S. hogsheads, 10% refill European wood. All Dewar's spirit filled and matured in Glasgow.

STYLE: Sweet and estery; heather honey and Ogen melon.

MATURE CHARACTER: Smooth and creamy; heather-honey, pears, melon and bruised apples; light maltiness. Taste is fresh, fruity and malty, predominantly sweet. Medium body.

Aberlour

REGION
Speyside
ADDRESS
Aberlour, Moray
PHONE
01340 881249
WEBSITE
www.aberlour.com
OWNER
Chivas Brothers
VISITORS
Welcome
CAPACITY
3.5m L.P.A.

HISTORICAL NOTES: A distillery was founded in the grounds of Aberlour House in 1825 by the laird James Gordon and a man named Peter Weir. By 1833 this venture had failed, and the distillery had been taken over by John and James Grant, in partnership with two brothers named Walker. When the lease ended in 1840, the Grants moved to Rothes and built Glen Grant Distillery – Peter Weir's son became their commercial traveller – and the Walkers went to Linkwood Distillery.

Today's Aberlour Distillery was built in 1879/80 by James Fleming, a local businessman who leased Dailuaine Distillery until that year, a mile from the original, using stone from the quarry used by Thomas Telford for his famous bridge at Craigellachie. It was enlarged in 1892, when ownership passed to the Greenock blenders, R. Thorne & Sons. It was largely destroyed by fire in 1898 and rebuilt.

The next owner was the English company W.H. Holt & Sons (Chorlton-cum-Hardy) Ltd, who bought Aberlour in 1921 and ran it for 20 years. In 1945 it was bought by S. Campbell & Son and re-equipped in 1973 (four stills), then sold to Société Pernod Ricard the following year. Pernod retained Campbell Distillers as its whisky division until acquiring Seagram's in 2001, including Chivas Brothers Ltd, which took over management of all its distilleries.

Sales of Aberlour single malt have increased dramatically since 2000, particularly in France, where it is the bestseller.

A new visitor centre was opened in August 2002, offering an excellent two-hour tour.

CURIOSITIES: Until the 1890s the distillery was entirely powered by water. In the grounds there is a holy well dedicated to Saint Drostan, a follower of Saint Columba who visited Speyside around 660AD, reputedly used by him for baptising wild Highlanders. He later established a monastery at Deer, Aberdeenshire, where the famous *Book of Deer* was later written. A small church dedicated to this saint opened in Rothes in 1931.

The name means 'the mouth of the chattering burn'.

Ian Mitchell, who died in 1992, worked at the distillery for 48 years, the last 27 of them as Manager. His grandfather, father and brother also worked there.

Aberlour a'bunadh ('original' in Gaelic) was introduced in 2000 – a natural strength, un-chill filtered expression from ex-sherry casks. To 2005 there have been 14 batches of this excellent single malt.

Aberlour House became a prep school, and it is now the headquarters of Walkers of Aberlour, the famous shortbread bakers.

EXPRESSIONS:
- Aberlour 10YO @ 40%
- Aberlour 15YO @ 40%
- Aberlour a'bunadh @ CS (no age statement)
- Aberlour 12YO Double Cask (France only)
- Aberlour 15YO Cuvee Marie d'Écosse (France only)

RAW MATERIALS: Unpeated malt from independent maltsters; own floor maltings closed in 1960. Process and reduction water from springs; cooling water from the Lour Burn.

PLANT: Semi-Lauter mash tun (12.12 tonnes); six stainless steel washbacks. Two plain wash stills (charge 12,500 each); two plain spirit stills (charge 16,000 litres each, requiring two wash distillations to charge one still). All indirect fired by steam. External shell-and-tube condensers.

MATURATION: Approximately half is first and refill sherry butts, the remainder refill hogsheads. The whisky to be bottled as single is matured on site in one of six bonded warehouses (capacity 27,000 casks); the rest at other sites in the Highlands and Central Belt.

STYLE: Sweet and fresh-fruity, medium bodied.

MATURE CHARACTER: Malty nose, with some fruits and spice. Viscous mouth feel. Honey, with a trace of nutmeg and a thread of smoke in the finish. Medium-bodied.

Ailsa Bay

Ai

REGION
Lowland
ADDRESS
Girvan, Ayrshire
PHONE
01465 716347
WEBSITE
No
OWNER
William Grant & Sons Ltd
VISITORS
No
CAPACITY
6m L.P.A.

HISTORICAL NOTES: William Grant & Sons announced their intention to build a new distillery within their Girvan grain spirit distillery in January 2007. By December the same year, spirit samples were being sent to potential customers. The project reputedly cost in excess of £10 million.

CURIOSITIES: 'The most outstanding natural feature of the area is the uninhabited island of Ailsa Craig, standing a few miles off the coast. It is the granite plug of a very old volcano. The granite from this extraordinary, steep-sided island is known as ailsite, and until recently was the sole source of curling stones for Scotland's national winter sport.' (Philip Morrice, The Whisky Distilleries of Scotland and Ireland, 1987)

This is the second pot-still malt distillery to have been built within William Grant's Girvan site. The first was Ladyburn (see entry), which operated from 1966 to 1975. The new distillery does not have exactly the same location as the old one, nor does it employ any of its equipment.

EXPRESSIONS:
The make will be used for Grant's blends.

RAW MATERIALS: Unpeated malt from independent maltsters. Soft water from Penwhapple Loch.

PLANT: Full-Lauter mash tun (12 tonnes); 12 stainless steel washbacks. The stills have been modelled on those at Balvenie: four straight-side boil-ball wash stills (12,000 litres charge); four boil-ball spirit stills (12,000 litres charge). All indirect-fired. Shell-and-tube condensers.

MATURATION: Mix of first-fill and refill ex-bourbon; small amount of European oak casks.

STYLE: Rich, complex, sweet. Balvenie style

Allt–a–Bhainne

REGION
Speyside
ADDRESS
Glenrinnes, by Dufftown,
Moray
PHONE
01340 783331
WEBSITE
No
OWNER
Chivas Brothers
VISITORS
No
CAPACITY
4m L.P.A.

The distillery looks out over to Corriehabbie, the haunt of many illicit distillers in the past, whose product was called leprach, after one of the neighbouring hills.

HISTORICAL NOTES: Built by Seagram's in 1975, Allt-a-Bhainne Distillery looks like a compact fortress crouching on the northern slopes of Ben Rinnes, the mountain that dominates northern Speyside.

The distillery itself is uncompromisingly modern, inside and out, but the six blocks that make up the building are cleverly heaped together, each with a different roofline, and the most forward block is clad with local stone, so that the overall effect is pleasing to the eye.

Production commenced with one pair of stills; a further pair were added in 1989, as specified by the original design. The whole operation was designed to be operated by one man, even in pre-computer days. The whisky made here is all carried to Keith by tanker and filled into cask there.

CURIOSITIES: Two years before Allt-a-Bhainne was commissioned, Seagram's had built Braeval as a result of the huge demand for Scotch at the time and anticipating that it would continue. Alas, this was not to be the case, and both distilleries have endured periods of closure, in the case of Allt-a-Bhainne from 2003 to 2005.

EXPRESSIONS:
Never bottled by its owner. Very occasional independent bottlings only.

RAW MATERIALS: Unpeated malt from independent maltsters. Unusually, the distillery has a Buhler five-roller malt mill. Water from 20 springs on the sides of Ben Rinnes, via the Rowantree and Scurran Burns, is collected in a dam behind the distillery.

PLANT: Traditional rake-and-plough mash tun (nine tonnes); eight stainless steel washbacks.

Two plain wash stills (22,000 litres charge); two tall boil-ball spirit stills (22,000 litres charge). The original spirit still has a straight neck, and was adapted in the 1980s. All steam fired. Shell-and-tube condensers.

MATURATION: Mainly refill U.S. hogsheads, matured off site.

STYLE: Sweet and grassy.

Ardbeg

REGION
Islay

ADDRESS
Haven Inches, Isle of Islay,
Argyll

PHONE
01496 302244

WEBSITE
www.ardbeg.com

OWNER
The Glenmorangie
Company

VISITORS
Centre, stylish shop and
excellent café/restaurant

CAPACITY
1.25m L.P.A.

HISTORICAL NOTES: Ardbeg has an old-fashioned, timeless atmosphere, with tasteful contemporary touches. It was resurrected from the dead by Glenmorangie, after they bought the distillery in 1997 for £7 million – over £6 million of which was for stock, the buildings and plant were so dilapidated.

The founders of the distillery were MacDougalls, tenant farmers in this part of Islay, and this family retained connections with Ardbeg until the 1970s. The first record of distilling on the site was in the 1790s, but the earliest commercial operation dates from 1815. By 1900 the village around the distillery housed the families of 40 workers (and two Excise officers); the school had over 100 pupils. However, it was in decline by the end of the 1920s. Ardbeg single malt was available by the small cask to private customers 'who had a credit account with the distillery'.

Alexander MacDougall & Company continued to own the distillery until the firm's liquidation in 1959, when Ardbeg Distillery Ltd was formed. This became the Ardbeg Distillery Trust in 1973 when the distillery was taken over by a joint venture between D.C.L. and Hiram Walker & Sons, the Canadian distiller. The latter acquired full control in 1976 (paying £300,000), but the distillery was mothballed five years later, with the loss of 18 jobs. This was the end of Ardbeg village.

Hiram Walker's distilling interests were bought by Allied Lyons (later Allied Distillers) in 1987 and production resumed in 1989 on a small scale. But Allied also owned Laphroaig Distillery, just down the road and producing a similarly smoky malt. Ardbeg was again mothballed in 1996 and discreetly offered for sale. The successful bidder was Glenmorangie, which took over in 1997 and spent £1.4m on restoration, new plant and a visitor centre. Production resumed the following year under the management of Stuart Thomson (until 2007), assisted by his wife, Jackie, who created the excellent visitor centre.

The Ardbeg Committee, a fan club founded in 2000, now has around 40,000 members.

CURIOSITIES: Alfred Barnard mentions the clan loyalty of the MacDougalls. When Alexander MacDougall of Ardbeg discovered that a kinsman had been found guilty of some misdemeanour, he immediately paid the fine, saying 'that it was impossible that a MacDougall could do anything wrong'.

Ardbeg was (and is) famously smoky whisky. Until 1977, it used its own kilns for drying malt, and it is said that the louvers in the kilns were manipulated so as to cause the smoke to linger and impart peatiness at 50ppm phenols. Since this date, malt has come from Port Ellen Maltings, specified at the same level. In spite of this high phenol level, the whisky itself does not taste as smoky as some other Islays, and this may be owing to the purifier pipe on the spirits still, which returns any liquid which has condensed in the lyne arm for redistillation.

Until the roll-on-roll-off ferry service to Islay was launched in 1968, Ardbeg's barley and coal arrived by sea, and its casks of whisky went out the same way. It was not always plain sailing. In December 1925 the puffer *Serb* was wrecked on the rocks at the entry to Ardbeg Bay, with a cargo of barley and malt. The crew were saved.

For two years after 1979 and between 1989 and 1996 Ardbeg produced an unpeated malt for blending purposes, called Kildalton – the equivalent of Caol Ila's 'Highland' style. A 1980 expression was bottled in 2004.

EXPRESSIONS:
Annual releases in small batches for the Ardbeg Committee are highly sought after.
• Ardbeg 10YO @ 46% (introduced 2000)
• Ardbeg Lord of the Isles 25YO @ 46% (released 2001)
• Ardbeg Still Young 1998 @ 56.2% (released 2002, limited to 3,000 bottles)
• Ardbeg Almost There 9YO @ 54.1% (2007)
• Ardbeg Uigeadail @ 54.2% (introduced 2003)
• Araigh nam Beist @ 46% (introduced 2006)
• Ardbeg 10YO Renaissance @ CS (introduced 2008)

- Ardbeg 1975 @ 54.2% (sherry butt, only available at the distillery, 2008)

RAW MATERIALS: Soft peaty water from Loch Arinambeist and Loch Uigeadail, three miles from distillery. Floor maltings until 1977 then heavily peated malt from Port Ellen Maltings (55ppm phenols).

PLANT: Stainless steel semi-Lauter mash tun (4.5 tonnes). Three larch washbacks and three of Douglas fir. One lamp-glass wash still (11,775 litres charge) and one lamp-glass spirit still (13,660 litres charge), both indirect fired by steam. Shell-and-tube condensers.

MATURATION: 98% bourbon barrels (first and second fill) and 2% sherry. 50% first-fill and 50% second fill used for single bottlings. Two dunnage and three racked warehouses on site (capacity 24,000 casks).

STYLE: Peaty.

MATURE CHARACTER: Peaty, medicinal, salty, dry, but the taste is surprisingly sweet, followed by a blast of smoke, with some liquorice. Full-bodied.

Ardmore

REGION
Highland (East)

ADDRESS
Kennethmont, by Huntly,
Aberdeenshire

PHONE
01464 831213

WEBSITE
www.ardmorewhisky.com

OWNER
Beam Global Spirits & Wine

VISITORS
By appointment

CAPACITY
5.1m L.P.A.

HISTORICAL NOTES: Ardmore is the heart malt of the Teacher's blends, and was built by Adam Teacher (son of the founder, who died shortly before the distillery was completed) in 1897/8. It was the family's first venture into distilling – in order to secure spirit supply for their successful *Highland Cream* blend (introduced 1884). The company would later buy Glendronach Distillery (1960).

The distillery stands deep in rural Aberdeenshire, between the historic villages of Spynie and Kennethmont, beside the main Inverness–Aberdeen railway line, off which the distillery had a siding (no longer used). Capacity was doubled to four stills in 1955, and eight stills in 1974 – all were direct fired by coal until 2002. The original steam engine, used to provide power, is still in situ and operational. Until 1976 malting in Saladin boxes was done on site.

William Teacher & Sons was acquired by Allied Breweries in 1976. The owner never bottled Ardmore as a single malt, and only a small amount found its way to Gordon & Macphail and Cadenhead's. When Allied Domecq was sold in 2006, Teacher's brands, together with Ardmore and Laphroaig Distilleries, were sold to the American distiller, Beam Global (owner of Jim Beam bourbon and a subsidiary of Fortune Brands). The company's Scotch Whisky Director, Douglas Reid, whose father worked at Ardmore for many years, and who was raised in one of the distillery cottages, plans to pursue a policy that 'provides continuity and builds on local knowledge, skill and experience gained over many years and generations'. How wise!

CURIOSITIES: Unusually smoky for a Highland malt, with a peating specification around 12–14ppm phenols. The peat comes from Saint Fergus in Buchan and has a different character to west coast peat, imparting a dry earthiness to the flavour of the whisky.

Before the invention of the stopper cork by William Manera Bergius, Adam Teacher's nephew, all whisky

Teacher's Highland Cream was the first whisky to use a stopper cork, introduced in 1913. The firm advertised under the slogan 'Bury the Corkscrew', and Teacher's was described as 'The Self-Opening Bottle (Patented)'.

bottles had driven corks, like today's wine bottles.

Ardmore was one of the last distilleries to fire its stills directly with coal. This was only abandoned in 2002, in favour of indirect firing by steam coils and pans. The only distillery to use coal today is Glendronach; Glenfiddich went over to direct firing by oil in 2002/03.

Ardmore and its sister, Laphroaig, pioneered the use of quarter cask finishing in first-fill American oak barrels of around 100-litres capacity.

EXPRESSIONS:
Only two bottlings have been done by the owner – the first now very rare.
- Ardmore Centenary 100th Anniversary Bottling 1977 21YO @ 43% (released 1999, exclusively for guests of the distillery)
- Ardmore Traditional Cask @ 46% (non-chill filtered, finished in quarter casks, introduced 2007)

RAW MATERIALS: Soft process water from 15 springs on Knockandy Hill. Cooling water from local sources. Medium-peated malt (12–14ppm phenols) from local independent maltsters.

PLANT: Traditional cast iron mash tun, semi-Lauter stirring gear, copper dome (12.5 tonnes). Fourteen Douglas fir washbacks. Four plain wash stills (15,000 litres charge each); four plain spirit stills, but narrower and slightly taller than the wash stills (15,500 litres charge each). All indirect fired since 2002. Shell-and-tube condensers with sub-coolers.

MATURATION: The majority of the spirit used for Teacher's is matured in European oak puncheons. The single malt is matured in ex-bourbon (Jim Beam) barrels, and finished in first-fill quarter casks.

STYLE: Sweet and smoky, with spice in the finish.

MATURE CHARACTER: Creamy, sweet and smoky on the nose; mellow and buttery, sweet and malty; distinctly smoky to taste. Unusual. Robust.

Arran

REGION
Highland (Island)
ADDRESS
Lochranza, Isle of Arran,
North Ayrshire
PHONE
01770 830264
WEBSITE
www.arranwhisky.com
OWNER
Isle of Arran Distilleries Ltd
VISITORS
Visitor centre, A/V presen-
tation and restaurant
CAPACITY
750,000 L.P.A.

HISTORICAL NOTES: The Isle of Arran Distillery was the brain-child of Harold Currie, former Managing Director of Chivas Brothers and later of Campbell Distillers. Some money was raised by a novel 'bond-holder' scheme, which invited subscribers to invest by guaranteeing them a certain amount of whisky – five cases of blended whisky in 1998, five cases of Arran Founder's Reserve in 2001, all for £450. The distillery, which stands above the picturesque village and sea loch of Lochranza, opened in 1995.

When the distillery opened, there was much speculation about which style of malt it would produce. Would it be Islay smoky, Campbeltown heavy or Lowland light? The distillery stands at the crossroads. Even by 1995, however, the influence of the location could largely be controlled by chemistry. Harold Currie was a Speyside distiller, and opted for that style. So it is impossible to classify Arran by regional style.

CURIOSITIES: The whiskies of Arran were rivalled only by those of Glenlivet by one nineteenth-century source, although there was only ever one licensed distillery on the island (at Lagg, in the southern part, closed 1837).

The visitor centre, which later won a top award from VisitScotland, was opened by H.M. The Queen in 1997 and is one of the island's main visitor attractions.

Arran also markets a range of blends and malts under the Robert Burns label, officially recognised by the International Burns Club network, of which the distillery is a patron. Unlike most distilleries, you may buy the Arran malt by the cask, as new-make spirit.

EXPRESSIONS:
The first release from Arran was a 3YO in 1998; a 4YO followed. Since then the distillery has released a number of cask finished malts @ 55%, and also occasional single casks at natural strength, including, in 2007,

Golden eagles are a familiar sight above the distillery, which is encircled by the high mountains of the north of Arran.

Gordon's Dram (1998 @ 46%, ex sherry-wood, to mark the retirement of Gordon Mitchell, Distillery Manager 1995–2007).

The core range comprises:
- Arran 10YO @ 46%
- Robert Burns Single Malt @ 40%
- Arran 100 Proof @ 57% (no age statement, introduced 2006)

RAW MATERIALS: Water from Loch na Davie, above the distillery via the Easan Biorach stream. 90% unpeated Scottish malt from Bairds (Black Isle). Each year a small amount of peated malt is taken in, for a future peated expression.

PLANT: Stainless steel full-Lauter mash tun (2.5 tonnes). Four Oregon pine washbacks. One plain wash still (6,500 litres charge) and one plain spirit still (3,695 litres charge), both indirect fired by steam coils. Shell-and-tube condensers.

MATURATION: Two modern dunnage warehouses, one racked on site, holding 5,000 casks – 80% of the make. The remaining 20% is matured on the mainland.

STYLE: Sweet and fruity, eau-de-vie.

MATURE CHARACTER: Speyside-like; pear drops, citric fruits, green apples. The taste is sweet, with some malt and citric acidity. Light-bodied.

Auchentoshan

REGION
Lowland

ADDRESS
Dalmuir, Dunbartonshire

PHONE
01389 878561

WEBSITE
www.morrisonbowmore.
co.uk

OWNER
Morrison Bowmore
Distillers

VISITORS
Visitor centre, conference
facilities, shop

CAPACITY
1.6m L.P.A.

HISTORICAL NOTES: Triple distillation was common among Lowland distilleries, many of which distilled other grains than malted barley in their pot stills. It increases the delicacy of the whisky, and its strength. Auchentoshan is the sole remaining Lowland distillery employing triple distillation, and one of only four surviving malt distilleries in the Lowlands.

It was founded by John Bulloch, corn merchant, in 1817 (as Duntocher), but he filed for bankruptcy in 1822. His son, Archibald, obtained a licence under the 1823 Act, but also went bust in 1826. In 1834 Duntocher was sold to John Hart (distiller for Bulloch & Co.) and Alexander Filshie, a local farmer whose family had lived in the district since the seventeenth century, on condition that John Bulloch be allowed to continue to live on the distillery grounds. (He died in 1846, aged 87.)

They changed its name to Auchintoshan (sic), which means 'the corner of the field'. Members of the Filshie family owned the distillery for 44 years. They rebuilt it in 1875 then sold it to C.H. Curtis & Company, whisky merchants in Greenock, following a disastrous grain harvest in 1877.

Curtis & Co. ran Auchentoshan until 1900, when it again changed hands, twice in three years; the second time going to John and George McLachlan Ltd, 'Brewers, Distillers and Wine & Spirits Merchants', who sold to Tennent's (Brewers) in 1960. Tennent's became part of Charrington in 1964 (later Bass Charrington), and in 1969 the distillery was sold to Eadie Cairns (for around £100,000). They re-equipped and refurbished, and sold it to its present owners in 1984. The Japanese distiller, Suntory, bought Morrison Bowmore in 1994.

CURIOSITIES: Auchentoshan's situation 20 minutes west of Glasgow makes it a popular place to visit, and the facilities here were refurbished in 2004 to enhance the experience. Its entire output is bottled as single malt and promoted as 'The Spirit of Glasgow'.

The Bulloch family went on to play an important

In 1941 Auchentoshan was badly damaged by enemy action, which destroyed three warehouses and almost one million litres of maturing spirit. Clydebank was levelled and 1,000 people killed, but miraculously the distillery survived. Today cooling water is collected from a bomb crater near the distillery. Production was resumed in 1948.

role in the whisky industry. Soon after they disposed of Auchentoshan, Bulloch & Company was founded (1830), and in 1855 John Bulloch's grandsons merged with the successful Glasgow whisky merchants, A. Lade & Company, to become Bulloch Lade & Company. Camlachie/Loch Katrine distillery was acquired next year, Caol Ila in 1863 and Benmore (Campbeltown) in 1868. The firm also offered a range of well-known blends, under the generic title 'B.L.', and by 1893 were sole agents for the Macallan-Glenlivet Distillery. Incorporated in 1898, Bulloch Lade joined D.C.L. in 1920.

Triple distillation works as follows: wash charges the wash still, and the low wines from here go to Feints Receiver 1, where they mix with the tails of the intermediate still (overall strength 18–19%). The smaller intermediate still is charged from this receiver, and the heads go to Feints Receiver 2, where they join the feints from the spirit still (overall strength 55%). The spirit still is charged from here, and distilled in the usual way, with foreshots and feints being returned to Feints Receiver 2, and spirit saved in the spirit receiver. Overall strength is an unusually high (for malt distilling) 82%.

A major revamp of packaging and liquids took place in 2008. Three Wood has featured in the finals of the Cuban Whisky and Cigar Challenge since its inception in 2003, and won in 2005 (paired with a Bolivar Imensas cigar).

EXPRESSIONS:
Current core expressions are:
- Auchentoshan Classic (no age statement) @ 40% (introduced 2008)
- Auchentoshan Select (no age statement) @ 40% (duty-free only, mid 1990s)
- Auchentoshan 12YO @ 40% (reintroduced 2005)
- Auchentoshan 18YO @ 43% (from American barrels, introduced 2008)
- Auchentoshan Three Wood @ 40% (a mix of ex-bourbon, ex-Oloroso and ex-Pedro Ximenez woods, introduced 1998)

- Auchentoshan 21YO @ 43% (limited edition; a mix of ex-bourbon and ex-sherry casks, mid 1990s)
- Occasional limited editions: 1976, 30YO @ 41.8%; 1965, 40YO @ 41.6%; 1957, 50YO @ 49.1% (all released 2007). Auchentoshan 1957, 50YO @ CS (released 2008).

RAW MATERIALS: Soft process water from Loch Katrine and cooling water from the Kilpatrick Hills, via the bomb crater dam where it is recyled through a fountain. Unpeated malt from independent maltsters.

PLANT: Stainless steel semi-Lauter mash tun, with copper canopy (6.82 tonnes). Four Douglas fir washbacks. One lamp-glass wash still (17,300 litres charge), one lamp-glass intermediate still (8,000 litres charge), one lamp-glass spirit still (11–12,000 litres charge). All indirect fired. External shell-and-tube condensers; those on the wash still are unusually large.

MATURATION: Ex-bourbon barrels, ex-sherry casks (Oloroso and Pedro-Jimenez), remade hogsheads and butts. Each expression has its own mix of casks/wood formula. Three dunnage and two racked warehouses on site hold 20,000 casks.

STYLE: Delicate, fruity and zesty.

MATURE CHARACTER: Floral-fragrant, with lemon zest and light cereal. Smooth mouth feel, sweet then dry with roast almonds, fruits and a trace of butterscotch. Short finish. Light-bodied.

Auchroisk

REGION

Speyside

ADDRESS

Mulben, Moray

PHONE

01542 885000

WEBSITE

www.malts.com

OWNER

Diageo plc

VISITORS

By appointment

CAPACITY

3.6m L.P.A.

HISTORICAL NOTES: Commissioned by Justerini & Brooks (J. & B.), building started at Auchroisk in 1972, on a site to the west of Keith with quantities of high-quality water available. The name comes from a nearby farm and means 'the ford of the red stream'. The distillery was designed by Westminster Design Associates and built by George Wimpey & Co.; it was completed by 1974.

The building won an award from the Angling Foundation for not interfering with the salmon's progress upstream.

A year before building started, water was tankered over to Glen Spey Distillery where a week's trial was conducted – the commissioners wanted a malt with a light style similar to Glen Spey for their leading blend, J. & B. Rare. J. & B. had been part of Independent Distillers and Vintners (together with W. & A. Gilbey & Sons) since 1962. In 1972, while Auchroisk was being built, I.D.V. was bought by the brewer, Watney Mann, and both companies were taken over by Grand Metropolitan within the year. Grand Metropolitan merged with Guinness to form U.D.V., then Diageo, in 1997.

Auchroisk is a large site and casks from other distilleries are matured here. It also acts as Diageo's collection centre in the North of Scotland: casks of mature whisky arrive here, are disgorged, blended and filled into road tankers for transportation to blending halls in the Central Belt.

CURIOSITIES: Jim Milne, J. & B.'s Master Blender, took the unusual step of reracking The Singleton into ex-sherry casks for two years after ten years' maturation in refill ex-bourbon. This was possibly the first example of 'wood finishing', although it was not stated on the label. These early bottlings covered themselves in international awards.

The Singleton brand name was dropped for Auchroisk in 2001, but was revived in 2006 for expressions of Glen Ord, Glendullan and Dufftown (see individual entries).

The Singleton brand name was adopted because the distillery name was deemed difficult to pronounce.

EXPRESSIONS:
Auchroisk is not common as a single, since J. & B. Rare continues to prosper in global markets, currently standing at number two. It was first bottled as a single malt in 1986, as The Singleton. Bottlings were released from 1976, 1980 (named Particular, for the Japanese market), 1981 and 1983 all at 12YO.
• Auchroisk 10YO @ 43% (Flora & Fauna series)
• Auchroisk 1974 28YO @ 56.8% (Rare Malts series)

RAW MATERIALS: Unpeated malt from Burghead. Soft process water from Dorie's Well; cooling water from Mulben Burn.

PLANT: Semi-Lauter mash tun (11.5 tonnes). Eight stainless steel washbacks. Four lamp-glass wash stills (12,700 litres charge); four lamp-glass spirit stills (7,900 litres charge). Indirect fired. Shell-and-tube condensers.

MATURATION: Mainly refill hogsheads matured on site, where there is warehousing for 265,000 casks.

STYLE: Grassy.

MATURE CHARACTER: Sweet and lightly honeyed, with Sugar Puffs breakfast cereal. Cooked apples in the taste, with a whiff of smoke. Light- to medium-bodied.

Aultmore

Au

REGION
Speyside
ADDRESS
Aultmore, by Keith, Moray
PHONE
01542 882762 or 01542 881800
WEBSITE
No
OWNER
John Dewar and Sons
VISITORS
By appointment
CAPACITY
2.9m L.P.A.

HISTORICAL NOTES: Alexander Edward of Forres, who had inherited Benrinnes Distillery from his father and led the consortium that built Craigellachie Distillery, built Aultmore in 1895, just outside Keith on the road to Buckie. The site, known as the Foggie Moss, was abundant in springs and rich in peat, and had been a favourite haunt of smugglers in the early nineteenth century. Aultmore went into production in 1897; so well-regarded was its make that capacity was doubled within a year (to 100,000 gallons per annum) and electric light installed, although all machinery in the plant was driven by either steam engine or water wheel. The wheel (which was used until about 1960) and an Abernethy 10hp steam engine are still there, although not in use.

Alexander Edward bought Oban Distillery next year and floated The Oban and Aultmore-Glenlivet Distilleries Ltd, which was over-subscribed. Alas, one of the Directors was closely involved in Pattison's of Leith, whisky blenders, which went dramatically bankrupt in 1900. Production was cut, but Aultmore survived, to be put up for sale in 1923 and bought by John Dewar & Sons.

Dewar's joined D.C.L. in 1925, and from then until 1998 (when Dewar's and its associated distilleries was sold to Bacardi) it was managed by S.M.D. and its successors. They converted the stills to steam heating in 1967, closed Aultmore's maltings in 1968 and added two more stills to the existing pair in 1971. The make was not bottled by its owners as a single until 1996, although it has been ranked Top Class by blenders from the outset.

CURIOSITIES: The name means 'the big river' in Gaelic.

The power supply was generated by a water wheel from 1890 until 1960, and the wheel is still in situ.

Well-respected but little known, Aultmore all went for blending. Professor Ronnie Martin, former Production Director at U.D., managed to secure some 10YO casks (both ex-sherry and ex-bourbon) for bottling by his son's company, Inverarity Vaults, in the late 1990s.

The illicit make from the Foggie Moss was popular among innkeepers in nearby Keith, Fochabers and Portgordon. One of the leading suppliers was Jane Milne. It was not uncommon for women to be illicit distillers in these days.

EXPRESSIONS:
Apart from a limited Centenary Edition (16YO @ 63%, which achieved £960 at auction in 2000), Aultmore was not bottled by its owner until:
• Aultmore 12YO @ 43% (Flora & Fauna range, introduced 1996)
• Aultmore 1974 21YO @ 60.9% (Rare Malts series, bottled 1996)
Under John Dewar/Bacardi's ownership:
• Aultmore 12YO @ 40%

RAW MATERIALS: Process water from Auchinderran Burn; cooling water from the Burn of Ryeriggs. Unpeated malt from Burghead.

PLANT: Stainless steel full-Lauter tun (ten tonnes). Six larch washbacks. Two plain wash stills (charge 15,500 litres each) and two lamp-glass spirit stills (charge 15,500 litres each). All indirect fired. Shell-and-tube condensers.

MATURATION: 90% of the wood is American and 10% European, with more use of sherry-wood in old stocks.

STYLE: Light and estery/fruity.

MATURE CHARACTER: Light and fragrant, with cut grass and green apples. The taste is sweet and floral – simple and easy. Light-bodied.

Balblair

REGION
Highland (North)
ADDRESS
Edderton, by Tain, Ross-shire
PHONE
01862 821273
WEBSITE
www.balblair.com
OWNER
Inver House Distillers
VISITORS
By appointment
CAPACITY
1.75m L.P.A.

HISTORICAL NOTES: Balblair is among the oldest distilleries in Scotland, and one of the prettiest. Founded in 1790, it was moved to its present site in 1894. Like many malts, the make was unknown beyond local farmers until relatively recently, but it is now – at last, for it deserves it – being nurtured and promoted as a brand by its owners.

The present distillery stands some distance from the original, six miles outside Tain, with its back to the Dornoch Firth. It was built around 1872, and expanded in 1894 (although it remains a small unit) to take advantage of the newly built railway line between Inverness and Wick.

Balblair was founded and run by members of the Ross family for just over a century. They had also leased Brora and Pollo Distilleries from the Duke of Sutherland, and it was to the latter that Andrew Ross moved in 1896 (the distillery stood south of Tain, and closed in 1903).

Balblair reverted to the estate. Alexander Cowan became tenant and was obliged to rebuild. He went bust in 1911, and the distillery closed until 1947 when it was bought by a Banff solicitor, Robert Cumming (known as 'Bertie', he also owned Pulteney Distillery). He expanded it in 1964, building more warehouses, and changed from direct to indirect fired stills. In 1970 he sold to Hiram Walker-Gooderham & Worts of Canada and retired. Balblair accordingly came under the ownership of Allied (in 1988). They sold to the current owners, Inver House, in 1996.

Inver House was bought by a subsidiary of Thai Beverages plc (ThaiBev plc), Southeast Asia's largest alcoholic beverage company, in 2001 and integrated into that company's international division, International Beverage Holdings Ltd (InterBev) in 2006.

CURIOSITIES: Edderton is reputed to have the cleanest air in Scotland; hence the brand name Elements.

The new packaging makes good use of imagery

related to the nearby Pictish stone, known as the Clach Biorach ('the sharp stone'), on the Eadar Dun (hence Edderton). It was the 'Gathering Place' for the local community – a term that has been adopted by the 'Friends of Balblair', the malt's fan club.

Founded and managed for many years by Rosses, currently four out of the distillery's nine employees bear this surname.

The usually taciturn Charles Craig (in his *Scotch Whisky Industry Record*) described Balblair as 'one of the most attractive small distilleries still standing'.

In March 2007 Balblair packaging was elegantly redesigned by Curious Group, Glasgow.

Inver House Distillers was named 'Distiller of the Year' in *Whisky Magazine*'s Icons of Whisky Awards, 2008.

EXPRESSIONS:

First bottled by its owner in the late 1990s, selected by long-term master blender Eddie Drummond, including a 33YO that won a gold medal from *Whisky Magazine* in 2003. Now bottled as limited edition 'vintages', with casks selected by current master blender, Stuart Harvey, by year, not age.

- Balblair 1979 @ 46% (limited release 2007, I.W.S.C. Gold 2007)
- Balblair 1989 @ 43% (limited release 2007, I.W.S.C. Gold 2007)
- Balblair 1997 @ 43% (limited release 2007)
- Balblair 1975 @ 46% (limited release 2008)
- Balblair 1985 @ 43% (limited release 2008 for France)
- Balblair 1986 @ 43% (limited release 2008 for travel retail)

RAW MATERIALS: Process and cooling water from the Allt Dearg Burn in the Struie Hills, piped five miles from the distillery. Floor maltings until the early 1970s, now unpeated malt from Portgordon Maltings.

PLANT: Semi-Lauter mash tun (4.6 tonnes). Six Douglas fir washbacks. One plain and dumpy wash still (19,600 litres charge) and one plain spirit still (11,800 litres charge), both indirect fired by steam. A heat converter system to pre-heat the wash was installed in 2006. The stillhouse also has a third small still, used as a model when the other stills were enlarged and converted to indirect firing. Shell-and-tube condensers.

Edderton was known as 'The Parish of Peats', such was the ready supply of that fuel.

MATURATION: Eight dunnage warehouses on site (one with a concrete floor installed by Norwegian troops during World War II, so it could be used as a canteen), with capacity for 28,500 casks. Mainly U.S. ex-bourbon hogsheads, some European oak. All single malt matured on site.

STYLE: Full-bodied, waxy-oily, nutty, leathery, but also green apples, floral notes and a natural spiciness.

MATURE CHARACTER: Nutty and sweet, with a trace of smoke and an elusive maritime note. The taste is medium-sweet, with fruity, nutty and spicy notes and an attractive thick mouth feel. Medium- to full-bodied.

Balmenach

Ba

REGION
Speyside
ADDRESS
Cromdale, Moray
PHONE
01479 872569
WEBSITE
www.inverhouse.com
OWNER
Inver House Distillers
VISITORS
By appointment
CAPACITY
2.7m L.P.A.

HISTORICAL NOTES: One of the earliest modern authorities on Scotch whisky is Sir Robert Bruce Lockhart (author of *Scotch*, 1951). His great-grandfather, James MacGregor, farmed at Balmenach and distilled illegally there until, in 1823, he received a warning from the local Excise officer and took out one of the first licences on Speyside. James died in 1878, and was succeeded by his brother (who came back from a successful career in New Zealand to take over).

When Alfred Barnard visited in the mid 1880s he described Balmenach as 'of the most antiquated type ... (with) picturesque old pot stills and vessels'. This was by design: John MacGregor refused to allow any changes for fear that the character and quality of the whisky might be altered.

When his son, another James, took over in 1897, he formed a limited company, Balmenach-Glenlivet Ltd, and made some improvements, including a branch railway line with a steam locomotive that operated until October 1968, a few days before the Speyside line itself was closed. In 1922 the MacGregors sold to a consortium of blenders, which became part of D.C.L. in 1925.

Under S.M.D.'s management, Balmenach was extended from four to six stills in 1960 (an indication of the quality of the make, which is ranked First Class by blenders). In 1964 the floor maltings were converted to Saladin boxes. The mashhouse was rebuilt in 1968 and a dark-grains plant installed ten years later. All this was to the standard 'Waterloo Street' plan, with the difference that Balmenach was conceived so as to run exclusively by gravity, avoiding the need for pumps at any stage between charging the wash still and filling the casks (see *Caol Ila*).

Balmenach was mothballed in 1993 and sold to Inver House Distillers in 1997. Production was resumed the following year. The new owner acquired no stock, which is why this excellent malt is not (yet) more readily available.

Inver House was bought by a subsidiary of Thai

In 1879, the same storm that collapsed the Tay Bridge blew down the distillery chimney and the whole place nearly went up in smoke.

Bev plc in 2001, and integrated into that company's international division, International Beverage Holdings Ltd (InterBev) in 2006.

CURIOSITIES: A battle was fought near the distillery on the Haughs ('heights') of Cromdale in 1690, where a Jacobite force was surprised at night by a detachment of government dragoons and routed.

While it was closed during World War II (as most malt distilleries were), Balmenach was used as a billet by the Royal Corps of Signals.

For a period in the 1990s, Balmenach was bottled under the label Deerstalker by the Glasgow firm of Aberfoyle & Knight. Inverarity Vaults also bottle the malt as Ancestral (14YO).

EXPRESSIONS:
Balmenach was only available (and rarely) through independent bottlings until the early 1990s Flora & Fauna release. It is not currently bottled by its owners.

RAW MATERIALS: Soft water from a private supply, via the Cromdale Burn. Saladin boxes were installed in 1964 and used until the 1980s; thereafter unpeated malt from independent maltsters.

PLANT: Large cast iron semi-Lauter mash tun with copper dome (8.25 tonnes). Six Douglas fir washbacks. Three boil-ball wash stills (10,000 litres charge), three boil-ball spirit stills (10,000 litres charge). All indirect fired by steam. Worm tubs, each with 85-metre long worms. Dunnage warehouses hold 8,000 casks in total.

MATURATION: Mainly U.S. refill hogs; some Spanish oak.

STYLE: Meaty, vegetal, oily, full-bodied, some say slightly sulphury.

MATURE CHARACTER: The rich style of Balmenach makes it appropriate for European oak maturation, and the best bottlings have a dried fruit, sherried style, with a whiff of smoke. Medium-sweet, rich and dry in the finish. Full-bodied.

Balvenie

REGION
Speyside
ADDRESS
Dufftown, Moray
PHONE
01698 843843
WEBSITE
www.thebalvenie.com
OWNER
William Grant & Sons
VISITORS
V.I.P. tours available (must
be booked in advance).
Bottle Your Own facility,
shared with Glenfiddich.
CAPACITY
6.4m L.P.A.

HISTORICAL NOTES: William Grant opened Glenfiddich Distillery in 1886, and, during the next decade, distillery building on Speyside was unprecedented. Developers were soon trying to buy or rent land adjacent to Glenfiddich itself, so the Grant family pre-empted them by buying 12 acres of adjoining land, including New Balvenie Castle and Mains of Balvenie Farm. The Old Castle of Balvenie is a massive medieval keep that stands close by, its walls veiled by trees.

The new distillery, called Glen Gordon during its early months, went into production on 1 May 1893, with the old mansion house, which had lain empty and derelict for over 80 years, being converted into a maltings. In 1929 the upper storeys were demolished, and the lower storey turned into Warehouse 24. In 1956 the whole Balvenie Estate was bought by the Grant family.

The following year the distillery was enlarged to four stills; a further two were added in 1965; two more in 1971; one in 1991; and three in 2008.

CURIOSITIES: New Balvenie 'Castle' was actually an Adam-style mansion, built about 1790 for James Duff, Earl of Fife, but only lived in for eight years (see also *Dufftown*). In 1895 the building was owned by his great-nephew, Alexander, who was created first Duke of Fife in 1900, upon his marriage to Princess Louise, a daughter of Queen Victoria.

'Old' Balvenie Castle is often missed by visitors to the Genfiddich/Balvenie complex, but is well worth a visit. Its origins are shrouded in the mists of the Pictish twilight. There may have been a fortification here by 1010, when Malcolm Canmore defeated a Danish army at the Battle of Mortlach, and it was certainly used as a base by King Edward I of England ('The Hammer of the Scots') in 1296, when he was subduing the province of Moray. By the mid 1300s the castle was controlled by Alexander Stewart, Earl of Buchan and son of King Robert II, described as a 'ruffianly paranoiac' and known as 'The Wolf of Badenoch' on account of his rapacious behaviour

– not least the burning of Elgin Cathedral, following a tiff with the Bishop of Moray.

Balvenie prides itself on 'doing everything in-house'. The distillery grows its own barley (albeit only a tiny amount) and has its own floor maltings (producing about 10% of its requirement), coppersmiths and bottling facility. Balvenie was first bottled as a single in the 1920s, then in the famous triangular bottle of the early 1970s (see *Glenfiddich*), followed by Founder's Reserve in a striking vintage champagne-style bottle in 1982.

In 2007 Grant's introduced a 'Bottle Your Own Balvenie' scheme, direct from the cask in Warehouse 24. There are three different casks to choose from – a sherry butt, a refill cask and a bourbon cask, all distilled in 1994. You draw the whisky with a 'dog', a copper tube sealed at one end with a coin and attached to a length of string. Such home-made devices were used by creative workers to steal whisky in days gone by. It was called a 'dog' on account of it being 'man's best friend', according to Dennis McBain, Balvenie's coppersmith! 'It was usually hidden down the trouser leg, tied to the belt, so that it would not slip down and be revealed (this would result in immediate dismissal)', he tells me.

EXPRESSIONS:

Balvenie Founder's Reserve was given a 10YO age statement in the early 1990s, when it was repackaged in the current dumpy bottle. In 2008 it was replaced by a 12YO signature package. In 2002 Balvenie released 83 bottles at 50YO from a sherry butt, RRP £6,000 the bottle.

The current core range comprises:

- Balvenie Doublewood 12YO @ 40% (re-racked into Oloroso sherry butts, introduced 1993)
- Balvenie Portwood 21YO @ 40% (re-racked into port pipes, introduced 1995)
- Balvenie Single Barrel Vintages 15YO and 25YO @ 50.4% and 46.9% (introduced 1993)
- Balvenie Vintage Casks @ around 32YO (varying strengths and very limited quantities released each year)

- Balvenie Rum Wood 14YO @ 47.1% (finished in ex-rum casks, released 2005)
- Balvenie New Wood 17YO @ 40% (finished in fresh American oak, released 2006)
- Balvenie Roasted Malt 14YO @ 40% (using dark roasted malt, released 2006)

RAW MATERIALS: Soft water from springs in the Conval Hills, some barley from Mains of Balvenie and the rest from independent maltsters. Peat from Tomintoul.

PLANT: Semi-Lauter mash tun (11.8 tonnes). Nine Oregon pine washbacks. Five boil-ball wash stills (three charged with 12,729 litres each and two with 9,092 each); four boil-ball spirit stills (charged with 12,729 litres each), all indirect fired. Shell-and-tube condensers.

MATURATION: Forty-four warehouses on site. American and European oak, with some port casks. For the 10YO, sherry-wood comprises 10% and ex-bourbon 90%.

STYLE: Fruity, full-bodied and honeyed.

MATURE CHARACTER: Rich and complex on the nose, with honeycomb, dried fruits (including orange peel) and some malt. Big mouth feel and a sweet taste, drying, with light acidity. Medium- to full-bodied.

Banff *Demolished*

REGION
Highland (East)

ADDRESS
Inverboyndie by Banff,
Moray

LAST OWNER
D.C.L./S.M.D.

CLOSED
1983

Banff Distillery was always known as Inverboyndie locally.

HISTORICAL NOTES: The elegant Royal Burgh of Banff was granted its charter by Robert the Bruce in 1324. During the seventeenth and eighteenth centuries many of the local landed gentry had town houses there, and the town retains an atmosphere of faded gentility.

The first distillery here was founded in 1824 at Mill of Banff, but closed in 1863. Its then owner moved to a site at Inverboyndie, a mile west of the town, overlooking Boyndie Bay, to take advantage of the recently opened railway line. The original buildings were largely destroyed by fire in 1877, but were rebuilt 'within a wonderfully short time' (six months).

The owner, James Simpson & Company Ltd, went into voluntary liquidation during the Depression of 1932, and the distillery was bought by S.M.D., who closed it.

Some improvements were made during the 1960s, although the exterior remained unaltered. S.M.D. closed Banff Distillery in May 1983.

CURIOSITIES: As well as the fire in 1877 and the attack in 1941, Banff Distillery suffered damage in 1959 when a still exploded. After decommissioning it was demolished section by section, the last part being cleared in 1991, following a further fire.

EXPRESSIONS:

Before World War I, Banff was bottled by its owners as Old Banff – Pure All-Malt Highland Whisky and supplied to the House of Commons.

Only one proprietary bottling in recent years, although there have been several independent bottlings:

• Banff 21YO @ 57.1% (Rare Malts series, released 2004)

Ben Nevis

REGION

Highland (West)

ADDRESS

Lochy Bridge, Fort William

PHONE

01397 702476

WEBSITE

www.bennevisdistillery.
com

OWNER

Ben Nevis Distillery Ltd
(Nikka, Asahi Breweries)

VISITORS

Visitor centre, museum,
exhibition, café

CAPACITY

2m L.P.A.

*'Long John'
Macdonald is
reputed to have
saved his brother
from being gored by
a bull by seizing its
horns, wrestling it
to the ground and
dislocating its neck.*

HISTORICAL NOTES: 'Long John' Macdonald, the
founder of the distillery, was a big man and proud,
and perhaps on account of his size and strength was
chosen by the Lochaber lairds to establish a legal
distillery near Fort William in 1825, when he was 27
years old. The original distillery produced only 200
gallons a week, but the make's reputation stretched
even to Buckingham Palace, which accepted a cask
in 1848, to be broached on the Prince of Wales' 21st
birthday in 1863. After the death of 'the Old Gael' the
business passed to his son, Donald Peter Macdonald.
Although not as flamboyant a character as his father,
it was Peter who really laid the foundations of the
distillery's success.

He expanded and refurbished – several of the
present-day buildings date from this time – and by
1864 was producing ten and a half times the amount
of whisky than his father. By 1877 he was employing
51 men and was marketing his product as Long John's
Dew of Ben Nevis Pure Highland Malt Whisky. The
following year he designed and built another larger
'model distillery' a mile away, at the mouth of the
River Nevis, after which it is named, and ran it in
tandem with its sister distillery.

Nevis Distillery had 'the largest Maltings under
one roof in the North of Scotland' (the malting floor
was 'so capacious that 3,000 persons could be seated
there with ease') and also a substantial joiner's
shop, a 'whole street of Workmen's Cottages' and a
'Warehouse and Stores' connected to the distilleries'
own harbour and wharf. All told, the distillery
employed 200 men.

On Peter Macdonald's death in 1891, the enterprise
passed to his sons but the 'whisky boom' was about
to turn to bust. Production at Nevis Distillery ceased
in 1908 (and never resumed), although the warehouses were used until they were demolished to
make way for sheltered housing in the mid 1990s.

Ben Nevis Distillery continued to operate off and
on, then the company was sold to the Canadian
entrepreneur, Joseph Hobbs , in 1941. He paid

£20,000 for the business, and the same day sold the warehousing at Nevis Distillery to Train & McIntyre (see below) for the same price! He only resumed production in 1955, having installed a continuous still alongside his pot stills, concrete washbacks and a novel malt handling system.

Production continued until 1978. In 1981 Hobbs' son sold it to Long John International, the spirits division of Whitbread plc, who embarked on a programme of modernisation, completed in 1984. The general downturn in the whisky trade at the end of the 1980s obliged Long John to sell in 1989. (Whitbread itself was taken over by Allied-Lyons the same year, to form Allied Distillers.) The new owner was Nikka Whisky Distilling Company of Japan, a company founded by Masataka Taketsuru, 'the Father of Japanese Distilling', who had trained in Scotland shortly after World War I.

CURIOSITIES: 'Long John' Macdonald, the founder of Ben Nevis Distillery, was a man who attracted tales. In one account, he routed a band of smugglers who ambushed him, resentful of his having 'gone legal', armed with nothing but a stout *cromach* (crook).

During the year 1884–85, when the two Nevis distilleries produced 260,000 gallons of whisky, Macallan Distillery produced around 40,000, Glen Grant 140,000 and The Glenlivet just under 200,000; in 1889 a newspaper article describes the Ben Nevis Distilleries as being 'almost double the size of their nearest rival'.

Joseph Hobbs made a fortune running Scotch into the United States from Canada during Prohibition. One of his main suppliers was Teacher's, for whom he shipped 137,927 cases of Highland Cream via Antwerp into San Francisco Bay on HMCS *Stadacona*, a converted Canadian naval vessel. Another of his steam ships *Ocean Mist* is now a rather drab floating night-club, permanently moored at The Shore in Leith. (See also *Glen Lochy*.)

Joe Hobbs pioneered the process of 'blending

at birth', that is, blending malt and grain new-make and maturing it together. When asked what malts he used, he is said to have replied, 'Oh, just whatever's around'! By the 1950s Dew of Ben Nevis had become a cheap blend.

Fascinating though the story of Ben Nevis Distillery is, the site itself has been sadly neglected. *Whisky Magazine* described it as reminiscent of 'a fading Siberian tractor collective'!

EXPRESSIONS:
Since the mid 1990s, there have been relatively frequent one-off bottlings from 1966, 1967, 1968 and 1971–75, at cask strength and mainly at 26YO.
- Ben Nevis 10YO @ 46% (since 1996)
- Glencoe 8YO (blended malt, since 1992/93)
- Ben Nevis 40YO @ 40.6% (released 2004)
- Ben Nevis 14YO ex-sherry @ 46% 1992 (limited edition, introduced 2007)

RAW MATERIALS: Water from Allt a'Mhuilinn (Mill Burn), which flows from Coire Leis and Coire na'Ciste near the top of Ben Nevis itself. Unpeated malt from independent maltsters.

PLANT: Stainless steel full-Lauter tun (8.5 tonnes). Six stainless steel washbacks, two Oregon pine. Two plain wash stills (21,000 litres charge), two plain spirit stills (12,500 litres charge). Indirect fired. Shell-and-tube condensers.

MATURATION: A combination of ex-bourbon and ex-sherry casks, on site in five traditional dunnage and one racked warehouse.

STYLE: Malty and robust, with a hint of smoke.

MATURE CHARACTER: Aromatic, fruity (cooked fruits), malty, with dark chocolate notes. Mouth feel creamy; sweet start with vanilla and caramels, a trace of sulphury smoke. Medium-to full-bodied.

BenRiach

REGION
Speyside

ADDRESS
Longmorn, by Elgin, Moray

PHONE
01343 862888

WEBSITE
www.benriachdistillery.
co.uk

OWNER
The BenRiach-Glendronach
Distilleries Company Ltd

VISITORS
By appointment

CAPACITY
2.8m L.P.A.

HISTORICAL NOTES: Until 2004, BenRiach's fortunes were closely linked to its larger and more famous neighbour, Longmorn. It was built by the owner of that distillery, John Duff, in 1897, designed by Charles Doig. Duff ran into financial trouble and sold it to Longmorn Distillers Company two years later. Mothballed in 1900 (although it continued to supply malt to its neighbour, to which it was connected by a quarter-mile-long rail link), it was only opened again in 1965, now owned by The Glenlivet Distillers Ltd, who had rebuilt it. Seagram's acquired The Glenlivet Group in 1977, and the licence was transferred to its subsidiary Chivas Brothers.

Seagram's whisky division was bought by Pernod Ricard in 2001, and BenRiach was again mothballed until 2004, when it was sold to a consortium of three entrepreneurs, led by veteran distiller Billy Walker, with backing from the South African company, Infra Trading. It went back into production in September that year.

Since it became independent there has been a slew of bottlings! As Mr Walker says: 'We can be creative in the range we bring to market because of the great inventory we acquired from Chivas'.

BenRiach was named Distillery of the Year in the 2007 Malt Advocate Whisky Awards.

CURIOSITIES: Billy Walker is one of the most experienced people in the trade today. Trained as an organic chemist, he joined Ballantine's in 1971. He then went to Inver House as a blender, then on to Burn Stewart Distillers. He was a member of the management buy-out team that acquired Burn Stewart in 1988 (see *Deanston*), becoming its Production Director. In July 2008 he bought Glendronach Distillery from Chivas Bros. (See *Glendronach*.)

Although mothballed for much of its existence, BenRiach's floor maltings were in almost continuous use until 1999, with peat rights on Faemussach Moor, near Tomintoul. Even during the Seagram ownership,

Billy Walker has been described (by Dave Broom) as 'the smartest man in the whisky industry.'

malt for Longmorn was made here, while BenRiach itself relied on malt from outside sources. After 1980, when the railway lines between the two distilleries were lifted, BenRiach used its own malt. The new owners plan to re-open the maltings in 2008, initially buying in 'green malt' and kilning on site.

Before 1965 BenRiach had one spirit still and one wash still. This was then doubled, and a third spirit still installed at a later date. This created an imbalance, however, so it was taken out (and ultimately sold to a Canadian business).

From 1983, BenRiach produced a quantity of peated malt as well as its usual unpeated style each year – a unique move at the time for a Speyside distillery, but one that allows the new owners to have aged peated Speysides in their portfolio.

EXPRESSIONS:
First bottled as a single by its owner @ 12YO in 1994. The new owner released a core range in August 2004 and has since added to it. Since then there have been numerous annual limited and single cask releases. The core range is:
- BenRiach Heart of Speyside @ 40% and 43%
- BenRiach 12YO @ 40% and 43%
- BenRiach 10YO Curiositas @ 40%, 43% and 46% (peated)
- BenRiach 16YO @ 40% and 43%
- BenRiach 20YO @ 40% and 43%
- BenRiach 21YO Authenticus @ 46% (peated, from 2005)
- BenRiach 15YO @ 46% (in four different finishes: Pedro Ximinez, Madeira, dark rum and tawny port, from 2006)
- BenRiach 25YO @ 46% (from 2007)
- BenRiach 30YO @ 46% (from 2007)
- BenRiach 12YO Heredotas Fumosas @ 46% (peated, finished in Pedro Ximinez casks, 2008)
- BenRiach 12YO Arumaticus Fumosas @ 46% (peated, finished in Jamaican dark rum barrels, 2008)
- BenRiach 12YO Heredotas Fumosas @ 46% (peated, finished in Pedro Ximinez casks, 2008)

RAW MATERIALS: Process water from deep springs about half a mile away, known as Burnside, shared with Longmorn;

cooling water from the Glen Burn (which also supplies Glen Elgin, Longmorn and Linkwood Distilleries). Currently peated (c. 35ppm phenols) and unpeated malt from independent maltsters.

PLANT: Traditional stainless steel mash tun with raised canopy (5.8 tonnes). Eight stainless steel washbacks. Two plain wash stills (15,000 litres charge), two plain spirit stills (9,600 litres charge). Indirect fired. Shell-and-tube condensers.

MATURATION: Now all filled into fresh ex-bourbon barrels for five to six years, then re-racked into refill hogsheads and butts.

STYLE: Sweet and fruity, Speyside style; sweet and smoky.

MATURE CHARACTER: (for the unpeated, un-finished malts) Fruity and estery, with apples and green bananas, some cereal notes. Sweet and creamy to taste, with vanilla and light caramel. Light- to medium-bodied.

Be

REGION
Speyside
ADDRESS
Aberlour, Moray
PHONE
01340 871215
WEBSITE
www.malts.com
OWNER
Diageo plc
VISITORS
By appointment
CAPACITY
2.6m L.P.A.

Benrinnes is ranked Top Class by blenders, and is extensively used in Diageo's blends.

Benrinnes

HISTORICAL NOTES: A distillery was established 700 feet above sea level on the northern slopes of Ben Rinnes, at Whitehouse Farm, by one Peter McKenzie in 1826. It was destroyed by the Great Flood of Moray three years later and another distillery was built at Lyne of Ruthrie some distance away by John Innes.

Innes went bankrupt in 1834. His successor, William Smith, also failed 30 years later (and was sent to prison), and the lease passed to David Edward, farmer, and then to his son Alexander, who became a well-known distiller, founder of Aultmore, Dallas Dhu and Craigellachie Distilleries, part-owner of Oban and Yoker and supporter of Benromach, which was built on his estate near Forres.

The distillery suffered what the *Northern Scot* described as a 'rather destructive fire' in 1896, but its fortunes were more severely hit by the failure of its agents, F.W. & O. Brickmann, in the fall-out of the Pattison crash of 1899, followed by the general recession in the whisky industry.

Alexander Edward sold to Dewar's in 1922, and the distillery passed to D.C.L. in 1925, with management by S.M.D. from 1930. It was rebuilt in 1955/56, and doubled in size to six stills ten years later. The 'new' half runs independently of the older half, and the two are vatted prior to filling into cask. Saladin boxes replaced floor malting in 1964, and operated for 20 years; steam heating replaced direct firing in 1970.

CURIOSITIES: Since 1956, Benrinnes has practised an unusual form of 'partial triple distillation', its six stills being arranged in two sets of three, so that some of the spirit is distilled three times and some of it twice.

Each wash still is charged with the contents of one washback. This distillation is split into heads and tails, the stronger heads being forwarded to the Strong Low Wines Receiver, and the weaker tails to the Weak Low Wines Receiver. The intermediate spirit still is charged from the Weak Low Wines Receiver and again the distillation is split: the heads going to the Strong Low Wines Receiver and the tails to the Weak Low Wines Receiver. The spirit still is charged from the Strong Low Wines Receiver, with the foreshots being transferred back to the same receiver, and the aftershots/feints being further split: strong feints going to the Strong Low Wines Receiver and weaker feints to the Weak Low Wines Receiver.

It might be expected that this would produce a light spirit, but the reverse is true, the effect of triple distillation being countered by the size and shape of the stills and the use of worm tubs.

EXPRESSIONS:
Dewar Rattray, the independent bottler from Ayrshire, use Benrinnes for their 12YO single malt, Stronachie – named after a Perthshire distillery which closed in the 1920s and selected as the malt which was closest in style to that whisky.

- The first proprietary bottling was in 1991, at 15YO (Flora & Fauna series).
- Benrinnes 1974 21YO @ 60.4% (Rare Malts series, released 1996).

RAW MATERIALS: Floor maltings until 1964, then Saladin boxes until 1984. Unpeated malt now comes from Burghead and Roseisle. Process water from the Scurran and Rowantree Burns, which rise high up on Ben Rinnes itself.

PLANT: Three-arm semi-Lauter mash tun (8.7 tonnes). Eight larch washbacks. Two plain wash stills (20,000 litres charge), two plain intermediary stills (5,243 litres charge), two plain spirit stills (7,000 litres charge). All indirect fired by steam. Worm tubs.

MATURATION: Mainly European oak and matured off site.

STYLE: Heavy, meaty.

MATURE CHARACTER: Benrinnes has a famously big, robust character. The nose is rich with burnt caramel, dried fruits, sherry notes. The texture in the mouth is big, filling, velvety. The taste is sweet, then drying, with a long finish. Full-bodied.

Benromach

REGION
Speyside

ADDRESS
Forres, Moray

PHONE
01309 675968

WEBSITE
www.benromach.com

OWNER
Gordon & Macphail

VISITORS
Malt Whisky Centre
opened 1999 (4* attrac-
tion awarded by the Scot-
tish Tourist Board). Fill
your own bottle facility

CAPACITY
750,000 L.P.A.

HISTORICAL NOTES: Benromach has had a chequered career, but is hopefully now on a sound footing.

The Benromach Distillery Company was founded in 1898 by Duncan MacCallum (of Glen Nevis Distillery, Campbeltown) and F.W. Brickmann (spirit dealer, Leith), with the support of Alexander Edward, who rented them the site on the northern edge of his Sanquhar Estate, Forres. (See *Aultmore*.)

As the distillery was nearing completion, Pattison's of Leith, one of the largest buyers of new-make spirit, suspended payments. Brickmann's firm was closely associated with Pattison's and ceased trading, with liabilities of over £70,000. Benromach did not go into production until 1909.

It was sold in 1911 to a London company, closed from 1914 to 1919, then acquired by Alloa brewer John Joseph Calder, who immediately sold it to Benromach Distillery Ltd (a company owned by Macdonald, Greenlees & Williams, of Leith, and six English breweries).

It worked for a spell in the mid 1920s, but 'had been silent for years' by 1937, when it was bought by Associated Scottish Distillers (a company formed by the colourful Joseph Hobbs (see *Ben Nevis, Glenesk* etc.), and sold next year to National Distillers of America. They sold to D.C.L. in 1953, and Benromach was transferred to S.M.D.

Benromach was refurbished in 1966, when the stills were converted to indirect firing; the floor maltings were removed in 1968. It was mothballed in 1983, and the plant removed. Ten years later it was sold to Gordon & Macphail (see *Leading Independent Bottlers*), and carefully refurbished. All plant was replaced except a spirit receiver. The new distillery was opened by Prince Charles, Duke of Rothesay, on 14 October 1998; the visitor centre opened the following year.

CURIOSITIES: Benromach is the smallest working distillery on Speyside. It was formerly a much larger affair, but by the time Gordon & Macphail bought it, nothing remained of the former plant except one receiver tank. During the five years between purchase and opening, the new owners did many experimental distillations before settling on the style they wanted. After they had gone into production, the former owner, Diageo, offered them a box of new-make samples from pre-1993. The spirit character was almost identical, and yet the distillery had been rebuilt. The only constants were the location and the water ...

In 1925 it had a rare (perhaps unique) wooden mash tun.

When S.M.D. took over, it was remarked that Benromach had a particularly good external appearance, enhanced by gardens laid out by the buccaneering Joe Hobbs. A key feature today is its smart red brick chimney, contrasting nicely the whitewashed walls of the distillery.

EXPRESSIONS:

G. &. M.'s aim was to produce a light style of Speyside, which could be enjoyed young. The current range comprises three young whiskies from the revived distillery, and a range of older malts from the original distillery:

- Benromach Traditional 5YO @ 40% (introduced May 2004)
- Benromach Organic 8YO (certified by the Soil Association, filled into new American oak casks, introduced 2006)
- Benromach Peat Smoke 9YO @ 46% (introduced 2007)
- Benromach 18YO @ 40% (introduced 2002)
- Benromach 22YO Port Wood Finish @ 45% (introduced 2002)
- Benromach 21YO @ 43% (introduced 2004)
- Benromach 1980 Cask Strength @ 58.6% (introduced 2004)
- Benromach 25YO @ 43% (introduced 2004)
- Benromach Vintage 1968 @ 41.8% (limited edition, released 2004)
- Benromach Classic 55YO @ 42.4% (limited to 70 bottles, released 2005)
- Benromach Latitude 53° @ 53% (limited edition to celebrate the partnership with the Clipper 2007/8 Round the World Yacht Race, released 2007)

'With its high-pitched gables and mullioned windows in the Scots vernacular style of the seventeenth century, [it] surprised and delighted the eye.'
Brian Spiller

- Benromach Latitude 55° @ 55% (limited edition as above, released 2007)
- Benromach Latitude 57° @ 57% (limited edition as above, released 2008)

RAW MATERIALS: Malt from independent maltsters in Scotland, peated to around 10ppm phenols, with some experimental distillations at heavier and lighter peating. Process water from Chapelton Spring; cooling water from the Burn of Mosset, which rises on Romach Hill.

PLANT: Semi-Lauter mash tun (1.5 tonnes); four Scottish larch washbacks. One plain wash still (7,500 litres); one boil-ball spirit still (5,000 litres). Both indirect fired; both shell-and-tube condensers. Spirit safe from Millburn Distillery. External shell-and-tube condensers.

MATURATION: Mainly refill U.S. hogsheads, some refill European wood. Matured on site and in Elgin.

STYLE: Fruity, with body.

MATURE CHARACTER: Light Speyside in style, with more body than some. Fresh and fruity/floral on the nose; creamy to taste; sweet overall with some sweet cereal notes. Light- to medium-bodied.

Be

Ben Wyvis Dismantled

REGION
Highland (North)
ADDRESS
Invergordon, Ross &
Cromarty
LAST OWNER
Invergordon Distillers
CLOSED
1977

*Only two bottles
of the original Ben
Wyvis (and one half-
bottle), dating from
the 1890s, have
appeared at auction.*

HISTORICAL NOTES: There were two Ben Wyvis distilleries. The first was built in 1879 on the outskirts of Dingwall – some of the buildings still stand, converted into flats. In 1893, its name was changed to Ferintosh, and it closed in 1927, although the warehouses were in use until 1980.

The second Ben Wyvis was situated within Invergordon grain whisky distillery, nearby. This malt distillery was installed in 1965, with two stills and a capacity of 750,000 L.P.A. It was silent from 1977 and has now been dismantled.

CURIOSITIES: Ben Wyvis was the model for Tamnavulin Distillery, also built by Invergordon, in 1966.

EXPRESSIONS:
Four limited bottlings of Ben Wyvis 1972 (all 27YO @ 43%, 43%, 43.1% and 45.9%) were released; one 1968 (@ 32YO) and one 1965 (37YO @ 44%, 200 bottles, signed by Richard Paterson, Master Distiller)

B1

Bladnoch

REGION
Lowland

ADDRESS
Bladnoch, Wigtown,
Wigtownshire

PHONE
01988 402235

WEBSITE
www.bladnoch.co.uk

OWNER
Co-ordinated Development
Services Ltd

VISITORS
Yes

CAPACITY
1m L.P.A.

HISTORICAL NOTES: Bladnoch was established as a farm distillery by the brothers Thomas and John McClelland in 1817, and operated by John's son, Charlie, until 1905 when production ceased. It was sold to the Irish distillers, Dunville & Company in 1911, and between that date and 1937 (when Dunville went into liquidation) it operated only intermittently. It was bought by Ross & Coulter of Glasgow, who dismantled it in 1941, sold the stock (89,000 gallons of whisky) at below its value – which led to the Inland Revenue imposing 100% 'excess profits tax' – and sold the plant to Sweden (one still is now in a museum). The distillery buildings went to A.B. Grant. Trading as Bladnoch Distillery Company, he installed two new stills in 1956 and sold to McGowan and Cameron, whisky blenders in Glasgow, ten years later, who doubled the distillery's capacity (to four stills).

Inver House owned the distillery for ten years until 1983, then sold it to Arthur Bell & Sons, so it became part of Guinness in 1985, and of U.D. in 1987. They reduced capacity in 1986 by disconnecting a pair of stills, then closed and decommissioned it altogether in June 1993. The local authority continued to manage some of the buildings as a 'heritage centre'.

This should have been the end of the road for Bladnoch. However, in 1994 it was bought by a developer from Banbridge, Northern Ireland, a family company directed by Raymond Armstrong, his brother Colin and their wives. The original plan was to develop the site as holiday cottages, but the new owners quickly realised what an important role the distillery had played in the local economy. Also, the distillery visitor centre was successful, yet without a distillery it would soon become pointless. U.D. had sold Bladnoch on the understanding that it would never be brought back into production, but they were prepared to waive this (to a degree) and help the new owner bring the distillery alive again. Bladnoch went back into production in December 2000.

CURIOSITIES: Wigtown is on the Solway Firth, at the southern extremity of Scotland, and Bladnoch is the most southerly of Scottish distilleries, well off the beaten track – although the district once boasted 11 distilleries. It describes its make as 'The Spirit of the Lowlands'.

In 1792 a schooner was arrested on the Solway Firth for smuggling contraband. Among the Excise officers involved was Robert Burns.

Bladnoch Distillery plays a crucial and integral role in the local community, welcoming around 25,000 visitors a year. As well as the usual shop and tours, the distillery hosts weddings, birthday parties, concerts, film evenings, book events (Wigtown is 'Scotland's Book Town') and an annual flower show, and sponsors numerous small-scale local charitable events. A camping/caravan site is available.

The Bladnoch Forum is an international group with a broad discussion forum. Members are able to buy casks, and annual bottlings at cask strength from other distilleries are made available to members at bargain prices. From time to time the distillery runs 'whisky schools'.

EXPRESSIONS:

Bladnoch was bottled by Bell's at 8YO, and by U.D. in their Flora & Fauna series at 12YO. Currently, the distillery bottles by hand in small batches and from single casks.

- Bladnoch 14–16YO @ 40–46% (introduced 2003)
- Bladnoch 15YO @ 55% min. (released 2003)
- Bladnoch 16YO @ 55% min. (Sheep label, from hogsheads, released 2004)
- Bladnoch 13YO (now 15YO) @ 55% min. (Belted Galloway label, bourbon barrels, released 2004)

RAW MATERIALS: Process and cooling water (soft and peaty) from the River Bladnoch. Mainly unpeated malt from independent maltsters. Very occasional medium-peated (18ppm phenols) malt, usually once a year.

PLANT: Semi-Lauter stainless steel mash tun (five tonnes). Six Oregon pine washbacks. One boil-ball wash still (13,500 litres charge), one boil-ball spirit still (10,000 litres charge) with sight glasses (it was once a wash still). Indirect fired by steam. Shell-and-tube condensers.

MATURATION: Thirteen dunnage-style warehouses on site. 80% first-fill bourbon barrels (4 Roses and Heaven Hill), sherry butts and hogsheads, and occasional ex-wine casks. Unusually high levels of evaporation.

STYLE: Sweet, grassy, malty, mellow.

MATURE CHARACTER: Pastoral and floral; reminiscent of hedgerows, with lemony/citric notes and some cereal. The taste echoes this. The overall impression is light and appetising. Short finish.

Blair Athol

REGION
Highland (South)
ADDRESS
Perth Road, Pitlochry
PHONE
01796 482003
WEBSITE
www.malts.com
OWNER
Diageo plc
VISITORS
Visitor centre built 1982
CAPACITY
2.3m L.P.A.

HISTORICAL NOTES: Adjacent to the distillery's rustic stone buildings, some thickly clad in Virginia creeper, flows the Allt Dour ('burn of the otter'), and this stream gave its name to the first distillery on the site, Aldour, founded in 1798. The name was changed to Blair Athol in 1825 when it was rebuilt and expanded.

In 1882 the distillery was bought and extended again by the Edinburgh blenders, Peter Mackenzie & Company (who later founded Dufftown Distillery). It was mothballed between 1932 and 1949, then tastefully restored by Arthur Bell & Sons, who had bought P. Mackenzie & Company in 1933. Professor McDowell described it in the 1960s as 'almost a model distillery'.

Bell's first refurbishment in 1949 cost £75,000; in 1970 they doubled the distillery's capacity, expanding from two to four stills and took out the floor maltings. Bell's Extra Special blended Scotch was by now the bestselling brand in the U.K.; the output of Bell's three distilleries quintupled between 1960 and 1970.

But Arthur Bell & Sons fell victim to its own success. In 1985 it was subject to a hostile take-over by Guinness plc and soon after it became part of U.D. (now Diageo).

CURIOSITIES: After the Battle of Culloden a local laird, Robertson of Faskally, who had been a captain in the Jacobite army, returned to his own country with a price on his head. He hid in Allt Dour farmhouse, then escaped down the Allt Dour Burn and sheltered in an old oak tree near the distillery until the red coats had passed on. Then he escaped to France.

With the acquisition of Blair Athol in 1933, via Peter Mackenzie & Company, Arthur Bell & Sons moved from being a small local blender to being a medium-sized distiller with the potential to become a major player.

Blair Athol is the heart-malt for the Bell's blends.

EXPRESSIONS:
Not common, since required for Bell's. Blair Athol 12YO was released in the Flora & Fauna series in 1991 (decorated, appropriately, with an otter) since 1991; a 27YO (1975 @ 54.7%) was released as a Rare Malt in 2003.

RAW MATERIALS: Floor maltings until 1960s; now unpeated malt from Glen Ord. Water from the Allt Dour, which rises as a spring in the heights of Ben Vrackie ('the speckled hill'), above the snow line.

PLANT: Semi-Lauter mash tun (eight tonnes). Four stainless steel washbacks; four Oregon pine washbacks (these came from Mortlach in the 1980s). Two plain wash stills (13,000 litres charge), two plain spirit stills (11,500 litres charge). Shell-and-tube condensers, run hot, with after-coolers.

MATURATION: Mainly ex-bourbon refills, some ex-sherry casks used in the proprietary single malt bottlings. Mainly matured in the Central Belt.

STYLE: Rich, nutty-spicy and cereal-like.

MATURE CHARACTER: Nutty and caramel-like on the nose, with rich maltiness, traces of leather and tobacco. A rich whisky, it takes European oak maturation well, adding to richness, with fruit cake, traces of wine and some sulphury notes. A curious mix of sweet and dry to taste, and not as long in the finish as the nose suggests. Medium-bodied.

Bowmore

Bo

REGION
Islay

ADDRESS
School Street, Bowmore,
Isle of Islay, Argyll

PHONE
01496 810441

WEBSITE
www.bowmore.com

OWNER
Morrison Bowmore
Distillers (Suntory)

VISITORS
New visitor centre opened
2007, cottages available
for let

CAPACITY
2.2m L.P.A.

HISTORICAL NOTES: Bowmore is the oldest distillery on Islay, and one of the oldest in Scotland. The usual date ascribed to its foundation is 1779, but the distillery may have been established a decade before this, when the model village of Bowmore was established by Daniel Campbell of Shawfield. David Simpson was brought over from Bridgend to build the distillery and was succeeded by his relation Hector Simpson. Hector sold to James and William Mutter, Glasgow merchants of German extraction, in 1837. They expanded the distillery and their sons retained ownership until 1892.

Ownership changed hands several times between then and 1925 when the distillery was purchased by a Skye man, Duncan MacLeod, trading as J.B. Sherriff & Company. (They had owned the distillery briefly, before going into liquidation in 1920, and had also owned Lochhead Distillery in Campbeltown and Port Charlotte Distillery, Islay.) Sherriff's sold to William Grigor & Son of Inverness, who had rebuilt Glen Albyn Distillery there in 1884.

During World War II the distillery was requisitioned by the Air Ministry to support Coastal Command's efforts to protect Atlantic convoys.

In 1963, the Glasgow whisky broker, Stanley P. Morrison, bought Bowmore for £117,000 and began modernising and expanding the site, including an innovative waste-heat recovery system, which was estimated to save just over £100,000 per annum at the time it was installed in 1983. Hot water from the condensers pre-heated the wash, heated the malt kiln and warmed the water for the local public swimming pool, located within a former bonded warehouse, donated to the community by Morrison Bowmore in 1983.

Suntory bought a 35% stake in the company in 1989 and whole ownership in 1994.

Bowmore whiskies are highly collectable. A bottle engraved 'W. & J. Mutter 1890' achieved £13,000 in 2001; another 'Mutter' bottle, allegedly from 1851, was bought for £25,000 in 2007.

CURIOSITIES: Bowmore is one of the few distilleries to retain its own floor maltings, producing around 30% of its malt requirement. It was one of the first distilleries to install shell-and-tube condensers, in 1886.

The whisky made here has long had a high reputation. As early as 1841, Walter Frederick Campbell of Islay, the laird, received an order from Windsor Castle to supply 'a cask of your best Islay Mountain Dew' for the Royal Household – cask size and price of no concern, 'but the very best that can be had'. The order was renewed two years later. The Mutter brothers owned a steamship to carry casks up to Glasgow, where they were bonded beneath the arches of Central Station.

The three bottlings of the legendary Black Bowmore, distilled in 1964, have achieved up to £1,600: the recommended retail price at the time of release was £100.

EXPRESSIONS:
Bowmore's range is among the largest on the market. Limited expressions that have been released recently are:
• Bowmore 1989 16YO @ 53.8% (bourbon cask, released 2005)
• Bowmore 1968 37YO @ 43.4% (released 2006)
• Bowmore 1990 16YO @ 53.8% (sherry-wood, released 2006)
• Bowmore 1991 16YO @ 53.1% (port-wood, released 2007)

The core range comprises:	Core range duty-free comprises:
• Bowmore Legend @ 40%	• Bowmore Surf @ 40%
• Bowmore 12YO @ 40%	• Bowmore Enigma @ 40%
• Bowmore 15YO @ 43%	• Bowmore Mariner @ 43%
• Bowmore 18YO @ 43%	• Bowmore Cask Strength @ 56%

RAW MATERIALS: Soft peaty water from River Laggan, seven miles from the distillery, for process and cooling. Three malting floors produce 30% of the malt requirement; the remainder comes from Simpson's of Berwick, peated to 25ppm phenols. 100% Scottish malt.

PLANT: Stainless steel semi-Lauter mash tun, with copper cover (eight tonnes). Old riveted 'coppers' to charge the mash tun. Six Douglas fir washbacks. Stainless steel wash charger, to free up a washback (for five to six hours) prior to charging the wash still. Two plain wash stills (20,000 litres charge each). Two plain spirit stills, with sight glasses (14,637 litres charge each). All indirect fired. External shell-and-tube condensers run very hot to provide the heat recovery system referred to above. Internal after-coolers to complete condensation.

MATURATION: Mix of first-fill American barrels and hogsheads, first-fill sherry butts and puncheons. Each expression has its own mix of cask-types. A three-floor dunnage warehouse on site, incorporating the ancient Bowmore Vaults on its ground floor, lies partly below sea level, and two warehouses (one dunnage, one racked) are on the Low Road outside Bowmore village. 27,000 casks in total.

STYLE: Smoky and floral.

MATURE CHARACTER: In a blind tasting, my identifier for Bowmore is 'lavender'. The character varies a lot, depending on cask selection (which varies from expression to expression). Behind the lavender/air-freshener note, it is sweet, rich, fruity (a combination of exotic fruits like mango, passionfruit and dried fruits), malty and scented – smoky on the nose. A good texture; sweet taste with a belt of smoke (especially in the younger expressions), and still this lingering perfume. Medium-bodied.

Braeval

REGION
Speyside
ADDRESS
Chapeltown, Ballindalloch,
Moray
PHONE
01542 783342
WEBSITE
No
OWNER
Chivas Brothers
VISITORS
No
CAPACITY
4m L.P.A.

HISTORICAL NOTES: At one time, 36 distilleries attached the suffix 'Glenlivet' – for example, Macallan-Glenlivet, Aberlour-Glenlivet – although there are only three distilleries in the glen of that name: The Glenlivet itself, Tamnavulin and Braeval.

Braeval is the highest distillery in Scotland.

Originally named Braes of Glenlivet, it was built by Seagram's in 1973 to produce fillings for the Chivas blends. Like its sister, Allt-a-Bhainne, it is attractively laid out – uncompromisingly modern, but with traditional elements such as a pagoda roof. It is highly automated and can be run by one person. To start with, it had three stills, each with a distinctive bulge in the neck known as a 'Milton Ball'; two more were added in 1975 and a further one in 1978. There are no warehouses on site, all the make being tankered to Keith Bond for filling into casks, then to other sites for maturation; pot ale used to go to The Glenlivet Distillery to be evaporated into pot ale syrup, and draff is sold to merchants.

Pernod Ricard bought Seagram's in 2001 and Braeval was mothballed the following year. It re-opened in July 2008.

CURIOSITIES: The district in which the distillery stands is known as Eskemulloch (which literally means 'headwater'). It is a mile north of the old Roman Catholic seminary of Scalan, one of the very few places in Scotland where priests could be trained after the Reformation. It was established by the (Catholic) owner of the glen, the Duke of Gordon, in 1717, but was destroyed by Hanoverian troops in 1746.

The Ladder Hills, from where Braeval draws its water, is crossed by the Whisky Road, used by smugglers in days gone by to carry their wares out of Glenlivet and down to the Lowlands.

Braeval is the highest distillery in Scotland.

Never bottled by its owner.

RAW MATERIALS: Unpeated malt from independent maltsters. Water from the Preenie and Kate's Well Burns and the burn at Ladderfoot (once popular with smugglers).

PLANT: Traditional rake-and-plough mash tun with copper canopy (nine tonnes); 15 stainless steel washbacks. Two plain and stocky wash stills (22,000 litres each). Two boil-pot spirit stills (7,500 litres) – one run from the wash still charges two spirit stills. All indirect fired by steam. Shell-and-tube condensers.

MATURATION: Mainly refill U.S. hogsheads, all at Mulben, near Keith.

STYLE: Sweet and grassy.

MATURE CHARACTER: Most of the independent bottlings of Braeval have come from ex-sherry butts, which cover the distillery character. The nose is sweet, with fruit cake, chocolate and sherry; the taste rich and full, with spicy notes.

Bottlings from ex-bourbon refills, which retain the distillery character, are lighter and drier, with Speyside character and a sweet, fresh-fruity flavour. Medium-bodied.

Brora Dismantled

REGION
Highland (North)

ADDRESS
Brora, Sutherland

LAST OWNER
D.C.L./S.M.D.

CLOSED
1983

HISTORICAL NOTES: For most of its life Brora Distillery was called Clynelish, but in 1967 a new distillery was built next door and given the same name. The original was mothballed for a year, then resumed production as Clynelish No. 2 until 1975 when it was renamed Brora. It was closed in May 1983 and most of its plant removed. The elegant old buildings still stand and the warehouses are used by Clynelish.

Clynelish/Brora was founded in 1819 by the Marquess of Stafford (later first Duke of Sutherland) as part of his plan to 'improve' his wife's vast northern estates – a plan which also required the clearing of some 15,000 tenants from the land to make way for sheep. Some of those cleared were moved to new coastal townships like Brora.

For the first 70 years of its existence the distillery struggled. Several of its licensees filed for bankruptcy. Then, in 1896, it was acquired and rebuilt by James Ainslie & Company, blenders in Glasgow, in partnership with John Risk (owner of Bankier Distillery, near Falkirk); in 1912 the latter acquired complete ownership, in partnership with D.C.L. and (after 1916) with John Walker & Sons. Risk was bought out in 1925, when Walkers (and Clynelish/Brora) amalgamated with D.C.L.

While Caol Ila Distillery was being rebuilt (1972–74), and for three years thereafter, Brora produced a heavily peated whisky.

By the early 1980s, Clynelish/Brora needed much work, and its owners resolved to build a new distillery on the site. (See *Clynelish*.) The buildings, stills, receiver and worm tubs are still in situ.

CURIOSITIES: The great Victorian connoisseur, Professor George Saintsbury, author of *Notes from a Cellar Book*, wrote highly of Brora/Clynelish.

EXPRESSIONS:

Brora's high reputation encouraged Diageo to issue several versions in its Rare Malts series, from 1972, 1975, 1977 and 1982. Since 2002 there have been annual releases at 30YO returned strength.

Bruichladdich

REGION
Islay
ADDRESS
Bruichladdich, Isle of Islay,
Argyll
PHONE
01496 850 221
WEBSITE
www.bruichladdich.com
OWNER
Bruichladdich Distillery
Company Ltd
VISITORS
Visitor centre, café, shop
and whisky school
CAPACITY
1.5m L.P.A.

HISTORICAL NOTES: Bruichladdich (pronounced Brewickladdie) has enjoyed a renaissance since 2000, when it was bought by a private concern led by Mark Reynier, a wine merchant in London, with the support of local investors. During the previous decade the distillery had operated only part-time (with periods of complete closure) under the ownership of Whyte & Mackay (J.B.B. Greater Europe), who had acquired it when they took over Invergordon Distillers in 1993.

Bruichladdich was purpose-built from scratch in 1881 by the Harvey brothers (owners of Dundashill and Yoker distilleries in Glasgow) using the then new material, concrete, to bind beach pebbles. When William Harvey died in 1937, the distillery was sold to the buccaneering Joseph Hobbs, who ran it through his company Associated Scottish Distillers (A.S.D.) until it was sold in 1952 to Ross & Coulter, whisky brokers in Glasgow and owners of Bladnoch Distillery, for £205,000 (the value of the stock). R&C had previously sold Fettercairn Distillery to A.S.D. The firm was absorbed by D.C.L. in 1954 and wound up in 1960, when Bruichladdich was sold to A.B. Grant & Co, who had bought Bladnoch from R&C in 1956. They sold the distillery to Invergordon in 1968.

CURIOSITIES: One of only three distilleries to bottle on site; only belt-driven mill in existence; cast iron mash tun; one riveted still; Victorian décor preserved where possible. As the distillery's Wikipedia entry remarks: 'It is, you might say, a museum of a distillery that is still in operation.' It is quirky and proudly independent.

James McEwan, Bruichladdich's Director of Production, is a legend in the whisky trade. He was trained as a cooper from 1963 at Bowmore Distillery and ran the warehouses there until 1977 when he moved to Glasgow to spend the next seven years as a blender. He returned to Bowmore as Distillery Manager in 1984 and was soon spending much of his time travelling the world, conducting talks and

At 80ppm phenols, Octomore is the most heavily peated spirit in the world!

tastings, spreading the whisky gospel, and that of Islay and Scotland. He was persuaded to join the team that took over Bruichladdich in 2000.

Bruichladdich became the focus of an intelligence operation by the (American) Defense Threat Reduction Agency who believed its distilling equipment could also be used to make chemical weapons. The distillery owners learned of this when a helpful American agent informed them that the webcams in the stillhouse, which she was using to monitor the facility, had broken down! Typically, Bruichladdich issued a limited run of commemorative bottles in her honour!

As well as the traditional style of very lightly peated malt, Bruichladdich also produces heavily peated whiskies, including Octomore and Port Charlotte. In 2006 it also produced the strongest malt whisky ever made (at least in modern times), triple-distilled Trestarig and quadruple-distilled Usquebaugh-baul, from an account by Martin Martin's *Description of the Western Isles* (1703). The latter translates as 'perilous whisky' and was filled into cask at 88% vol.

Plans to build a separate distillery nearby, a revival of the old Port Charlotte Distillery (closed 1929), are well-advanced. The new distillery will employ stills from the dismantled Inverleven Distillery and should be in operation in 2009, if all goes according to plan.

EXPRESSIONS:

Until the current owners took over, Bruichladdich was bottled at 10YO; since then a bewildering number of limited edition bottlings (over 200!) have been released. A small amount of make is set aside each year for sale by the cask.

- The current core range is:
- Bruichladdich 12YO @ 46%
- Bruichladdich 15YO @ 46%
- Bruichladdich 18YO @ 46%
- Bruichladdich 20YO @ 46%
- Bruichladdich Rocks @ 46% (multi-vintage, lightly peated c. 3ppm phenols)

- Bruichladdich Waves @ 46% (multi-vintage, medium peated *c.* 15ppm phenols)
- Bruichladdich Peat @ 46% (multi-vintage, heavily peated *c.* 35ppm phenols)
- Bruichladdich Valinch Series (bottled by hand, only available at the distillery; single casks, at cask strength, from 1970, 1983, 1986, 1988, 1990)
- Bruichladdich Legacy Series @ CS (32, 33, 34, 35, 36 and 37YO)
- Bruichladdich Links Series @ 46% (a range of bottlings featuring Scottish golf courses, launched 2003)
- Port Charlotte PC5 @ 63.5% (heavily peated, distilled 2001, bottled 2006)
- Port Charlotte PC6 @ 61.6% (heavily peated, distilled 2001, bottled 2007)

RAW MATERIALS: Bruichladdich reservoir for process water (soft and acidic/peaty), Bruichladdich burn for the cooling water and James Brown's spring (clear water) at Octomore for reduction water. Floor maltings closed 1961; then malt from Port Ellen; now malt from mainland maltings.

PLANT: Cast iron rake-and-plough mash tun (6.2 tonnes). Six Oregon pine washbacks. Two tall plain wash stills (charge 12,000 litres each). Two tall plain spirit stills (charge 7,100 litres each). All indirect fired by steam. Shell-and-tube condensers.

MATURATION: 25% in first-fill and refill ex-sherry hogsheads, 65% in first-fill bourbon barrels, and other types of casks (rum and wine). Eight bonded warehouses on site and another four at Port Charlotte. Most are dunnage, with two racked; 35,000 casks in total.

Bottling Hall named after the Harvey brothers, opened May 2003. Cooperage opened May 2004.

STYLE: Malty, with peaty variations.

MATURE CHARACTER: 'Traditional' (i.e. unpeated) Bruichladdich is fresh, grassy and malty on the nose, with fragments of wild flower notes. The taste is sweet to start, with cereal and citric notes; dry and short in the finish. Light-bodied.

Bunnahabhain

REGION
Islay

ADDRESS
Near Port Askaig, Islay,
Argyll

PHONE
01496 840646

WEBSITE
www.bunnahabhain.com

OWNER
Burn Stewart Distillers (CL
World Brands)

VISITORS
Welcome. Holiday
cottages

CAPACITY
2.5m L.P.A.

HISTORICAL NOTES: William Robertson of Robertson & Baxter, whisky blenders and brokers in Glasgow, founded Bunnahabhain Distillery in 1881, in partnership with the Greenlees Brothers from Campbeltown (owners of the very successful Lorne, Old Parr and Claymore blends, and of Hazelburn Distillery) and with the name Islay Distillers Company Ltd. This became the Highland Distilleries Company Ltd in 1887, when it merged with Glenrothes-Glenlivet.

The distillery's situation is among the most remote in Scotland, and building here was not without its difficulties: two large boilers were blown off the beach, where they waited to be fitted, during the first winter of building. The decision to build here was on account of Robertson & Baxter's close relationship with Bulloch Lade & Company, who were rebuilding Caol Ila at the time, just up the road, and also because of the copious water from Loch Staoinsha and good sea access. As well as the distillery itself, a pier and a mile-long road up a cliff had to be built to connect the place to the nearest track. The spirit first flowed in January 1883.

The original distillery had one pair of stills. This was doubled in 1963, at which time the floor maltings were removed. Although its capacity was reported to be 3.4 million litres per annum in 1987, it had been closed from 1982 to 2004, and production was down to 750,000 litres by 2002.

Highland Distilleries changed its name to Highland Distillers in 1998 and then took the name of its parent company, The Edrington Group, in 1999. Somewhat surprisingly, the company sold Bunnahabhain to Burn Stewart Distillers in April 2003 for £10 million.

CURIOSITIES: Bruichladdich was built and Caol Ila rebuilt at the same time as Bunnahabhain, using the novel material, cement, but the builders of the latter opted for traditional stone, quarried locally. As well as the distillery itself, a mile-long road had

Over 250 ships have foundered off the coast of Islay, four of them within sight of Bunnahabhain.

to be constructed up the steep cliff to join the track to Port Askaig, a pier built out into the fast flowing waters of the Sound of Islay, and houses erected for the workforce. The total cost was estimated at £30,000.

When completed, the distillery was much admired. Alfred Barnard, who visited five years after it opened described it as ... fine pile of buildings in the form of a square and quite enclosed. Entering by the noble gateway one forms an immediate sense of the compactness and symmetrical construction of the work'. The appearance is little altered today.

Bunnahabhain is Islay's most remote and most northerly distillery. Its make is often described as the mildest Islay malt. This light style was adopted to provide whisky for blending, especially for Cutty Sark and Black Bottle (the latter was also sold to Burn Stewart).

Bunnahabhain is traditionally lightly peated (2–3ppm phenols), but trials with heavily peated malt (35–40ppm) were conducted in 1997, and under Burn Stewart's ownership, a batch of smoky Bunnahabhain has been produced. The first, called Moine (Gaelic for 'peat'), was offered for sale at 6YO during the Islay Festival 2004.

Since it was first bottled as a single in the late 1970s, Bunnahabhain labels have been illustrated with a sailor behind a ship's wheel and the motto 'Westering Home'. The words come from the well-known Scots song:

Westering Home, with a song in the air,
Light in the eye and it's goodbye to care;
Laughter o' love and a welcoming there,
Isle of my heart my own one.

EXPRESSIONS:
First released by its owners in the late 1970s @ 12YO.
Core range:
- Bunnahabhain 12YO @ 40%
- Bunnahabhain 18YO @ 43%
- Bunnahabhain 25YO @ 43%

RAW MATERIALS: Very slightly peated and unusually hard process water from a spring in the Margadale Hills, piped from source so as to keep peat content down. Cooling water from Loch Staoinsha. 10% of malt from Port Ellen Maltings, the rest from Simpson's of Berwick. A portion peated to around 38ppm phenols; the majority unpeated.

PLANT: Large stainless steel rake-and-plough mash tun (12.5–13 tonnes). Six Oregon pine washbacks. Two plain pear-shaped wash stills (charge 16,625 litres each) and two plain onion-shaped spirit stills (charge 9,000–9,600 litres each). All indirect fired by steam. Shell-and-tube condensers.

MATURATION: Mainly refill ex-bourbon hogsheads, with a percentage of 10% first- and second-fill sherry casks. Six dunnage and one racked warehouses on site; approximately 21,000 casks in total. All matured on site.

STYLE: Sweet and fruity, with a smoky batch each year, at 35–40ppm phenols (trialled in 1997; resumed 2003).

MATURE CHARACTER: 'Traditional' Bunnahabhain (i.e. unpeated) is sweet, lightly fruity and faintly maritime on the nose, sometimes with a whiff of peat smoke. The mouth feel is smooth, the taste mild, lightly sweet, then drying, with a hint of smoke. Light- to medium-bodied.

Caledonian Grain Distillery (Redeveloped)

ADDRESS
Haymarket, Edinburgh
LAST OWNER
D.C.L./S.G.D.
CAPACITY
Unknown
CLOSED
1988

Caledonian was capable of producing as much spirit in a day as a small malt distillery produces in a year.

HISTORICAL NOTES: The Caledonian Distillery – for a year it was known as The Edinburgh Distillery – was built in 1855 by Graham Menzies & Company (owners of Sunbury Distillery in Edinburgh, which closed when Caledonian went into full production), near Haymarket railway station. Now only minutes from the centre of the town, in the 1850s it was beyond the city boundary, but it was close to both the Caledonian and the Edinburgh and Glasgow Railways (both of which ran sidings to the distillery. It is believed that it was one of the first distilleries to take advantage of rail access). Process water came from the city mains supply and cooling water from the nearby Forth and Clyde Canal. It was described as 'the model distillery of Europe'.

Caledonian joined the first Lowland distillers' 'Trade Arrangement' the following year (see *Carsebridge*). This allocated the trade between six distillers, in order to control prices; of the six, Menzies & Company had the largest stock of whisky and were allocated 41.5% of the trade (the next largest was John Bald of Carsebridge, with 15%). However, Graham Menzies held back from joining the nascent D.C.L.: his son had just become a partner in the family business and wanted to retain family ownership. They joined Distillers in 1884.

In common with other grain distilleries, Caledonian operated both pot and patent stills. In the mid 1880s it had three large pot stills (two of which were used for producing 'Irish' whiskey. They were removed about 1900); its Coffey still was the largest in Europe.

In 1966 the distillery came under the ownership of D.C.L. production subsidiary, Scottish Grain Distillers (S.G.D.). Nearly 400 people were employed at that time. The distillery was closed in 1988, the site being sold and partially demolished in 1997. The remaining buildings – 'externally little changed from the 1880s' (Morrice) – were restored and have been converted into flats.

Caledonian was the largest distillery in the world for many years – certainly between 1897 and 1930.

CURIOSITIES: *Old and New Edinburgh* by James Grant (1882): 'The Caledonian Distillery contains the greatest still in Scotland. In order to meet the growing demand for the variety of whisky known as "Irish" the proprietors of Caledonian distillery about 1867 fitted up two large stills of an old pattern, with which they manufacture whisky precisely similar to that which is made in Dublin.'

William Dudgeon Graham Menzies (1857–1943) became Chairman of D.C.L. in 1897, at the same time as the legendary W.H. Ross became General Manager and Secretary. They made a formidable team, and Menzies served for 28 years, handing over chairmanship to Ross in 1925, but remaining on the board for a further 20 years. 'Together Menzies and Ross built D.C.L.' (Charles Craig). He left a personal fortune of £1.4 million.

'Caledonian has always been a one Coffey-still operation, but with a wash pipe diameter of 4⅜th inches and a height of 45 feet, it produces 4,000 litres of alcohol an hour.' (Morrice)

EXPRESSIONS:
Never bottled as a single by its owner, except in 1986 to commemorate the Commonwealth Games being held in Edinburgh.

Cambus Grain Distillery (Dismantled)

ADDRESS
Tullibody, by Alloa,
Clackmannanshire
LAST OWNER
United Distilleries
CAPACITY
20m L.P.A.
CLOSED
1993

HISTORICAL NOTES: Alloa has been a centre of brewing and distilling, glass-making and textiles for over 200 years. Cambus Distillery was built in 1806 by John Moubray, on the banks of the River Devon close to where it joins the Forth. The name comes from Gaelic *camas*, for a creek or small bay, and the site had formerly been a flour mill.

John was succeeded by his son and grandson; pot stills were abandoned in favour of Stein stills in 1826, to be replaced by Coffey stills in 1851. The grandson, Robert Moubray, took Cambus into D.C.L. on its foundation in 1877 (see *Cameronbridge*, *Carsebridge*), and expanded the distillery in 1882 by the acquisition of the Cambus Old Brewery. Alas, most of the buildings were destroyed by fire in September 1914, and for the next 24 years it functioned only as a bonded warehouse and as a maltings for Carsebridge Distillery nearby.

The ruins of the original structure were demolished, except for a small part of the stillhouse, which was incorporated within a new building in 1937. Production was immediately interrupted by the outbreak of World War II, but resumed in 1945. In 1964 the first by-products recovery plant at any grain whisky distillery was installed at Cambus, converted to a dark-grains plant in 1982.

It was closed by U.D. in 1993; the plant has been removed and the buildings are used for cask filling and maturation.

CURIOSITIES: In 1905 an English court ruled that 'whisky', whether malt, grain or blended, must be made in a pot still. At appeal the next year, the court was equally divided. On the day this result was announced, 25 June 1906, D.C.L. cheekily launched an advertising campaign for 'Cambus: A Brand of Pure Patent Still Whisky. Not a headache in a gallon'! The 'What is Whisky?' question was only settled by the appointment of a Royal Commission in 1908, which found that patent still spirit could also be called whisky.

A former Excise
man at the distillery,
Philip Snowden,
became Chancellor
of the Exchequer
in the first Labour
government of 1947.

The distillery had its own train for taking in cereals
and a yeast house for making 'German' yeast. Casks
came in and went out by sea from the distillery's
own dock. A CO_2 processing plant was built in 1953,
a draff drying plant in 1964 and a dark-grains plant
in 1982. In 1952 a rectification plant was installed at
Cambus to make gin and augment D.C.L.'s production
from Wandsworth Distillery. This was an indication
of things to come. Today, around 70% of U.K. gin
is made in Scotland, mainly at Cameronbridge
Distillery.

Cambus drew water from three sources: process
water from the Lossburn Reservoir, deep in the Ochil
Hills which rise steeply behind the distillery, cooling
water from the River Devon and reduction water
from Loch Turret.

In 1957/58 the Forth Brewery next door was
converted to patent-still whisky production. During
its first two years of existence it produced patent-
still malt whisky, but then went over to making
grain whisky. It was bought by D.C.L. in 1982 and
demolished to make way for the dark-grains plant.

EXPRESSIONS:
Cambus has been bottled by its owners on at least three
occasions: 13yo @ 63.6%, 15yo @ 63% and no age @ 40%;
the last in the early 1990s by U.D.

Cameronbridge Grain Distillery

ADDRESS
Windygates, Leven, Fife
PHONE
01333 350377
OWNER
Diageo plc
CAPACITY
70m L.P.A. grain whisky;
30m L.P.A. grain neutral
spirit

HISTORICAL NOTES: Cameronbridge is the oldest grain whisky distillery, and the largest. It was also the first distillery in Scotland to produce grain whisky in column stills – prior to this many Lowland distilleries made grain spirit in pot stills.

It was founded in 1824 by John Haig. According to family tradition, in 1822 (aged 20), he was riding with an 'old servant' past the site of the Cameron Mills on the River Leven by Windygates in Fife. For two centuries this mill had enjoyed 'thirled' privileges (local tenants were obliged to have their corn ground there). John turned to the old retainer and said: 'D'ye ken Sandy. There is money to be made here – aye from whisky.'

He leased the land from its owner, his friend Captain Wemyss, the lease being taken in his father's name since he was a minor, and Cameron Bridge Distillery was licensed in October 1824.

He installed one of the first Stein stills within a year of its invention (by his cousin, Robert Stein, in 1828), paying the Steins 1d per gallon royalty, to make 'malt aqua'. Two years later he switched to the more efficient Coffey still. This led to a glut of grain whisky, and as early as the mid 1830s Haig was trying to interest the Eastern Lowland distillers in a scheme to regulate prices.

This came to fruition in the 1865 with the foundation of the Scotch Distillers Association, a trade agreement between eight grain distilleries to divide up the market according to their production capacity, and to fix prices and conditions of sale. This was the forerunner of D.C.L., established in April 1877 as a combination of grain whisky distillers (Port Dundas, Carsebridge, Cameronbridge, Glenochil, Cambus and Kirkliston) which together controlled 75% of grain whisky production. The nominal capital was £2 million, and its stated purpose was 'to secure the benefits of combined experience and the advantage (which manufacturing and trading on a large scale alone can command) of reduced expenses and increased profits'. John's son, Hugh Veitch Haig,

In August 1877 the River Leven burst its banks and the distillery was 'completely surrounded by water, and a rapid stream ran through the centre court, drowning out the boiler fires ... The main entrance gate gave way under pressure ... and with its demolition empty casks rolled away on the turbulent surface of the waters ... Much difficulty was experienced in saving the lives of horses and pigs.'

took over the management of Cameronbridge on his father's death in 1878.

Cameronbridge was expanded in 1903 when Drumcaldie malt distillery, nearby, was bought by D.C.L. and absorbed. Until the 1920s it had a combination of Coffey, Stein and pot stills: the last two were removed by 1930.

In 1989 the distillation of Gordon's, Booth's and Tanqueray London Dry Gins was transferred to Cameronbridge from Wandsworth. Today, around 70% of U.K. gin is made in Scotland, mainly at Cameronbridge.

In 2007 Diageo allocated £40 million to expanding the site. This phased development will include a new tun room, new fermenters, three new mash tuns and an effluent treatment plant, which will supply energy (methane) to run the plant.

CURIOSITIES: An earlier distillery at Cameronbridge had been worked by John Edington and Robert Haig from about 1813 to 1817. John himself had been born in Cameron House in 1802.

John Haig was a scion of the great Haig distilling dynasty. His father was William Haig, licensee (after 1795) of Kincaple Distillery, close to Saint Andrews, and founder (in 1810) of Seggie Distillery at Guardbridge – also Lord Provost of Saint Andrews for twelve years. Young John attended Saint Andrews University, where he won a silver medal for mathematics, and then served an apprenticeship at Seggie Distillery.

All his uncles were distillers: James (1755–1833) at Canonmills, and later Lochrin, Edinburgh – the spokesman for the whisky industry from the 1790s; John (1758–1819) at Bonnington Distillery, Edinburgh; George (1760–74) who had an interest in Inverkeithing Distillery; Robert (1764–1834) founded Dodderbank in Dublin, and later took over Seggie, and Andrew (1769–1824) who took over Kilbagie Distillery at Alloa.

When Alfred Barnard visited Cameronbridge in the 1880s he found 'two Coffey's patent stills, handsome machines with their cooper tubes brilliantly polished

... two of Stein's Patent Steam Stills ... an old Pot Still.' He concluded: 'The whisky made here is said to have no rival in the world. There are several kinds manufactured. First "Grain Whisky", second "Pot Still Irish", third "Silent Malt" and fourth "Flavoured Malt".'

EXPRESSIONS:
Choice Old Cameron Brig is one of only two proprietary bottled single grain whiskies available in the U.K., and one of only three available in the world.

RAW MATERIALS: Wheat from the East Coast of Scotland; Wanderhaufen malting system on site until 1997, now dried malt from Burghead. Process water from bore-holes on site.

PLANT: Three Coffey stills, and one Patent still with nine columns for making neutral spirit, for gin and vodka.

MATURATION: Mainly first-fill and refill ex-bourbon casks; at Leven, nearby, and Blackgrange, Alloa, in racked warehouses.

STYLE: Light and clean, but fruity and flavourful.

Caol Ila

Ca

REGION
Islay

ADDRESS
Port Askaig, Isle of Islay,
Argyll

PHONE
01496 302760

WEBSITE
www.malts.com

OWNER
Diageo plc

VISITORS
Yes

CAPACITY
3.6m L.P.A.

During the period 1970–74, when the distillery was rebuilt, peating levels were raised at Brora Distillery to make up for the potential shortfall of smoky whisky.

HISTORICAL NOTES: The distillery takes its name (pronounced 'Cull-eela') from the strait between the islands of Islay and Jura, the Sound of Islay. The first distillery on this site – a small bay just north of the ferry point at Port Askaig – was built in 1846 by Hector Henderson who took advantage of copious water from Loch nam Ban. The site had previously been used for washing lead ore. It enjoys splendid views across to Jura and its mountainous Paps. A number of houses were built on the hillside above the distillery, with a shop and Mission Hall for the employees.

In 1857 Caol Ila was bought by the Glasgow blending firm, Bulloch Lade & Company, who built a pier capable of withstanding the 12-foot tide-fall and the strong currents of the Sound, which allowed small cargo ships (puffers) to supply coal and barley and uplift whisky.

In 1927 D.C.L. acquired a controlling interest in Bulloch Lade, and ownership went to S.M.D. in 1930. They bought their own puffer, the *Pibroch*, to service their three Islay distilleries.

In 1972 the original distillery was demolished (apart from the large, three-storey warehouse, which is still in use) and replaced by a larger and more efficient building in S.M.D.'s so-called 'Waterloo Street' style. It resumed production in 1974, with six stills (where formerly it had two).

CURIOSITIES: The 'Waterloo Street' style was named after the Glasgow address of S.M.D.'s engineering department. The design was for a six-still distillery and specified that the outside wall of the still-house be of glass, with windows that could open, making them light-filled and airy – and in Caol Ila's case providing a stunning view across the Sound of Isla to the Isle of Jura.

The mashhouse and tun-room were arranged in such a way as to make the best use of gravity, thus saving unnecessary pumps, and the overall plan was both efficient and aesthetically pleasing, while also

The current Manager, Billy Stichell, is the fourth generation of his family to have worked here.

being pleasant to work in. The design was the brainchild of Dr Charlie Potts, S.M.D.'s Chief Engineer, and was applied in the following distilleries: Balmenach (1962), Caol Ila (1974), Clynelish (1968), Craigellachie (1965), Glendullan (1972), Glen Ord (1966), Glentauchers (1966), Linkwood (1970), Mannochmore (1971) and Teaninich (1970).

EXPRESSIONS:

Caol Ila has always been a blending whisky, and continues to be such, although since 1989, when a 15YO expression was released in the Flora & Fauna series, it has been bottled by its owner. Later it was bottled four times in the Rare Malts series: 1975 @ 20YO, 1975 @ 21YO, 1977 @ 20YO and 1977 @ 21YO.
- Current proprietary bottlings:
- Caol Ila 12YO @ 43% (released in 2002)
- Caol Ila 18YO @ 43% (released in 2002)
- Caol Ila Cask Strength (non-age, but about 10YO, released in 2002)
- Caol Ila 25YO @ CS (distilled 1978, released in 2003)
- Caol Ila 1979 25YO @ 58.4% (Special Release, 2005)
- Caol Ila Distiller's Edition @ 43% (distilled 1993, finished in ex-Moscatel casks, released in 2006)
- Caol Ila 8YO Unpeated @ 43% (distilled 1993, released in 2006)

RAW MATERIALS: Heavily peated malt (30–35ppm phenols) from Port Ellen Maltings, and, for around four months of the year, unpeated malt from Port Ellen. Water from Loch nam Ban.

PLANT: Cast iron semi-Lauter mash tun (11.5 tonnes). Eight larch washbacks. Three plain wash stills (35,340 litres charge), three plain spirit stills (29,550 litres charge). Indirect fired by steam throughout. Shell-and-tube condensers.

MATURATION: Refill ex-bourbon hogsheads. Mainly matured in the Central Belt, some on site in the original warehouse.

STYLE: Peaty, but with a lighter body than its sister Lagavulin.

MATURE CHARACTER: Sweet and lightly fruity on the nose, with smoked ham or smoked cheese, and some seaweed. The taste is sweet, with fragrant smoke and antiseptic cream. Medium length.

CAOL ILA
ISLAY SINGLE MALT SCOTCH WHISKY
AGED 8 YEARS
"Unpeated Style"
BOTTLED IN 2007

Caperdonich

REGION
Speyside
ADDRESS
Rothes, Moray
PHONE
01542 783300
WEBSITE
No
OWNER
Chivas Brothers
VISITORS
No
CAPACITY
2.1m L.P.A.

HISTORICAL NOTES: At the height of the Whisky Boom, the demand for Glen Grant malt was such that the distillery's owner, Major James Grant, built another distillery 'across the road', which he imaginatively named Glen Grant Number Two (see *Glen Grant*). It was designed to augment supplies of Glen Grant, the make of each being considered the same, and there was a pipe connecting the two. However, it is said that from the outset, the product of Number Two was quite different from Number One.

It opened in 1898, two years before the Boom turned to bust, and the distillery was closed in 1902, the floor maltings and two kilns being used to supply malt to Glen Grant Distillery, and warehouses used to store materials.

It remained silent until 1965, when it was rebuilt by The Glenlivet Distillers Ltd, expanded in 1967 to four stills and renamed Caperdonich after the well which supplies its reducing water. In 1977 it was acquired by Seagram when they bought Glenlivet Distillers, and by Pernod Ricard when that company bought Seagram's whisky interests in 2001. The following year Chivas Brothers, Pernod Ricard's operating company, mothballed the distillery. Currently, there are no plans to re-open.

CURIOSITIES: The stills installed in 1965/67 contained large parts of the original Glen Grant No. 2 stills, identifiable by their riveted seams, but they have now been replaced. Although it uses the same malt and water, Caperdonich's make is lighter.

Glen Grant No. 2 was connected to its sister by a pipe, so new make was pumped up the hill to be filled into cask at the larger distillery.

EXPRESSIONS:
Apart from some 5YO bottled for Italy in the 1970s and labelled the same as Glen Grant, with two kilted Highlanders, Caperdonich was only once bottled by its owners:
• Caperdonich 1988 16YO @ 40% (released 2005).

The 'whisky pipe' which connected Caperdonich to Glen Grant was a popular source of free spirit among the 'free spirits' of Rothes!

RAW MATERIALS: Process and cooling water from Glen Grant Burn; reducing water from the Caperdonich Well .

PLANT: Traditional rake-and-plough mash tun (4.62 tonnes); two stainless steel washbacks, six of steel. The original two stills were duplicates of the old small stills at Glen Grant; in 1965 two more stills were installed and all changed to boil-pot design; in the 1980s they were changed again to the 'German helmet' design found at Glen Grant. All indirect fired by steam. Shell-and-tube condensers.

MATURATION: Taken by tanker to other Chivas sites, for filling and maturing in mainly refill casks, except for a peaty variety of make once made at the distillery, which was filled into cask on site.

STYLE: Sweet and grassy.

MATURE CHARACTER: Speyside style – pear drops and hedgerows, with floral notes and hints of oak and vanilla. The taste is sweet, with tropical fruits and nutty-nougat notes. Light-bodied.

Cardhu

REGION
Speyside
ADDRESS
Knockando, Aberlour,
Moray
PHONE
01340 872556
WEBSITE
www.malts.com
OWNER
Diageo plc
VISITORS
Visitor centre – the 'brand home' of Johnnie Walker, with memorabilia
CAPACITY
2.3m L.P.A.

HISTORICAL NOTES: Like many others, Cardhu (the spelling was for many years Anglicised to Cardow, pronounced 'Cardoo') was a farm with a still. John Cumming, the son of a hill-farmer and grazier, became tenant here around 1810, and soon turned his hand to illicit whisky-making. The location, in hilly country to the north of the Spey, was, in those days, remote. He took out a licence in 1824; much of his make was taken by horse and cart to Burghead and shipped to Leith.

John died in 1846 and was succeeded by his son, Lewis Cumming, and Lewis by his wife, Elizabeth – a faded photograph of whom is in the distillery. At this time the output of the distillery was 240 gallons a week (623 litres).

In 1884 she rebuilt the distillery, selling the old stills to William Grant, who was building Glenfiddich Distillery at the time. By 1888 her whisky was being sold as a single malt in London, proudly claiming to be the only whisky from Speyside that did not need to affix the name Glenlivet to its own.

Elizabeth Cumming sold to John Walker & Sons in 1893, on condition that her son, John, joined the Board of the company. Her grandson, Ronald, would ultimately rise to be Chairman of both Walkers and D.C.L., and a Knight of the Realm.

In 1897 the distillery was expanded to four stills, and in 1925 Walkers joined D.C.L. Sir Ronald Cumming (re-)introduced the make as a single malt in 1981, under the original distillery name, Cardhu – it was the first single malt to be promoted by D.C.L.

Around this time, the company took the unusual step (for them) of allowing journalists and non-whisky trade V.I.P.s to visit the distillery.

Cardhu stands among the top six bestselling malts in the world, and is number one in Spain.

CURIOSITIES: John Cumming's wife, Helen, aided her husband and others in their illicit distilling ventures by boldly offering accommodation in the farmhouse to visiting excisemen, there being no inn for miles around. As soon as they were safely at table, she hoisted a red flag over the barn at the back as a warning.

Barnard had a high regard for the make from Cardow, describing it as "of the thickest and richest description and admirably suited to blending purposes". Charles Mackinlay & Co in Leith were agents, and it commanded a premium price.

Alfred Barnard visited Cardow shortly before Elizabeth Cumming rebuilt the distillery. He reported that the buildings were 'of the most straggling and primitive description and although water power existed, a great part of the work was done by manual labour. It is wonderful how long this state of things existed, considering the successful business that was carried on for so many years.'

In 1924 a trade journal reported that the 'two larger stills' at Cardhu were fired by 'oil and steam pressure on the jet system' – i.e. direct fired by oil – while the two smaller stills continued to be heated by coal fires. This was an experiment far ahead of its time. The experiment was abandoned after two years, on account of the cost of oil, not the quality of spirit.

In many ways, Sir Alexander Walker was an innovator, but in others he was very conservative. He subscribed to the widely held belief that it was unlucky to interfere with spiders in the tun room, as being beneficial to fermentation. On his orders they were a protected species, so when a new brewer at Cardhu unwittingly cleaned and repainted the room ... 'Sir Alexander's anger, when he discovered this act of impiety, was long remembered' (Brian Spiller).

Cardhu is so popular in Spain that there is not enough to supply the demand. In 2002 Diageo sought to solve the problem by introducing a 'pure malt' (a blend of malts – in this case only two) version of Cardhu. It was named Cardhu and offered in the same style of bottle, with a very similar label, although the difference between 'pure' and 'single' malt was explained

Elizabeth Cumming was a formidable character who became known as 'The Queen of the Whisky Trade'.

on the carton, and it was planned to revert to the original name Cardow for the single malt. The move caused an uproar in the whisky industry, unprecedented in modern times, and led to a tightening of the definitions of malt whisky (the word 'pure' was banned, for example, as being misleading to consumers). Cardhu Pure Malt was withdrawn.

EXPRESSIONS:

- Cardhu 12YO @ 40% (relaunched 2005)
- Cardhu 1973 25YO @ 60.5% (Rare Malts series, released 1998)
- Cardhu 1973 27YO @ 60.02% (Rare Malts series, released 2000)
- Cardhu 22YO @ 57.8% (Special Release, 2005)
- Cardhu Special Cask Reserve @ 40% (released 2006)

RAW MATERIALS: Unpeated malt from Burghead Maltings. Soft water from springs on Mannoch Hill and from the Lynne Burn, both collected in a dam near the distillery.

PLANT: Full-Lauter mash tun (seven tonnes). Eight larch washbacks. Three plain wash stills (18,000 litres charge); three plain spirit stills (11,000 litres charge). Indirect fired since 1971. Shell-and-tube condensers.

MATURATION: Refill ex-bourbon hogsheads.

STYLE: Floral.

MATURE CHARACTER: Fragrant and floral (Parma Violets, dried rose petals), and Speyside-fruity (pear drops, fresh apples) on the nose. Sweet and fresh to taste. Light-bodied.

Ca

Carsebridge Grain Distillery (Redeveloped)

ADDRESS
Alloa, Clackmannanshire
OWNER
Diageo plc
CAPACITY
Unknown
CLOSED
1983

Carsebridge once had its own fire brigade, employing 40 firemen.

HISTORICAL NOTES: Clackmannan was the cradle of brewing and distilling in Scotland during the late eighteenth century. Alloa stands in the shadow of the Ochil Hills, at the junction of the Stirling Plain and the fertile lowlands of Fife; it was close to some of the earliest coal pits in Scotland, and had access to the Forth for the import of coal and grain from East Lothian.

Here were found 'the largest manufacturing undertakings of any kind to emerge during the first decade of the industrial revolution in Scotland' (Michael Moss) – Kilbagie and Kennetpans Distilleries, owned by the Stein family, and associated trades, such as coppersmiths, glass works and cooperages (all of which still exist).

Carsebridge was built in 1799 by John Bald, who left the running of it to his son, Robert. In 1845 it passed to Robert's brother, John. It began as a pot still malt whisky distillery, but switched to patent stills and grain whisky production in 1860.

John Bald II (described as 'the politic Bald') was a leading light in the move towards promoting the collective interests of the Lowland distillers. This first took the form of a 'Trade Arrangement for one year', signed in 1856 by the owners of Caledonian, Cambus, Carsebridge, Glenochil, Haddington and Seggie Distilleries. This was extended by a second Trade Arrangement in 1865, when Cameronbridge replaced Seggie and Port Dundas replaced Haddington; later the same year Yoker and Adelphi Distilleries joined.

But all this was but a prelude to the formation, in April 1877, of D.C.L. (see *Cameronbridge*).

Carsebridge was transferred to the ownership of D.C.L. subsidiary S.G.D. in 1966, at which time it was the largest grain distillery in the group, employing 300 people, with three Coffey stills and a large dark-grains plant. It was closed and dismantled in 1983 and the site is now used by Diageo's Spirit Supply, Scotland division, which is responsible for all the company's spirits production. The site also houses the company's principal cooperage and 'bodega'

111 | CARSEBRIDGE

– the latter for seasoning casks with sherry or other wines.

CURIOSITIES: The first steam engine in Scotland was installed in the 1770s at Kennetpans, while Kilbagie had the first steam-powered threshing mill. One of the earliest railway lines in Scotland connected the two distilleries, so that goods could easily be moved from Kilbagie to the wharf at Kennetpans, a mile distant.

EXPRESSIONS:
Never bottled as a single by its owner. Occasional bottlings by independents.

Clynelish

C1

REGION
Highland (North)

ADDRESS
Brora, Sutherland

PHONE
01408 623000

WEBSITE
www.malts.com

OWNER
Diageo plc

VISITORS
Visitor centre and shop

CAPACITY
3.26m L.P.A.

HISTORICAL NOTES: The present-day Clynelish Distillery was built in 1967/68, close to the original Clynelish Distillery, which was renamed Brora (see this entry for the early history), as part of D.C.L.'s expansion policy at that time. Architecturally, it bears a resemblance to Caol Ila, Mannochmore and Craigellachie – all of which were rebuilt at around the same time, in the so-called 'Waterloo Street' style (see *Caol Ila*).

It was equipped with six stills, all steam heated from an oil-fired boiler.

It is the third largest distillery in Diageo's estate.

CURIOSITIES: The old Clynelish Distillery was officially closed in 1967, but continued in production. From 1972 to 1977 it produced heavily peated whisky, to make up for the loss of peaty spirit from Caol Ila Distillery, which was being rebuilt at the time. Its name was only changed to Brora in 1975, so for seven years Clynelish was being made at both distilleries.

Clynelish is unusual in having spirit stills larger than its wash stills. Its spirit style is uniquely 'waxy', and this flavour comes through in the mature whisky. Until recently it was a mystery where this prized waxiness came from. A full investigation was prompted by a temporary change in spirit character and it was discovered that the characteristic was contributed by deposits of greasy matter which built up in the receivers and piping. Its temporary absence was on account of the piping having been cleaned when a receiver was replaced. Such are the mysteries of where flavour comes from in malt whisky!

EXPRESSIONS:
Clynelish is highly prized by blenders, and forms a key component in the Johnnie Walker blends. As a result it has been uncommon as a single until recently: now it has been included in Diageo's extended Classic Malts series.
• Clynelish 14YO @ 43% (Flora & Fauna series, since 1991)
• Clynelish 14YO @ 43% (Hidden Malts series, released 2002)
• Clynelish 1972 22YO @ 58.95% (Rare Malts series)

Clynemilton Burn has supplied the town of Brora since 1819 and is said to contain particles of gold; certainly gold can be panned for in neighbouring rivers.

- Clynelish 1972 24YO @ 61.3% (Rare Malts series)
- Clynelish 1972 23YO @ 57% (Rare Malts series)
- Clynelish 1974 23YO @ 59.1% (Rare Malts series)
- Clynelish 14YO @ 46% (extended Classic Malts of Scotland series, from 2006)

RAW MATERIALS: Unpeated malt from Glen Ord. Soft water from the Clynemilton Burn.

PLANT: Full-Lauter mash tun, with copper canopy (12.5 tonnes). Eight larch washbacks. Three boil-pot wash stills (17,000 litres charge); three boil-pot spirit stills (20,000 litres charge). All indirect fired. Shell-and-tube condensers.

MATURATION: Mainly ex-bourbon refill casks, with some ex-sherry. Two dunnage warehouses on site (7,000 casks). Most matured in the Central Belt.

STYLE: Waxy, with heather notes.

MATURE CHARACTER: An outstanding example of the 'Highland' style, Clynelish is scented with heather flowers and moorland herbs, candlewax and fragrant smoke. The texture in the mouth is waxy, teeth-coating; the taste creamy, lightly fruity and spicy, with tobacco notes. Medium-bodied. Complex.

Coleburn Dismantled

REGION
Speyside
ADDRESS
Longmorn, by Elgin,
Moray
LAST OWNER
D.C.L./S.M.D.
CLOSED
1985

*'In a snug corner ..
complete in itself,
compact and clean'*
Moray & Nairn
Express

HISTORICAL NOTES: Coleburn was built in 1896 by John Robertson & Son Ltd, blenders in Dundee, designed by Charles Doig. It has an attractive situation within the Glen of Rothes, chosen to take advantage of a branch-line of the Great North of Scotland Railway, and the distillery had its own small station and siding (closed in 1966). The name recollects that charcoal was made nearby.

The distillery closed in 1913 and was sold three years later to Clynelish Distillery Company Ltd (itself owned by D.C.L., John Walker & Sons and John Risk), passing to full D.C.L. ownership in 1925. It was licensed to J. & G. Stewart, and the make was a key filling in the Usher's blends. It closed in 1985. The attractive site was sold to Dale and Mark Winchester in 2004 for development.

CURIOSITIES: Dale and Mark Winchester starred in the film *Local Hero*, with Dale on accordion and Mark on fiddle.

They have plans to develop Coleburn as an entertainment centre and concert venue, with music studios, restaurant, travel lodge and shops. Hopefully planning permission will have been granted by the time this book goes to press.

EXPRESSIONS:
Only once bottled by its owner as a single, although at least four independent bottlings have appeared.
• Coleburn 1979 (Rare Malts series, released 2000, 21YO @ 59.4%)

Convalmore Dismantled

REGION
Speyside
ADDRESS
Dufftown, Moray
LAST OWNER
William Grant & Sons
CLOSED
1985

HISTORICAL NOTES: Convalmore was the fourth distillery to be built in Dufftown, next door to Balvenie and Glenfiddich (the buildings, now used as storage and warehousing, are owned by William Grant & Sons, owners of the adjacent distilleries). Building commenced in 1893 and production started next year.

The owner was the Convalmore-Glenlivet Distillery Company, a group of Glasgow blenders, with Peter Dawson (a Dufftown man, and a well-known wholesale whisky merchant) as Managing Director. In spite of this ready market for its make, the company failed in 1905 and was bought by W. P. Lowrie & Company, blenders in Glasgow and suppliers of whisky to James Buchanan & Company, which acquired Lowrie's in 1907. Many of the buildings were destroyed by fire in 1909, but they were rebuilt the following year (incorporating a continuous still, but this was abandoned in 1915).

Buchanan's joined D.C.L. in 1925, and ownership went to S.M.D. in 1930. Convalmore was closed in 1985, and the buildings sold to William Grant & Sons in 1990.

CURIOSITIES: The distillery name comes from the Conval Hills, from which the process water was drawn. Cooling water came from the River Fiddich. During the fire of 1909, the heat was so intense that the distillery's hoses could not be connected and workers had to resort to carrying buckets of water up from the Fiddich. 'While it was at its height the flames rose to between 30 and 40 feet high ... To add to other discomforts, snow commenced to fall, and the effect of the burning building on the white landscape provided a striking picture.'

EXPRESSIONS:
Bottlings of Convalmore are rare:
- Convalmore 1978 (Rare Malts series, 24YO @ 59.4%)
- Convalmore 1977 (Special Release, 28YO @ 57.9%)

Cragganmore

REGION
Speyside
ADDRESS
Ballindalloch, Moray
PHONE
01479 874700
WEBSITE
www.malts.com
OWNER
Diageo plc
VISITORS
Yes
CAPACITY
1.6m L.P.A.

HISTORICAL NOTES: A distillery at Ballindalloch, deep in Speyside, was only made possible by the opening of the Strathspey railway in 1863. Its founder, John Smith, was acknowledged to be one of the most experienced distillers of his day, having formerly managed Macallan, Glenlivet, Glenfarclas and Wishaw Distilleries; he was also a keen railway enthusiast and a moving force behind the building of the Speyside line.

The site he chose for his distillery was on Ballindalloch Estate, and he built it with the support of Sir George Macpherson Grant, the laird, whose family had owned Ballindalloch Castle since the fifteenth century (and continues to do so).

The distillery opened in 1869. On John's death in 1886, it passed to his brother, and then to his son, Gordon Smith, when he came of age in 1893. He refurbished it in 1901, employing Charles Doig, the famous distillery architect; between his death in 1912 and its sale in 1923, Cragganmore was managed by his widow Mary Jane.

The new owner was a partnership between Macpherson Grant and White Horse Distillers; the latter's 50% passed to D.C.L. in 1927, and in 1965 S.M.D. bought out the remaining share, having doubled the capacity (to four stills) the previous year.

CURIOSITIES: For reasons unknown, John Smith designed his stills with flat tops, rather than the usual swan necks. This may increase reflux, the spirit vapour condensing on the flat surface and dripping down to be redistilled. Any lightness of body this might contribute is countered by the use of worm tubs. The result is a medium-bodied Speyside of unusually complex character.

John Smith himself was a very large man – he weighed 308 lbs (140 kg) – and was too wide to enter a railway carriage. Accordingly, he was obliged to travel in the guard's van.

Cragganmore is a very attractive distillery, compact and neat. It is built around a courtyard, one side of

Cragganmore is ranked Top Class by blenders. In 1988 it was chosen by its owners to represent the Speyside style in their Classic Malts series.

which houses the 'Club Room' (used for entertaining guests), which is furnished in Edwardian style, with memorabilia including John Smith's desk and (large!) chair.

EXPRESSIONS:
- Cragganmore 12YO @ 40% (Classic Malts series, from 1987/88)
- Cragganmore Distillers Edition @ 40% (port cask finish)
- Cragganmore 1973 29YO @ 52.5% (Special Release, 2004)
- Cragganmore 1993 10YO @ 60.1% (Special Release, 2005)
- Cragganmore 1988 17YO @ 55.5% (Special Release, 2006)

RAW MATERIALS: Lightly peated malt from Roseisle. Hard process water from a spring on Craggan More Hill via the Craggan Burn; cooling water from the River Spey.

PLANT: Full-Lauter mash tun with copper canopy (seven tonnes). Six Oregon pine washbacks. Two lamp-glass wash stills (18,500 litres charge); two boil-ball spirit stills (6,000 litres charge), with unusual flat tops, all indirect fired. Unusual rectangular worm tubs, with worms from both wash and spirit stills in the same tub.

MATURATION: A mix of refill ex-bourbon and ex-sherry casks.

STYLE: Big, rich and meaty.

MATURE CHARACTER: A multi-layered nose of polished leather and saddle-soap, green bananas, tobacco, nuts, dried fruits and herbs. The taste is dryish overall, with walnuts, hard toffee and dried fruits. Medium-bodied.

Cr

Craigellachie

REGION
Speyside
ADDRESS
Craigellachie, Aberlour,
Moray
PHONE
01340 872970
WEBSITE
No
OWNER
John Dewar & Sons
(Bacardi)
VISITORS
By appointment
CAPACITY
3.6m L.P.A.

HISTORICAL NOTES: Craigellachie Distillery was substantially rebuilt and expanded from two stills to four in 1964/65 by D.C.L., its then owner to the 'Waterloo Street' design (see *Caol Ila*).

All that remains of the earlier distillery are parts of the warehouses. The original was designed by Charles Doig and built in 1891 (but did not start production until 1898) for a consortium of blenders and merchants, led by Peter Mackie of White Horse and Alexander Edward, owner of Benrinnes and Aultmore Distilleries. The latter pulled out in 1900, and Mackie & Company took over complete ownership in 1916. 'From that date (1900) onwards the annual general meeting of the company provided the Chairman, Peter Mackie, with a platform for strongly held opinions on the state of the whisky industry, the nation and the British Empire.' (Brian Spiller)

Sir Peter Mackie died in 1924; the company changed its name to White Horse Distillers and joined D.C.L. three years later.

In 1998 U.D.V. (successor to D.C.L.) was obliged to sell Craigellachie, with three other distilleries, to Bacardi along with the Dewar's brands. Further expressions of Craigiellachie are planned for 2008.

CURIOSITIES: Peter Mackie was one of the leading characters of the whisky industry. Among his eccentricities was the invention of a 'power flour' called B.B.M. (Bran, Bone and Muscle), mixed to a secret recipe under the boardroom at Craigellachie, which all employees were required to use at home. Staff were also required to tend their gardens carefully, and an annual prize was offered, after a tour of inspection by the Directors. He was an ardent Conservative, but was made a baronet in 1920 for his war work by a Liberal Prime Minister.

The distillery was lit by paraffin lamps until 1948, and a water wheel was used to drive the wash still rummager until 1964, when the distillery was completely rebuilt.

Peter Mackie was described as 'one third genius, one third megalomaniac and one third eccentric'.

EXPRESSIONS:
• Craigellachie 14YO @ 43% (Flora & Fauna series)
• Craigellachie 1973 22YO @ 60.2% (Rare Malts series)
• Craigellachie 14YO @ 40% (introduced 2004 by John Dewar & Sons)

RAW MATERIALS: Floor maltings until 1964; thereafter lightly peated malt from Burghead. Soft process water from springs on Little Conval Hill; cooling water from the River Fiddich.

PLANT: Full-Lauter mash tun (ten tonnes) installed 2001. Eight larch washbacks. Two plain wash stills (22,730 litres charge); two plain spirit stills (22,730 litres charge). All indirect fired since 1972. Worm tubs.

MATURATION: Mainly refill ex-bourbon hogsheads, some ex-sherry butts; matured in the Central Belt.

STYLE: A big-bodied and very slightly smoky Speyside style.

MATURE CHARACTER: Craigellachie is unusual as a Speyside in adding a thread of smoke to the familiar floral-fruity characteristic of the region. Sweet and creamy in the mouth, with citric notes, light acidity and a trace of smoke in the finish. Medium-bodied.

Da

Daftmill

REGION
Lowland
ADDRESS
Daftmill Farm, Cupar, Fife
PHONE
01337 830303
WEBSITE
www.daftmill.com
OWNER
Francis and Ian Cuthbert
VISITORS
By appointment
CAPACITY
20,000 L.P.A.

Daftmill is currently the smallest distillery in Scotland.

HISTORICAL NOTES: Daftmill is among the most attractive distilleries in Scotland. It is a neat, sensitively converted meal mill, built around three sides of a square, with the glass-fronted stillhouse at the base, a warehouse to the right and mashhouse/tun room in the left-hand range. The mill building itself dates from the late seventeenth to nineteenth centuries (the date on the gablestone reads 1809).

The conversion, which was done between 2003 and 2005, was the work of brothers Ian and Francis Cuthbert, whose family has been farming the land hereabouts for six generations. They also own a gravel quarry nearby; income from which provided the money to convert the mill.

CURIOSITIES: All the work done to convert the mill was done by men from within a five-mile radius of Daftmill Farm, except for the stills and mash tun, which were made by Forsyth's of Rothes.

The brothers have their own barley, malted by Crisp of Alloa.

The Daft Burn, which gave its name to the mill, is so called because it appears to flow uphill.

EXPRESSIONS:
Not yet available; first bottling 'when it's ready' (F. Cuthbert).

RAW MATERIALS: Unpeated malt from Crisp, Alloa. Process and cooling water (hard) from a spring on site.

PLANT: Semi-Lauter mash tun with copper canopy (one tonne). Two stainless steel washbacks. One plain wash still (2,500 litres charge); one plain spirit still (1,500 litres charge); both indirect fired. Shell-and-tube condensers.

MATURATION: A mix of first-fill ex-bourbon (from Heaven Hill Distillery) and ex-sherry casks.

STYLE: Light and fruity, with cereal notes.

Dailuaine

REGION
Speyside
ADDRESS
Carron, Moray
PHONE
01340 872500
WEBSITE
www.malts.com
OWNER
Diageo plc
VISITORS
Visitor centre and shop
CAPACITY
3.2m L.P.A.

HISTORICAL NOTES: The distillery was built in 1851 by William Mackenzie, in a small wooded glen a mile off the main road, at the other (northern) end of Ballindalloch Estate from Cragganmore. Access to market was given a terrific boost 12 years later by the arrival of the Speyside Railway on the opposite bank of the river, with the village of Carron connected by a road bridge.

The distillery was rebuilt in 1884, and when Alfred Barnard visited in 1887 he noted: 'Within the last few years, nearly the whole of the distillery has been re-built on a larger and more modern style, and the work now contains all the latest improvements in the art of distilling.' It was now one of the largest Highland distilleries.

Mackenzie & Company became a limited company in 1890, and merged with Talisker to become Dailuaine-Talisker Distilleries Ltd in 1898. By this time the business was in the hands of Mackenzie's son, Thomas, who had built Imperial Distillery the previous year. When Thomas died without heirs in 1915 Dailuaine-Talisker was bought by its principal customers, Walkers, Dewar's, W.P. Lowrie and D.C.L. A fire destroyed much of the property in 1917, and it was rebuilt.

A major reconstruction took place in 1959/60, when the floor maltings were converted into a Saladin box system, the number of stills increased from four to six and mechanical coal-stoking was introduced (the distillery went over to indirect firing in 1970). A dark-grains plant was also installed at this time. Malting on site remained until 1983.

Always designed to be a blending whisky, Daluaine was not bottled as a single by its owners until 1991.

CURIOSITIES: The pagoda roof, which has since become the *leitmotif* of a malt whisky distillery, was destroyed by the fire in 1917. There was another fire in 1959, and this prompted the refurbishment referred to above.

A 0–4–0 saddle locomotive, built by Barclay of

Charles Doig of Elgin, the pre-eminent distillery architect of his day, installed his first pagoda at Dailuaine in 1889.

Kilmarnock, was bought in 1897 to run goods down to Carron Station. It operated until 1939, when it was replaced by another engine from the same works, named Dailuaine No. 1 – described by a former driver as 'truly a joy to behold', with its bright paintwork and polished brasswork. When the Speyside line was closed in 1967, it was donated to the Railway Museum in Aviemore. It was later returned to U.D. and is now on display at Aberfeldy Distillery.

EXPRESSIONS:
The few proprietary bottlings are drawn from ex-sherry refills.
- Dailuaine 16YO @ 43% (Flora & Fauna series, introduced 1991)
- Dailuaine 22YO 1973 @ 60.92% (Rare Malts series)
- Dailuaine 16YO @ CS (released 1997)

RAW MATERIALS: Floor maltings until 1959 then Saladin boxes until 1983; thereafter unpeated malt from Burghead. Soft process water from Balliemullich Burn, flowing down from Ben Rinnes; cooling water from the Green Burn or the River Spey.

PLANT: Full-Lauter mash tun (11.5 tonnes). Eight larch washbacks. Three lamp-glass wash stills (19,000 litres charge); three plain spirit stills (21,000 litres charge). All indirect fired. Shell-and-tube condensers, unusually two of them made from stainless steel – one wash and one spirit.

MATURATION: Mainly refill ex-bourbon hogsheads, with some ex-sherry butts; all spirit now tankered for maturation in the Central Belt.

STYLE: Full-bodied, rich and meaty.

MATURE CHARACTER: The style of the new-make spirit makes it eminently suitable for sherry-wood maturation, and these flavours emerge in the mature whisky. The nose is redolent of dried fruits and fruit cake, moist with sherry. A hint of rubber immediately after water is added. A thick, unctuous texture in the mouth, with a taste that starts sweet in the mouth and finishes slightly tannic, with dark chocolate. Full-bodied.

Da

REGION
Speyside

ADDRESS
Mannachie Road, Forres,
Moray

PHONE
01309 676548

WEBSITE
www.historic-scotland.
gov.uk

OWNER
Historic Scotland

CLOSED
1983

Dallas Dhu Museum

HISTORICAL NOTES: This is the only distillery 'preserved in aspic' as a museum, an admirable time warp back to the 1950s, and a chance to see (albeit in a somewhat sanitised setting) what distilleries used to be like before modern changes took place.

The ubiquitous Alexander Edward (see *Benromach* etc.) granted the site at the other end of his estate to the well-known Glasgow blenders, Wright & Greig Ltd. They instructed Charles Doig in 1898, and Dallas Dhu (originally named Dallasmore) went into production the following June.

Ownership passed to J.P. O'Brien & Company (distillers in Glasgow) in 1919, and then to a consortium of English brewers called Benmore Distilleries Ltd. The latter was acquired by D.C.L. in 1929. Closed during the 1930s, the stillhouse was destroyed by fire in 1939, and then the distillery was closed for the duration of World War II, resuming production in 1947. In 1963 the coal-fired stills were equipped with mechanical stokers, and converted to internal heating by steam in 1971.

Dallas Dhu was terminally closed in May 1983, and sold to Historic Scotland in 1986.

CURIOSITIES: Dallas Dhu derives from the Gaelic 'Dail eas dubh' ('the field by the black/dark waterfall').

Wright & Greig's key brand was Roderick Dhu, named after a character in Walter Scott's *The Lady of the Lake*. In the 1880s and 1890s this was a big export Scotch, particularly in India and the Antipodes. Dallas Dhu was built to supply fillings for it.

The parish and ancient church of Saint Michael were granted in 1279 to one William de Ripley, who changed his name to 'de Dallas'. Dallas, Texas, was named after one of his descendants, the U.S. Vice-President George M. Dallas in 1845.

EXPRESSIONS:

Dallas Dhu has been bottled several times by its former owner as a Rare Malt, and also in special bottlings for Historic Scotland.

- Dallas Dhu 24YO @ 58%, 59.91%, 60.54%, 60.6% (Rare Malts series, all bottled 1995)
- Dallas Dhu 21YO @ 57.1%, 61.9% (Rare Malt series, bottled 1997)

Dalmore

Da

REGION
Highland (North)
ADDRESS
Alness, Ross and Cromarty
PHONE
01349 882362
WEBSITE
www.thedalmore.com
OWNER
Whyte & Mackay Ltd
VISITORS
New visitor centre opened in 2004; cottages available
CAPACITY
3.2m L.P.A.

HISTORICAL NOTES: Alexander Matheson, who founded Dalmore in 1839, was a partner in the famous Far East trading company, Jardine Matheson, established by the 'shogun' William Matheson who made a vast fortune out of trading opium from China. Matheson leased it to the Sutherland family, and in the 1850s the distillery was being run by Mrs Margaret Sutherland.

The brothers Charles, Alexander and Andrew Mackenzie took over in 1878; their descendants ran Dalmore until 1960, when they amalgamated with Whyte & Mackay, a company with which they had friendly relations from the outset.

The name means 'the Big Meadow', and the situation, on the alluvial plain overlooking the Cromarty Firth, supports this. During World War I the distillery warehouses were requisitioned by the Admiralty for the manufacture of mines. The pier below the distillery was built by them and is known as the Yankee Pier.

Ownership of Dalmore Distillery passed to the United Breweries Group of India in 2007, when that company acquired Whyte & Mackay.

CURIOSITIES: Dalmore has several unusual or unique features. The large wash charger – around six metres across – is made of pine. Formerly, it was equipped with two paddles connected to a long wooden tiller; the operator would walk round the vessel, pushing the tiller and driving the paddles, in order to agitate the wash and prevent sediment entering the wash stills before the wash itself.

It is claimed that the stills are the oldest in the Highlands. Part of one of them dates from 1874. Four (the wash stills) have flat tops, rather than the usual 'swan necks'. This makes for a heavier, more characterful spirit. The other four (the spirit stills) have unique water-jackets around their necks (first fitted in 1839), so the copper is continually cooled, increasing reflux and making for a lighter spirit. Curiously, the condensers for the spirit stills

One of a dozen bottles of Dalmore 62YO sold privately in April 2005 for £32,000 – the current world record. (In truth the bottle contained whisky from 1868, 1878, 1926 and 1939.) The purchaser opened and drank the bottle immediately, with friends.

are mounted horizontally, outside the stillhouse.

Furthermore, one of the spirit stills is twice as big as the other three – another unique feature. The spirit coming from this still has a different character to that from the others – citric fruits and aromatic spices, while the smaller stills create rich and robust musky flavours.

There are four spirit safes in the stillhouse, one of them of unusual design and considerable antiquity.

The 12-point (or 'royal') stag which embellishes bottles of Dalmore was adopted in 1886 and recollects the fact that this emblem was granted to an ancestor of the Mathesons and Mackenzies, who rescued King Alexander III from being gored by a stag 750 years ago.

Drew Sinclair, who retired as manager in 2006 (and died soon after) worked at Dalmore for 40 years.

EXPRESSIONS:

Until recently, only the standard bottling at 12YO was available, although a bottling at 20YO was made in 1978 for Eduardo Giaccone. The core range is now at 12, 15 and 18YO, with special editions:

- Dalmore 12YO @ 40% and 43%
- Dalmore 15YO @ 43%
- Dalmore 18YO @ 43%
- Dalmore 21YO @ 43%
- Dalmore Cigar Malt @ 43% (first released 2001)
- Dalmore Gran Reserva @ 43% (replacing Cigar Malt from 2007, 60% ex-Oloroso casks)
- Dalmore 30YO Stillman's Dram (U.S. only, released 2002)
- Dalmore 50YO @ 52% (limited to 25 bottles)
- Dalmore 62YO @ 40.5% (limited to 12 bottles)
- Dalmore 1966 Vintage @ 44.6%
- Dalmore 1973 Vintage @ 52.3% (Gonzales Byass Sherry Cask Finish, released 2003)
- Dalmore Black Isle @ 40% (released 2004)
- Dalmore Black Pearl @ 40% (six years in Madeira casks, released 2005)
- Dalmore Cabernet Sauvignon Finish @ 45% (released 2006)
- Dalmore 40YO @ 40% (limited edition, released 2007)

Dalmore is reputed to be the first single malt whisky exported to Australia (in 1870).

RAW MATERIALS: Floor maltings until 1956, then converted to Saladin boxes until 1982. Now unpeated malt from Bairds, Inverness. Process water from Loch Kildermorie, on the slopes of Ben Wyvis; cooling water from River Averon or Alness.

PLANT: Semi-Lauter mash tun (9.2 tonnes); eight Oregon pine washbacks. Four lamp-glass, flat-top wash stills (three of 13,411 litres, one of 30,000 litres); four boil-pot spirit stills, fitted with water jackets to cool the necks of the stills (three of 8,865 litres, one of 19,548 litres). All indirect fired by steam. Shell-and-tube condensers.

MATURATION: Mix of ex-sherry, ex-bourbon and refill hogsheads. Matured on site mainly in dunnage warehouses and in Leith.

STYLE: Heavy, oily and musky (from the smaller stills); lighter and more citric (from the larger still).

MATURE CHARACTER: The overall style of Dalmore new-make is appropriate for sherry-wood maturation. The nose is rich and sherried, with sweet malt, fruit cake, orange peel and marzipan. Medium- to full-bodied, the texture is mouth-filling and the taste sweet rather than dry. Long finish.

Dalwhinnie

REGION
Highland (Central)

ADDRESS
Dalwhinnie, Inverness-shire

PHONE
01540 672219

WEBSITE
www.malts.com

OWNER
Diageo plc

VISITORS
Visitor centre and shop

CAPACITY
2m L.P.A.

HISTORICAL NOTES: Dalwhinnie is 'the meeting place', the place where drove roads from the north and west met those coming out of Strathspey and headed south; in the 1730s these were replaced by military roads, under the supervision of General Wade who also built a straggling village here.

The distillery itself was originally named Strathspey. It was built in 1897 by three men from the neighbouring town of Kingussie, but they soon ran into financial difficulties and sold up. The new owners changed the name to Dalwhinnie and employed Charles Doig to make improvements, then sold in 1905 to Cook & Bernheimer, the largest distillers in America at that time. This was the first time a Scottish distillery came under foreign ownership, but it was to last only 14 years, when Prohibition was announced in the U.S.A. Dalwhinnie was sold again, to the well-known blending firm Macdonald, Greenlees & Williams. The latter joined D.C.L. in 1926, and Dalwhinnie was licensed to James Buchanan & Company.

The distillery was badly damaged by a fire in 1934 – until that year there was no electricity in the village and the distillery was lit by paraffin lamps. It was rebuilt and opened again in April 1938, the original stillhouse becoming the present day tun-room, only to be closed again during World War II.

There was another refit in the 1960s. The stills were converted to indirect heating by steam in 1961 (originally a coal boiler, converted to oil 1972); malting on site ceased in 1968; British Rail closed the private siding off the main line, which runs at the back of the distillery, in 1979. Between 1992 and 1995 the distillery was closed for a major refurbishment.

Dalwhinnie single malt became well-known when it was selected by U.D. to represent the Highland style in the Classic Malts series.

CURIOSITIES: Until Braes of Glenlivet (now Braeval) was built in 1973, Dalwhinnie was the highest distillery in Scotland, at 1,073 feet above sea level. It

The distillery's priorities are 'Family, Friends and Flavour'.

is a remote spot (in spite of the nearness of the main north trunk road, the A9), and the coldest distillery, with an average annual temperature of 6°C. Since 1973 Dalwhinnie has operated as a 'Climatological Station'. Every day, including Christmas and New Year, readings of temperature, wind strength, humidity, visibility, frost and hours of sunshine must be recorded and sent to Edinburgh. This job used to be the (unpaid) responsibility of the manager, but is now shared by the operators.

Hamish Christie, stillman, after recalls playing football in 1963 on a pitch covered with five feet of hard-packed snow, using as goalposts the single visible foot of the six-foot tall poles which marked the roadway.

'Its wind-blasted location made a visit, even in May, seem like a major expedition to a forgotten outpost', wrote Philip Morrice in 1987. It is not uncommon for Dalwhinnie to be snowbound for weeks – but this may change with global warming.

In 1986 the worm tubs here were replaced by shell-and-tube condensers (from Banff Distillery), but this changed the spirit character so much that the move was reversed and the worms reinstated, in 1995.

In such a remote spot, it is common for families to work here generation after generation. Maureen Stronach, Head Guide, who has worked at the distillery for 32 years, succeeded her father and grandfather (both of whom were brewers) and three uncles. Her late husband was a stillman, and now her brother Hamish (with 18 years' service) and son are both stillmen/operators at Dalwhinnie.

EXPRESSIONS:
- Dalwhinnie 15YO @ 43% (Classic Malts series since 1988)
- Dalwhinnie Distillers Edition @ 43% (re-racked into Oloroso sherry casks, introduced 1998)
- Dalwhinnie 36YO 1966 @ 47.2% (Special Releases, 2002)
- Dalwhinnie 29YO 1973 @ 57.8% (Special Releases, 2003)
- Dalwhinnie 20YO 1986 @ 56.8% (Special Releases, 2006)

RAW MATERIALS: Floor maltings until 1968; now lightly peated malt from Roseisle. Soft water from Lochan an Doire-uaine (2,000 feet) via Allt an t'Sluie Burn.

PLANT: Full-Lauter mash tun (7.3 tonnes). One Oregon pine washback and five Siberian larch washbacks. One plain wash still (17,500 litres charge); one plain spirit still (16,200 litres charge). Direct fired until 1961, now indirect. Worm tubs. The lye pipe from the spirit still is sprayed with cold water before it enters the worm tub, to encourage early condensation, and thus lack of copper uptake.

MATURATION: Mainly ex-bourbon refill casks, matured in the Central Belt.

STYLE: Full-bodied, sweet, heather-honey.

MATURE CHARACTER: Dalwhinnie is a remarkably viscous malt, with a big mouth feel. The nose is sweet, with heather pollen, even heather honey, and moorland scents. The taste is soft and smooth, starting sweet and drying out with a whiff of peat smoke.

Deanston

De

REGION
Highland (South)

ADDRESS
Doune, Perthshire

PHONE
01786 841422

WEBSITE
www.burnstewartdistill-
ers.com

OWNER
Burn Stewart Distillers plc

VISITORS
By appointment

CAPACITY
3m L.P.A.

HISTORICAL NOTES: Deanston Distillery was created within an historic cotton mill, designed in 1785 by Richard Arkwright (pioneer of steam-powered spinning). It is the classic example of a mill-distillery, of which there are several in Scotland, for the simple reason that both require copious supplies of fast-running pure water. It stands on the edge of the River Teith, near the picturesque Doune Castle, and operated until 1965.

The distillery conversion was the brainchild of Brodie Hepburn Ltd (whisky brokers in Glasgow, owners since 1953 of Tullibardine Distillery and builders of Macduff Distillery in 1963). They took a 30% share, in partnership with the owners of the mill, James Findlay & Company. A water turbine and stand-by generator were already in place, but four solid floors had to be removed and two pairs of stills installed. Production commenced in October 1969, and the first Deanston Single Malt was released in 1974.

The original plan was to link production to the development of a major brand of blended whisky (Old Bannockburn), but this never happened, and in 1972 Invergordon Distillers took control. The distillery was silent from 1982 to 1990, when it was sold to Burn Stewart Distillers for £2.1 million in cash and brought back into production. Burn Stewart was acquired in 2002 by C.L. World Brands (based in Trinidad), owners of Angostura Bitters, Hine Cognac and Rhum Rum.

CURIOSITIES: 'Dean' and 'Doune' come from the Gaelic 'dun', a hill-fort. Doune Castle is 'one of the largest, best-preserved and best-restored examples of late fourteenth-century military-domestic architecture in Scotland' (*The Blue Guide to Scotland*).

Doune Castle was used in *Monty Python and the Holy Grail* (1974) as Camelot, Castle Anthrax and Swamp Castle!

Brodie Hepburn claimed in an advertisement in the *Scottish Licensed Trade News* (1966) to be 'the

A gin distillery was commissioned within Deanston in 1995; still in place and capable of being brought back into service if required.

oldest established whisky broker'. The company was bought by Invergordon Distillers in 1971.

Burn Stewart dates back to the 1940s, but it was a management buy-out led by Bill Thornton in 1988 that created the present company. They paid £7 million; the company went public three years later, with a capitalisation of £83 million, which allowed the Directors to build offices and bottling facilities at East Kilbride in 1992/93 (expanded 1995) and buy Tobermory Distillery in 1993. Bunnahabhain Distillery was acquired in 2003 (along with the successful Black Bottle blend). The company's blends are prepared at Airdrie, which also has an extensive warehousing.

EXPRESSIONS:
Around 15% of Deanston make is bottled as single malt, the rest goes into Burn Stewart's blends, particularly Black Prince and Scottish Leader. Current bottlings:
• Deanston 12YO @ 40%
• Deanston 17YO @ 40%
• Deanston 30YO @ 40% (released 2006)
• Deanston 35YO @ 50.7% (limited edition, released 2003)

RAW MATERIALS: Unpeated malt from independent maltsters. Soft water from the River Teith.

PLANT: Cast iron mash tun (11.2 tonnes). Eight Corten steel washbacks. Two boil-ball wash stills (8,500 litres charge); two boil-ball spirit stills (6,500 litres charge). Indirect fired. Shell-and-tube condensers.

MATURATION: 40,000 casks on site in a former weaving shed known as Adelphi Mill; remainder at Airdrie.

STYLE: Waxy, light, fruity.

MATURE CHARACTER: Lightly oily on the nose, with cereal notes. The taste is malty and fruity and lightly nutty, starting sweetish and finishing dryish. Light- to medium-bodied.

Dufftown

REGION
Speyside
ADDRESS
Dufftown, Moray
PHONE
01340 822100
WEBSITE
www.malts.com
OWNER
Diageo plc
VISITORS
No
CAPACITY
4.5m L.P.A.

HISTORICAL NOTES: The distillery was converted from a meal mill in 1895/96. It is located just outside Dufftown in the Dullan Glen, and the site was chosen by Peter Mackenzie and Richard Stackpole, of P. Mackenzie & Company, wine and spirits brokers in Liverpool (owners of The Real Mackenzie blend). Peter Mackenzie was born in Glenlivet, and his firm had bought Blair Athol Distillery in 1882. The founders included a local farmer and owner of the original mill, John Symon (who also supplied barley from his Pittyvaich Farm), and John Macpherson, a local solicitor. A year after its foundation, Peter Mackenzie formed a limited company to acquire full ownership of Dufftown-Glenlivet and the other assets of Mackenzie & Company.

In 1933 Mackenzie & Company (Distillers) Ltd was bought by Arthur Bell & Sons, and Dufftown-Glenlivet became a key filling for Bell's Extra Special. The distillery was expanded from two to four stills in 1968, to six in 1974 and to eight in 1979 (later reduced to six again).

Bell's was acquired by Guinness plc in 1995; Guinness went on to take over D.C.L. in 1997, so Dufftown now falls within Diageo's estate.

Dufftown is Diageo's largest malt whisky distillery, with a capacity of four and a half million litres of pure alcohol a year.

CURIOSITIES: Dufftown-Glenlivet was the sixth distillery to be built at Dufftown.

Unusually, the spirit stills are larger than the wash stills.

Dufftown village itself was founded in 1817, by James Duff, fourth Earl of Fife, as a means of finding employment for men returning from the Napoleonic Wars. He had distinguished himself during the Peninsula War, achieving the rank of Major General, and was M.P. for Banffshire 1818–27. The town was originally named Balvenie after the large medieval castle that stands on its edge, but soon changed its name to that of its founder. (See *Balvenie*.)

The men of Mortlach (Dufftown's original distillery) resented the arrival of a newcomer and sought to divert Dufftown's water supply on more than one occasion.

EXPRESSIONS:
Some Dufftown was bottled as a single by Bell's. Since Guinness took over:
- Dufftown 15YO @ 43% (Flora & Fauna series, released 1990)
- Dufftown-Glenlivet 20YO @ 55.8% (Centenary Bottling, released 1996)
- Dufftown 21YO 1975 @ 54.8% (Rare Malts series, released 1997)

RAW MATERIALS: Floor maltings until 1968, now unpeated malt from Burghead. Soft process water from Jock's Well in the Conval Hills (supplemented by the Convalley Springs), cooling water from the River Dullan.

PLANT: Full-Lauter mash tun (11 tonnes). Twelve stainless steel washbacks. Three plain wash stills (13,000 litres charge); three plain spirit stills (15,000 litres charge). All indirect fired, and run hot. Shell-and-tube condensers, with after-coolers.

MATURATION: Ex-bourbon refills, with a small amount in ex-sherry refills.

STYLE: Malty, nutty.

MATURE CHARACTER: The nose is Speyside-sweet, fruity and cereal-like (bruised apples, pears), with some butterscotch. The taste is predominantly sweet, with cereal notes and light toffee. Medium-bodied.

Dumbarton Grain Distillery (Demolished)

ADDRESS
2 Glasgow
Road, Dumbarton ,
Dunbartonshire
OWNER
Allied Distillers
CAPACITY
25m L.P.A.
CLOSED
2002

The stills, designed in North America and built in Scotland, were the first to challenge the supremacy of the Coffey still.

HISTORICAL NOTES: Dumbarton Distillery was built in the town of the same name by Hiram Walker (Scotland) Ltd in 1938 from millions of red bricks, an unusual material in Scotland. The site was formerly MacMillan's shipyard, and the distillery was designed in North America, the continuous stills coming from the Vulcan Copper & Supply Company of Cincinnati. In its day it was the largest grain distillery in Scotland.

Inverleven (malt whisky) Distillery was built within the Dumbarton complex at the same time as the grain distillery, and in 1959 a Lomond still was added. In 1965 the first dark-grains plant in the U.K. was installed (based on the American system).

Hiram Walker was bought by Allied Lyons in 1987, and Dumbarton Distillery was closed in 2002. It has now been demolished.

CURIOSITIES: Water came from Loch Lomond, which gave its name to the Lomond still.

Only maize was used, and this ambition was a qualified success: the stills could not process other grains, producing a heavy style of make, and it was quickly realised that to make good-quality grain whisky it was essential that at least part of the stills must be made from copper, a purifying and lightening catalyst. The maize came mainly from the U.S.A. and France.

Hiram Walker Gooderham & Worts Ltd was the largest distiller in Canada (Canadian Club was its leading brand). Keen to enter the Scotch whisky market, the company bought Ballantine's in 1935, together with extensive stocks of mature whisky but no distilleries. It was imperative to acquire production facilities, so Glenburgie and Miltonduff Distilleries were acquired in 1936 (see entries), and then Dumbarton was built.

EXPRESSIONS:
Never bottled by its owner; used for Ballantine's blends.
Occasionally bottled by independents.

Ed

Edradour

REGION
Highland (Perthshire)

ADDRESS
Milton of Edradour, near
Pitlochry, Perthshire

PHONE
01796 472095

WEBSITE
www.edradour.com

OWNER
Signatory Vintage Scotch
Whisky Co. Ltd.

VISITORS
Visitor centre, shop and
tasting bar

CAPACITY
96,000 LPA

HISTORICAL NOTES: Edradour is a classic farm distillery, was the smallest in Scotland until 2005, and remains among the prettiest. It stands as a reminder of how many distilleries will have looked, and operated, during the 19th century.

In all likelihood it was established by one Duncan Forbes in 1825 (named Glenforres), but the foundation on the present site was in 1837, when a group of farmers leased a strip of land beside the Edradour Burn from the Duke of Atholl. Their leader was Mungo Stewart; Duncan Forbes and six other farmers joined the co-operative.

After 1841 they were led by John McGlashan, who continued to manage the distillery until 1877, although after 1853 the license was in the name of another local farmer, James Reid.

In 1885 the distillery was transferred to John Mackintsh, son of one of the original founders. He increased production and transformed Edradour into a successful commercial enterprise. When he died in 1907 he left the distillery to his nephew Peter, whose father (John's brother) was the excise officer at Ord Distillery.

These were difficult times for the whisky industry, and Peter was further hindered by bad health. Between 1920 and 1932 cask sales dropped from 90 to 21. In early 1933 he sold the distillery and two cottages to William Whiteley for £1,050.

Whiteley's subsidiary, J.G. Turney & Sons, was a customer of Edradour, and used the make in his blends House of Lords and King's Ransom (the latter introduced in 1928 and reputed to be the most expensive whisky of its day). He quickly developed the American market, getting around the problem that Prohibition was still in place by building relationships with the highest levels of the Mafia.

He retired in 1938 and sold the company and distillery to his American distributor, Irving Haim, who left Edradour as it was, except for installing electricity in 1947. On his death in 1976, the distillery was briefly owned by a consortium, then bought by Campbell

Edradour is one of the most popular distillery destinations in Scotland, welcoming around 100,000 visitors a year.

Distillers (a subsidiary of Pernod Ricard) in 1982. Four years later Edradour was bottled as a single malt for the first time, at 10 years old, and the former malt barn was developed into a visitor centre and shop.

In July 2002, Edradour was bought for £5.4 million (£3 million of which was maturing stock) by Andrew Symington, owner of Signatory Vintage Malt Whisky Company. Many improvements have been made, including the building of a bottling hall in 2007.

CURIOSITIES: William Whitely (1861–1942) was a tough Yorkshireman and a canny marketeer. He had started as a salesman for a wine and spirits company, but was dismissed in 1908 for acting beyond his remit. In 1914 he purchased J.G. Turney & Son, another wine and spirits merchant, based in Leith, but selling mainly in export markets. With the introduction of Prohibition in the U.S., Whiteley appointed Frank Costello as his 'U.S. Sales Consultant' with an annual salary of $5,000. It may have been Costello who described Whiteley as 'The Dean of Distillers', and the name stuck.

Costello was a leading figure in the Mafia, becoming its Capo di tutti Capi (and the model for 'The Godfather' in Mario Puzo's books). Described as a 'visionary gangster' he was a major bootlegger and controlled numerous speakeasies and clubs in New York. Whiteley's business was handed by Costello's side-kick, Irving Haim, and when Whitely retired in 1938, he acquired J.G. Turnery & Son.

EXPRESSIONS:

The new owner has greatly increased the product range, including many wood finishes and limited editions. A smoky range (over 50ppm phenols), named Ballechin (after a local distillery which closed in 1927), was first released in 2006.

• Edradour 10YO Distillery Edition 40% (U.S.A. 43%)

• Edradour Straight From The Cask Range - Cask strength bottled by hand – (Typically 10–12 years old in 50cl bottles. Single sherry casks or wine finishes which have spent between 6 and 24 months in finishing cask. 12 varieties to date, more in pipe-

line. Wood finishes include Maderira, Sauternes, Chardonnay, Burgundy, Bordeaux, Cotes de Provence, Marsala, Barolo, Super Tuscan, Grand Arome Rum, and Port wood)
- Edradour 10YO @ 46% (non-chill filtered, first released in 2002)
- Edradour Natural Cask Strength (12–14YO single sherry casks at cask strength)
- Edradour 30YO @43% (limited edition, released 2003)
- Edradour 30YO @53.4% (limited edition, sherry butt released 2003)
- Edradour 1983 Portwood Finish @ cask strength (bottlings from a small batch of casks recasked into port casks in 2002. 21yo, 22yo, 23yo and 24yo releases to date)
- Edradour 1984 Pedro Ximinez Finish @ cask strength (21 and 22YO bottlings)
- Edradour 1984 and 1985 Chateau d'Yquem Finish @ cask strength (limited bottlings at 21 and 22yo)
Ballechin Discovery series are limited releases from the various casks used to mature the peated version of the Edradour, each limited to 6,000 bottles:
- Ballechin Discovery Series #1 3YO @46% (from ex-Burgundy barrels, released 2006)
- Ballechin Discovery Series #2 4YO @ 46% (from Madeira casks, released 2007)
- Ballechin Discovery Series #3 5YO @46% (from Port casks, released 2008)

RAW MATERIALS: Un-peated malt from Bairds, Edinburgh; peated malt from Inverness. Pre-1975 the malt was ground on site by mill-stones; between 2002 and 2007 it arrived ready milled. Soft process water from a spring on Moulin Moor, cooling water from Edradour Burn.

PLANT: Cast iron, rake and plough mash tun made in 1910 (1.1 tonnes). Wort cooled by a Morton Refrigerator (the last left in the whisky industry; made in 1933 and installed in 1934). Two Douglas fir washbacks. One plain wash still (4,200 litres charge); One boil-ball spirit still (2,000 litres charge), equipped with a purifier. Both indirect fired. Worm tubs on both stills.

MATURATION: Edradour is matured in a combination of refill U.S. oak hogsheads and European oak butts; Ten different kinds of first fill wine casks are also used, either for maturing or finishing. Ballechin is primarily matured in first-fill ex-bourbon barrels, with some first fill sherry and refill sherry. In both makes, no cask is used more than twice.

STYLE: Edradour fruity, pear-like, with a good body. Ballechin peaty.

Fettercairn

REGION
Highland (East)
ADDRESS
Fettercairn, Laurencekirk,
Angus
PHONE
01561 340244
WEBSITE
www.whyteandmackay.
com
OWNER
Whyte & Mackay
VISITORS
Visitor centre
CAPACITY
2m L.P.A.

HISTORICAL NOTES: Fettercairn is in the heart of the fertile Mearns district, celebrated by the writer Lewis Grassic Gibbon (*Sunset Song* etc.). The distillery was established by the laird of Fasque, Sir Alexander Ramsay, in 1824. He sold the estate to Sir John Gladstone, father of Prime Minister William Ewart Gladstone in 1830. Although managed by tenants, the Gladstone involvement remained until 1923, when the distillery was sold to Ross & Coulter, whisky brokers since 1919 (and later owners of Bladnoch and Bruichladdich Distilleries). They mothballed it from 1926 to 1939, then sold it to a subsidiary of National Distillers of America (which would ultimately own Ben Nevis, Bruichladdich, Lochside, Glenesk and Glenury Royal Distilleries). Extended from two to four stills in 1966/67.

Fettercairn was bought by Tomintoul-Glenlivet Distillery Company in 1971, and the latter was acquired by the Scottish & Universal Investment Trust, owner of Whyte & Mackay Distillers, two years later. They built an extensive effluent disposal plant adjacent to the distillery in 1980. In 2007 Whyte & Mackay was acquired by the Indian brewer and distiller, U.B. Group.

CURIOSITIES: The water-cooling system on the spirit stills is unique. Cold water cascades down the necks of the stills from a collar, collecting in a trough above the shoulder to be drawn off and re-used in the boiler. A further curiosity is the fact that each pair of stills has its own spirit safe – referred to as No. 1 Side and No. 2 Side – although the makes of each are mixed.

The product of the distillery was sold as Old Fettercairn until 2002, when the core expression was rebranded and repackaged as Fettercairn 1824.

EXPRESSIONS:
In spite of the distillery's size, Fettercairn has never been common, even in independent bottlings. Current bottlings include:
• Fettercairn 1824 12YO @ 40% (introduced 2002)

Some single cask bottlings on site are for sale exclusively through the visitor centre.

RAW MATERIALS: Floor maltings until 1960; now unpeated malt from independent maltsters, and, since 2005, heavily peated (55ppm phenols) for a couple of weeks a year for blending purposes. Process water from springs in the Grampian Hills which rise behind the town; cooling water from the Caulecotts Burn.

PLANT: Cast iron traditional mash tun (4.88 tonnes); eight Oregon pine washbacks.

Two plain wash stills (13,000 litres charge); two plain spirit stills (13,500 litres and 11,500 litres charge), both with water jackets. All indirect fired. Shell-and-tube condensers (all stainless steel until 1995).

MATURATION: Mix of ex-sherry, ex-bourbon and refill hogsheads. Matured mainly at Invergordon; some in dunnage warehouses on site, where there is capacity for 30,000 casks.

STYLE: Butterscotch, walnuts and spice.

MATURE CHARACTER: The nose is sweet and malty, with traces of damp wool and mixed nuts. The taste is sweetish to start, drying with nuts, biscuits and a whiff of smoke. Slightly oily. Medium-bodied.

Girvan Grain Distillery

ADDRESS
Girvan, South Ayrshire
PHONE
01465 713091
OWNER
William Grant & Sons Ltd
CAPACITY
77m L.P.A.

The distillery has an austere appearance, influenced by the Bauhaus design style.

HISTORICAL NOTES: The post-war boom in demand for Scotch, combined with grain rationing – the industry was not completely deregulated until 1958 – and an acute shortage of aged whiskies, meant that the larger companies (notably D.C.L.) limited the amount of both malt and grain whisky available to smaller producers.

During the late 1950s/early 1960s several companies built new grain whisky distilleries to meet the demand: Invergordon (Invergordon Distillers Ltd, 1959), Strathmore (North of Scotland Distilling Company, 1960) and Moffat/Garnheath (Inver House Distillers, 1965). William Grant & Sons, owners of Glenfiddich and Balvenie Distilleries, and of the successful blend Standfast, built Girvan in 1963/64. Within a year they had added a malt whisky distillery to the site, named Ladyburn (closed 1975).

Key reasons for choosing the small Ayrshire port of Girvan were the water supply, the availability of labour and access to both the sea and Lowland blending houses.

CURIOSITIES: In 1962 the ever enterprising Grant's of Glenfiddich proposed running an advertising campaign for their popular Standfast blend on the nascent commercial TV channel in the U.K. The mighty D.C.L. responded by threatening to cut off their supply of grain whisky, and it is said that this influenced the family's decision to build their own grain whisky distillery.

The dark-grains plant which was also installed has the largest filter presses in the world for separating solids and yeast debris.

EXPRESSIONS:
• Black Barrel Single Grain Whisky @ 40% (duty-free and export only)
• Girvan 1964 @ 48% (limited to 1,200 bottles, released 2000)

RAW MATERIALS: The cereal base is home-grown wheat and malted barley. Water from Penwhapple Loch.

PLANT: The continuous mashing plant, which integrated cooking and mashing, was replaced in 1995. The patented distillation systems operate a unique vacuum distillation process in the mash column, heated by the vapour off the rectifier. There are three distillation plants, two of the above type and a modified Coffey still which is today used only rarely.

MATURATION: On site.

STYLE: Clean, estery, sweet.

G1

Glen Albyn Demolished

REGION
Highland (North)
ADDRESS
by Muirtown Basin,
Merkinch, Inverness
LAST OWNER
D.C.L./S.M.D.
CLOSED
1983

Glen Albyn had a reputation as being 'the classic example of Highland style'.

HISTORICAL NOTES: The distillery was built on the ruins of Muirtown Brewery, beside the Caledonian Canal, in 1840 by James Sutherland, Provost of Inverness. The site provided easy access to southern markets by sea, but the distillery was badly damaged by fire nine years after it opened, and in 1855 Sutherland was sequestrated. Briefly used as a flour mill, the buildings lay unoccupied for 20 years, before being bought (in 1884) by William Grigor, a grain merchant, who built a new and larger distillery on the site.

Manager John Birnie, in partnership with Charles Mackinlay & Company, bought the site across the road and built Glen Mhor Distillery in 1892 (see entry). Mackinlay & Birnie bought Glen Albyn in 1920, and the company was acquired by D.C.L. in 1972 and transferred to S.M.D. Both distilleries were closed in 1983, and the Glen Albyn site is now a supermarket.

CURIOSITIES: During World War I, Glen Albyn became a U.S. naval base for the manufacture of mines, according to one source, and an Admiralty depot making boom defences according to another.

The distillery's floor maltings were replaced by Saladin boxes in 1954.

Although only a matter of yards from each other, the make from Glen Albyn was entirely different from that of Glen Mhor, and rated more highly.

EXPRESSIONS:
Uncommon as a single malt.
• Glen Albyn 1975 @ 54.8% (Rare Malts series, released 2002)

Glenallachie

REGION
Speyside
ADDRESS
Aberlour, Moray
PHONE
01340 871315
WEBSITE
www.maltwhisky
distilleries.com
OWNER
Chivas Brothers
VISITORS
No
CAPACITY
3m L.P.A.

HISTORICAL NOTES: The 'Glen of the Rocky Place' (*Gleann Aleachaidh*) runs up behind Aberlour towards Edinvillie. It is not very rocky, although the mass of Ben Rinnes rises close beside the distillery, which draws its production water from springs on the mountainside.

It was commissioned by Mackinlay-Macpherson (then a subsidiary of Scottish & Newcastle Breweries) in 1967, primarily to contribute Speyside fillings to the Mackinlay blend, which at that time was among the top five bestsellers in the U.K., and designed by William Delmé-Evans. The architect was Lothian Barclay, son of the whisky entrepreneur, James Barclay (see *Strathmill*). The design is modern and efficient, and very 1960s.

Mackinlay's was sold to Invergordon Distillers in 1985, and Glenallachie was mothballed, then closed. In 1989 it was sold to Campbell Distillers (Pernod Ricard), and went back into production. Chivas Brothers became Pernod Ricard's distilling division in 2001.

CURIOSITIES: William Delmé-Evans has been compared to Charles Doig, the greatest distillery architect of the late nineteenth century. Having completed Tullibardine and Jura Distilleries, he turned to Glenallachie, his last project.

He was such a stickler for efficiency that he even marked the light-bulbs in the distillery with the date on which they were installed, to monitor how long they lasted!

EXPRESSIONS:
A small amount of Glenallachie was bottled as a single in 1982, for export.
• Glenallachie 1989 16YO @ 56.7% (from ex-sherry-wood, released 2005)

RAW MATERIALS: Unpeated malt from independent maltsters. Water from springs on Ben Rinnes via two dammed streams flowing into the Lour Burn. Cooling water is collected in an attractive pond by the distillery.

Glenallachie comes from Glen Aleach-aidh – the glen of the rocky place.

PLANT: Semi-Lauter mash tun (9.2 tonnes); six stainless steel-lined washbacks.

Two lamp-glass wash stills (23,000 litres charge); two plain spirit stills (16,000 litres charge). All designed by Delmé-Evans. Indirect fired. Horizontal shell-and-tube condensers.

MATURATION: Mainly refill U.S. hogsheads, some first-fill. Twelve racked and two palletised warehouses on site, the rest matured at other Chivas sites.

STYLE: Sweet, grassy and estery.

MATURE CHARACTER: Speyside sweetness, with fruity-floral notes. Some detect a whiff of smoke. Light and fresh. Similar to taste, starting very sweet, with vanilla and apples; clean and smooth, with a scented finish. Light-bodied.

Glenburgie

REGION
Speyside

ADDRESS
Mains of Burgie, Forres,
Moray

PHONE
01343 850258

WEBSITE
No

OWNER
Chivas Brothers

VISITORS
By appointment

CAPACITY
4.2m L.P.A.

HISTORICAL NOTES: Glenburgie bore the name
Kilnflat, a place in the parish of Alves, between Elgin
and Forres, until the 1870s. It was built in 1829 by
William Paul, the son of a distinguished surgeon,
who had formerly been involved in Grange Distillery
(somewhere nearby and founded 1810, hence the
foundation date adopted by Glenburgie). In 1871, Paul
sub-let to Charles Hay, who changed the name to
Glenburgie and sold to Alexander Fraser & Company,
in about 1882.

The new owner went bankrupt in 1925 and the
receiver, a well-known character named Donald
Mustard, took over but did not resume production
and sold to the blending firm, James & George
Stodart Ltd of Dumbarton (owners of the Old
Smuggler brand) two years later.

The giant Canadian distiller, Hiram Walker, bought
60% of Stodart's in 1930 – Walker's first move into
Scotch – and took full control in 1936, when they
also bought Miltonduff Distillery. They had acquired
George Ballantine & Son Ltd the year before from
James Barclay (see *Strathisla*), and Glenburgie and
Miltonduff became (and remain) the key malts for
the Ballantine's blends.

In 1987 Allied Lyons bought Ballantine's and its
associated distilleries, and in 2005 they passed to
Pernod Ricard and its operating division, Chivas
Brothers.

Glenburgie Distillery was demolished in 2004 and
rebuilt on an adjacent site at a cost of £4.3 million.
The new owners immediately installed an extra pair
of stills and the distillery came into production in
June 2005.

CURIOSITIES: Remarkably, the original distillery
building of 1829 still stands, now isolated in a car
park, but tastefully refurbished as a nosing room.
It is tiny: a two-windowed, stone-built cottage, about
80 feet by 30, with an outside stair leading to a single
room and a low-ceilinged cellar beneath.

Between 1958 and 1981, two Lomond stills were in

The distillery stands on a slight eminence, the tail end of Burgie Hill, which was the 'blasted heath' where Macbeth met the witches.

operation here, producing Glencraig single malt – named after William Craig, Ballantine's Production Director at the time. (See *Inverleven, Miltonduff.*) His son, who still works for the company, reports that the name was given to placate his father, who was sceptical about their effectiveness! The stills were converted to plain stills in the 1980s, by replacing the heads.

In his seminal book *Scotch Whisky* (1930), Aeneas Macdonald lists Glenburgie among his Top 12 Highland Malts.

The novelist Maurice Walsh was the Excise officer at Glenburgie during the 1940s. His books *The Quiet Man* and *Trouble in the Glen* were made into Hollywood movies; the first in 1950 (starring John Wayne and Maureen O'Hara), the second in 1954 (starring Orson Welles and Margaret Lockwood). His grandson is Jameson's master blender.

The views from the gallery in the malt loft across the Laich o' Moray to the Moray Firth are stupendous.

EXPRESSIONS:
Only bottled once by its owner (Allied) at 15 years old, in 2002. Not currently bottled by its owner as a single.

RAW MATERIALS: Unpeated malt from independent maltsters; own floor maltings removed 1958. Production water from springs on Burgie Hill; cooling water from a burn.

PLANT: Full-Lauter mash tun (eight tonnes); 12 stainless steel washbacks. Three plain wash stills (12,000 litres each charge); three plain spirit stills (14,000 litres each charge). Indirect fired by steam since 1958 (the riveted base of No. 1 wash still dates from the days of direct firing). Shell-and-tube condensers .

MATURATION: Mainly refill U.S. hogsheads, some first-fill. Dunnage, racked and palletised warehouses on site with capacity for 60,000 casks. The remainder matured at Mulben.

STYLE: Sweet, grassy and estery.

MATURE CHARACTER: The 15YO is light and grassy, with sweet vanilla sponge notes. The taste is sweet, with hints of vanilla, toffee and tinned pears, and a trace of smoke. Light-bodied.

G1

Glencadam

REGION
Highland (East)
ADDRESS
Park Road, Brechin, Angus
PHONE
01356 622217
WEBSITE
www.angusdundee.co.uk
VISITORS
By appointment
OWNER
Angus Dundee plc
CAPACITY
1.5m L.P.A.

HISTORICAL NOTES: Situated about a mile outside the ancient Royal Burgh of Brechin, Glencadam (the name means 'the glen of the wild goose') was founded in 1825 by Messrs Thomas & Ruxton. In 1852 Alexander Milne Thompson took over, and in 1893, when Glencadam Distillery Ltd was incorporated, it was under the control of the Glasgow blenders Gilmore Thomson & Company. Thomas, Thompson, Thomson … I have been unable to establish connections. However, the Directors of Gilmore Thomson & Company sold the distillery to Hiram Walker for £83,400 in July 1954, the same year in which the Canadian company bought Scapa; Pulteney would be acquired in 1955.

When he visited in 1985, Philip Morrice noted: 'It is trimly furnished – in keeping with all the distilleries belonging to Hiram Walker – and is in no way dulled by its proximity to its nearest neighbour, the municipal cemetery'. Two years later Hiram Walker was bought by Allied Lyons (whose spirits division became Allied Distillers the same year). Glencadam became the heart malt for Stewart's Cream of the Barley. Allied mothballed the distillery in 2000, then sold it to Angus Dundee Ltd, a well-established family firm of blenders, based in London, in 2003. A large blending plant was installed at the distillery in November 2007.

CURIOSITIES: Glencadam has ascending lyne arms on both stills (by 14°), which increases reflux and makes for lighter spirit. Another uncommon feature is that the wash is heated externally in a heat exchanger attached to the wash still, then pumped back into the still where it is forced through a 'diffuser' to heat the rest of the wash. This greatly increases copper uptake so also makes for a lighter spirit.

EXPRESSIONS:
A few independent bottlings only, until Angus Dundee took over.
• Glencadam 15YO @ 40% (released 2004)

149 | GLENCADAM

Gilmore Thomson's 'Royal', for which blend Glencadam was a key malt, was a favourite of King Edward VII – a man who generally preferred champagne.

RAW MATERIALS: Unpeated malt from independent maltsters. Soft cooling and process water from Moorans water supply (a tributary of the North Esk), which used to supply the Royal Burgh of Brechin.

PLANT: Rake-and-plough mash tun (4.9 tonnes); six stainless steel washbacks. One plain wash still (12,600 litres); one plain spirit still (12,260 litres). Wash still has an external heater-diffuser. Indirect fired. Shell-and-tube condensers.

MATURATION: All ex-bourbon barrels. 20,000 casks on site.

STYLE: Soft, light, boiled sweets, pear drops.

MATURE CHARACTER: The 15YO has a pleasant 'peaches and cream' nose, with almonds and vanilla. The taste is sweet and creamy, with nuts and a trace of malt. Some detect asparagus and aniseed. Medium-bodied.

Glendronach

REGION
Speyside

ADDRESS
Forgue, near Huntly,
Aberdeenshire

PHONE
01466 730202

WEBSITE
www.theglendronach.com

VISITORS
Visitor centre

OWNER
The BenRiach-Glendronach
Distilleries Company Ltd

CAPACITY
1.3m L.P.A.

HISTORICAL NOTES: Glendronach is one of the most charming and old-fashioned distilleries in Scotland. It was built in 1825 by a group of local farmers and businessmen, led by James Allardice, who so impressed the local laird, the Duke of Gordon, that he was introduced by the Duke to London society, among whom he established something of a reputation for his 'Guid Glendronach'. Alas, a fire in 1837 largely destroyed the distillery, and this was followed five years later by Allardice's bankruptcy.

Most of his partners withdrew at this time, to be replaced by others who rebuilt the distillery during the 1850s (much of the present distillery dates from this time). The managing partner was Walter Scott, of Falkirk, who became sole proprietor in 1881. On his death in 1886, Glendronach was taken over by another partnership, this time of Leith wine merchants and a Campbeltown distiller. They managed it successfully until 1920 (even providing Teacher's Ardmore Distillery with its first Manager), when it was bought by Captain Charles Grant, youngest son of the founder of Glenfiddich Distillery (for £9,000).

His son sold to William Teacher & Sons in 1960, together with the distillery's 1,000-acre farm, and a herd of Highland cattle. The make had long been a key filling for the Teacher's blends. Glendronach was extended from two to four stills in 1966/67, then mothballed between 1996 and May 2002; and when Allied was split up in 2005, Teacher's went to Fortune Brands, and Glendronach Distillery to Pernod Ricard/Chivas Brothers.

On 25 July 2008, it was announced that the distillery had been sold to Billy Walker of BenRiach Distillers.

CURIOSITIES: On one occasion, when he had dined at Gordon Castle, Mr Allardice, somewhat the worse for drink, was over-effusive in his praise of the Duchess of Gordon's piano playing. The following morning the Duke informed him that his wife was not amused,

'Redcurrant jelly is good for the belly. Ginger and nuts are good for the guts. But the wine of Glendronach is good for the stomach!'

to which he replied: 'Well, Your Grace, it was just the trash of Glenlivet you gave me yesterday after dinner that did not agree wi' me. If it had been my ain guid Glendronach, I would have not have been ony the warr.' A cask of Glendronach was ordered immediately.

EXPRESSIONS:
In 1991 Allied took the novel step of offering two versions of Glendronach 12YO: Traditional (from ex-sherry casks) and Original (from a mix of ex-sherry and ex-bourbon casks). These were included in their Caledonian Malts series.
Current proprietor's bottlings:
• Glendronach 12YO Original (double matured)

RAW MATERIALS: Production water from Dronac Burn, which flows through the distillery. Lightly peated malt from independent maltsters; own floor maltings, but not used since 1996.

PLANT: Unusually small cast iron, rake-and-plough mash tun (3.72 tonnes). Nine Oregon pine washbacks. Two boil-ball wash stills (9,000 litres charge); two boil-ball spirit stills (6,000 litres charge). Direct fired by coal until September 2005, when converted to indirect firing by steam. Shell-and-tube condensers.

MATURATION: Combination of ex-sherry and ex-bourbon casks.

STYLE: Rich, sweet, creamy.

MATURE CHARACTER: Richly sherried in style, but also showing the contribution (sweetness, vanilla, trace of coconut) of American oak. The taste is both sweet (with dried fruits, malt and toffee) and tannic-dry. Full- to medium-bodied.

Glendullan

REGION
Speyside
ADDRESS
Dufftown, Moray
PHONE
01340 820250
WEBSITE
www.malts.com
VISITORS
By appointment
OWNER
Diageo plc
CAPACITY
3.7m L.P.A.

HISTORICAL NOTES: Glendullan Distillery was founded in 1897 by William Williams & Sons, blenders in Aberdeen, in a wooded glen beside the River Fiddich. Water from the river drove all the machinery in the distillery, via a huge water wheel – 'a great saving, compared to distilleries which have to use steam engines', wrote *Harper's*. It also shared a private railway siding with its neighbour, Mortlach. All supplies came by rail until 1968, when the branch line was closed.

The distillery was very well-built, and most of the original plant was still being used in the 1930s.

It was the seventh distillery built in Dufftown and gave rise to the rhyme:

'Rome was built on seven hills, but Dufftown stands on seven stills'.

In 1919 Williams amalgamated with Greenlees Brothers Ltd, Glasgow and London, makers of the Old Parr blends. This company had already merged with Alexander & Macdonald Ltd of Leith and now became Macdonald Greenlees & Williams. The company joined D.C.L. in 1925 and Glendullan was transferred to S.M.D. in 1930. The distillery was closed from 1940 to 1947, and rebuilt in 1962, the stills being converted to indirect heating at that time.

Ten years later a new and larger (six stills) distillery was built nearby, in S.M.D.'s 'Waterloo Street' style (see *Caol Ila* etc.). Between 1972 and 1985 the two distilleries operated in parallel, the makes of each being vatted together, then the original distillery was closed and dismantled. The buildings are now used as workshops by Diageo. Glendullan is the company's second largest distillery.

CURIOSITIES: Small amounts of Glendullan single malt were supplied to the Royal Household of Edward VII in 1902.

The spirit character from the original Glendullan Distillery was quite different from that of the 1970s distillery, and is esteemed more highly. The current spirit character is similar to Cardhu, a fact which led to it being used in the infamous Cardhu Pure Malt (see *Cardhu*).

EXPRESSIONS:

- Glendullan 12YO @ 43% (Flora & Fauna series, since 1992)
- Glendullan 22YO 1972 @ 62.6% (Rare Malts series, released 1995)
- Glendullan 23YO 1972 @ 62.4% (Rare Malts series, released 1996)
- Glendullan 23YO 1973 @ 58.6% (Rare Malts series, released 1997)
- Glendullan 16YO 1982 @ 62.6% (Centenary Bottling, released 1998)
- Glendullan 23YO 1974 @ 63.1% (Rare Malts series, released 1999)
- Glendullan 26YO 1978 @ 56.6% (Rare Malts series, released 2005)
- The Singleton of Glendullan 12YO @ 40% (North America only, introduced 2007)

RAW MATERIALS: Floor maltings until 1962, now unpeated malt from Burghead. Soft process water from springs in the Conval Hills; cooling water from the River Fiddich. Previously, Fiddich water was used for mashing as well – one of the reasons for choosing the site was its proximity to the river.

PLANT: Full-Lauter mash tun (12 tonnes). Three plain wash stills (15,500 litres charge); three plain spirit stills (16,000 litres charge). Until 1972, two stills only. All indirect fired. Shell-and-tube condensers. The original distillery had worm tubs, in use until 1985.

MATURATION: Ex-bourbon refill hogsheads, some European oak (for The Singleton). Matured in the Central Belt.

STYLE: Floral/grassy.

MATURE CHARACTER: Typical light/medium-style Speyside. The nose is sweet and estery, with apples and pears and cut grass; the taste is sweet throughout with a smooth texture and light mouth feel. Medium- to light-bodied.

Glen Elgin

REGION
Speyside

ADDRESS
Longmorn, Elgin, Moray

PHONE
01343 860212

WEBSITE
www.malts.com

OWNER
Diageo plc

VISITORS
By appointment

CAPACITY
1.9m L.P.A.

HISTORICAL NOTES: Charles Doig, the famous distillery architect who designed Glen Elgin, prophesised that it would be the last distillery to be built on Speyside for 50 years. He was spot on: the next was Glen Keith, which opened in 1958.

Glen Elgin was founded by a former Manager at Glenfarclas, William Simpson, in partnership with a banker, James Carle. Building started in 1898, but following the crash of Pattison's – a major blending house and buyer of fillings – it was down-sized, and within six months of its opening in 1900 it closed and was sold for £4,000. Production resumed for a year, then Glen Elgin was sold again in 1906 (for £7,000) to John J. Blanche & Company, a wine and spirit company in Glasgow. Blanche died in 1929 and again the distillery was sold, this time to D.C.L., who licensed it to White Horse Distillers – it had long been a key constituent of the White Horse blend.

Until the 1950s the distillery was entirely operated and lit by paraffin; all machinery was driven by a paraffin engine and water turbine. Like other D.C.L. distilleries, Glen Elgin was extensively refurbished in 1964, and expanded from two stills to six; it closed again for refurbishment between 1992 and 1995.

Glen Elgin is ranked Top Class by blenders, and it has been described as 'the distillers' dram of drams'.

CURIOSITIES: Brian Spiller remarks that: 'It took almost the whole of one man's time to keep the paraffin lamps in working order.' Glen Elgin was only connected to the electricity grid in 1950.

EXPRESSIONS:
A 12YO was introduced by White Horse Distillers as early as 1977, and the first distillery bottling (Flora & Fauna series) was introduced in the early 1990s. This was withdrawn in 2002 and replaced by the same whisky in the Hidden Malts series. In 2006, Glen Elgin became part of the extended Classic Malts series (12YO @ 43%).
• Glen Elgin 12YO @ 43% (Hidden Malts series, released 2002)
• Glen Elgin 32YO @ 42.3% (Special Edition, released 2003)

Glen Elgin's site was chosen for the quality of its water supply and proximity to the railway. Unfortunately, the water source proved unreliable and permission for a railway siding was refused by the Board of Trade!

RAW MATERIALS: Floor maltings until 1964, now unpeated malt from Burghead. Soft process water from springs near Millbuies Loch; cooling water from the Glen Burn.

PLANT: Full-Lauter tun, with an octagonal canopy (8.2 tonnes). (The earlier rake-and-plough mash tun was only removed in 2000.) Six larch washbacks. Three plain wash stills (6,800 litres charge); three plain spirit stills (8,100 litres charge). All indirect fired (direct fired by coal until 1970). Worm tubs.

MATURATION: Mix of ex-bourbon and ex-sherry refill casks.

STYLE: Fruity and full-bodied.

MATURE CHARACTER: Glen Elgin is subtle and complex. At first sight it is a typical Speysie – estery, fruity, grassy – but there is interesting depth to these aromas, traces of tangerine, light honey, vanilla, even a hint of cloves. Medium-bodied.

Glenesk Dismantled

REGION
Highland (East)
ADDRESS
Kinnaber Road, Hillside,
Montrose, Angus
LAST OWNER
D.C.L./S.M.D.
CLOSED
1985

No distillery has been known by so many names!

HISTORICAL NOTES: When it was founded in 1897, within a converted flax mill on the bank of the River South Esk, it was named 'Highland Esk'. By 1897 it was 'North Esk'; between 1938 and 1964 it was called simply 'Montrose'; then its name changed to 'Hillside' (1964); finally it became 'Glenesk' in 1980.

The mill conversion was done by James Isles, a wine merchant in Dundee, in partnership with Septimus Parsonage & Company. They lasted only two years, when the distillery was taken over. Closed during World War I, it did not operate again until 1938, when it was bought by Joseph Hobbs for National Distillers of America (see *Ben Nevis*). A patent still was installed and Glenesk/Montrose was converted to grain distillation. When D.C.L. bought it in 1954 they continued to distill grain whisky intermittently, then resumed malt whisky distilling in 1964.

A drum maltings was built beside the distillery in 1968 (enlarged in 1973 to 24 drums) – Montrose's situation is on the edge of the fertile Mearns district, good barley-growing country. The maltings was bought by Pauls Malt Ltd in 1996, and is now owned by the Irish company Greencore, the sixth largest malt producer in the world.

The distillery closed in 1985, although the distilling licence was only cancelled in 1992. All the distilling equipment has now been removed.

CURIOSITIES: 'Esk' derives from 'uisge', the Gaelic for 'water'.

Glenesk was licensed to William Sanderson & Sons during its D.C.L. days, and supplied fillings for VAT 69.

EXPRESSIONS:
A few independent bottlings have appeared, and Hillside has been popular as a rare malt.
- Glenesk 24YO @ 60% (to celebrate the 25th anniversary of the Maltings, released 1994)
- Hillside 25YO @ 60–62% (six bottlings at cask strength in the Rare Malts series, released between 1995 and 1997)

Glenfarclas

REGION
Speyside
ADDRESS
Ballindalloch, Moray
PHONE
01807 500257
WEBSITE
www.glenfarclas.co.uk
OWNER
J. & G. Grant
VISITORS
Visitor centre, shop (with
panelling from SS *Empress
of Australia*)
CAPACITY
3m L.P.A.

HISTORICAL NOTES: The distillery was not actually founded by the Grants of Glenfarclas: the first licence for the site was granted in 1836 to Robert Hay of Rechlerich Farm (there had been an unlicensed enterprise here since 1797), and when he died in 1865 his neighbour John Grant bought the distillery for £512. He leased it to John Smith, who had managed The Glenlivet Distillery, went on to build Cragganmore, and was reckoned one of the best distillers of the day.

In 1896, a second pair of Grants, John and George (grandsons of the founder) took over and rebuilt the distillery.

It was expanded in 1960 by the third pair of J. & G. Grants (great-grandsons, who took over in 1949), when a second pair of stills was added; this was increased to three pairs in 1976. George S. Grant served 52 years as Chairman of the family company (1949–2001), when he was succeeded by his son John. John's son is now Global Ambassador for Glenfarclas, and set to take over one day ... His name? Why, George, of course!

CURIOSITIES: 'Glenfarclas' means 'the valley of the green grass'; it stands in meadows at the foot of Benrinnes. The distillery has the largest stills on Speyside and was the first to release a cask strength single malt, in 1968, later named '101' (one degree over proof).

It was also one of the first distilleries to build a visitor centre, in 1973, which included a tasting room fashioned from the stateroom of RMS *Empress of Australia* (built 1913, broken up 1952).

Glenfarclas was named Distiller of the Year in the Icons of Whisky Awards 2006.

EXPRESSIONS:
A huge number of expressions have been released by Glenfarclas, particularly since the late 1990s, and the company is very touchy about allowing independents to use the distillery name.

• THE CORE RANGE: 8 and 10YO @ 40%; 15YO @ 46%; 12, 21, 25,

'Of all the whiskies, malt is king – of all the kings, Glenfarclas reigns supreme!' (1912, quoted by a rival distiller!)

30 and 40YO all @ 43% and Glenfarclas 105 @ 60%.
The company also offers a range of vintages, at natural strength from 1952 to 1994 – 'The Family Casks'. This is being added to annually, and in some cases variations are available, for example, the 1990 expression is available at 46% from Oloroso first-fill, from Fino first-fill and from plain oak first-fill.

RAW MATERIALS: Floor maltings until 1972, now lightly peated malt from independent maltsters. Soft process and cooling water from springs above the snow line on Benrinnes.

PLANT: Largest semi-Lauter mash tun on Speyside (16.5 tonnes per mash). Twelve stainless steel washbacks. Three large boil-ball wash stills (25,000 litres charge), equipped with rummagers; three boil-ball spirit stills (21,000 litres charge). All direct fired by gas (with oil as back-up). Shell-and-tube condensers.

MATURATION: Now mainly Oloroso ex-sherry casks, used up to three times. 60,000 casks matured on site, with about a third refill bourbon (so-called 'plain' casks).

STYLE: Delicate, sweet and fruity – gains weight during maturation.

MATURE CHARACTER: Glenfarclas ages very well, especially in sherry-wood. Above 15YO it develops complexity which is not apparent in the younger expressions – combining sherry, fruit cake and orange marmalade with sweet malt, nuts and tannic dryness, in a wholly satisfactory way, and rarely with the sulphury notes associated with sherry-wood.

Glenfiddich

REGION
Speyside
ADDRESS
Dufftown, Moray
PHONE
01340 820373
WEBSITE
www.glenfiddich.com
OWNER
William Grant & Sons Ltd
VISITORS
Reception centre, large
shop, conference facilities,
restaurant
CAPACITY
10m L.P.A.

For many years, Sir Compton Mackenzie (author of the bestseller Whisky Galore!) featured in the print advertising for Grant's Standfast.

HISTORICAL NOTES: In the autumn of 1886 William Grant, son of a Dufftown tailor and Manager of Mortlach Distillery, bought the distilling equipment from Elizabeth Cumming of Cardhu for £120 (including stills and a water mill). Since his annual salary was £100, it had taken him many years to amass enough to go it alone. With his wife and nine children he set about carting stone from the bed of the River Fiddich and building his distillery on a site on the edge of the town named Glenfiddich, 'the valley of the deer'. The first whisky ran from its stills on Christmas Day 1887.

His family all joined William Grant in the enterprise, and the company is still controlled by his descendents, now the fifth generation. Fortunately, soon after Glenfiddich began production, William Williams & Company, blenders in Aberdeen, placed an order for 400 gallons a week – the entire output of the nascent distillery. Soon the family were offering their own blends, including Standfast (the motto of Clan Grant), and selling them overseas as well as in the U.K. By 1914 the company had established 63 agencies around the world.

In 1963 the Directors of William Grant & Sons took the unprecedented step of bottling Glenfiddich Pure Malt (Straight Malt in the U.S.A.) and marketing it in the same way as blended Scotch had always been marketed; at first in England, then overseas. The venture was a huge success, export sales alone rising from 4,000 cases in 1964 to 119,500 cases in 1974. That year the company was granted the Queen's Award for Export Achievement, the first whisky company to be so honoured.

CURIOSITIES: In spite of having the largest number of pot stills in the world, the distillery is traditional in many ways. All the stills are direct fired (by gas since 2003, previously by coal); it has its own cooperage and coppersmiths; maturation is done on site; and until recently all bottling was also done at the distillery (from 2007 the bottling of 12YO has been

For many years Glenfiddich has been the bestselling single malt in the world, commanding around 18% of the market and outselling its nearest rival by 2–1.

done at Bellshill, near Glasgow, although the spirit is still reduced with process water from the Robbie Dubh spring).

Glenfiddich was the first distillery to open a visitor centre, in 1969. Today, it has five stars from VisitScotland and the summer staff of 40 (speaking 11 languages) welcomes around 80,000 visitors a year. Grant's invested £2 million in visitor facilities in recent years, and in 2007 visitors came from 101 countries.

Unveiled in spring 2008, Glenfiddich commissioned a magnificent life-size bronze stag from the eminent sculptor, Tessa Campbell Fraser. The red deer stag has long been the emblem of the distillery: 'fiddich' derives from the Anglicisation of the Gaelic 'fiadh', meaning deer.

The unique triangular-shaped bottle commissioned by Grant's in the 1960s for their Standfast blend, and later used for Glenfiddich single malt, was designed by Hans Schleger. Ever innovative, the family saw the opportunity offered by the emergence of duty-free shops in airports (the first opened in Shannon around 1968). As a result, English tourists' first encounter with malt whisky was often while on holiday, which gave it happy associations.

Another simple but effective promotion was to offer Standfast bottles filled with tinted water as stage props. As a result it became a common sight in TV dramas of the 1960s!

EXPRESSIONS:

The core range comprises:

- Glenfiddich 12YO @ 40% (no age statement prior to 2002)
- Glenfiddich Caoran Reserve 12YO @ 40% (a peated expression, introduced 2002)
- Glenfiddich 15YO @ 40% (a mix of four wood types, introduced 1998)
- Glenfiddich 18YO @ 40% (introduced 1980s)
- Glenfiddich Gran Reserva 21YO @ 40% (finished in Cuban rum casks, introduced 2002)
- Glenfiddich 30YO @ 40% (introduced 1999)

- William Grant & Sons also release occasional limited edition vintages, such as:
- Glenfiddich Vintage Reserve 1965 35YO @ 47.8% (480 bottles only, released 2001)
- Glenfiddich Vintage Reserve 1973 31YO @ 49.2% (440 bottles only, released 2003)
- Glenfiddich Vintage Reserve 1991 13YO @ 40% (released 2004)
- Glenfiddich Vintage Reserve 1972 31YO @ 48.9% (519 bottles only, released 2004)
- Glenfiddich Vintage Reserve 1973 33YO @ 40% (861 bottles only, released 2006)
- Glenfiddich Toasted Oak 12YO @ 40% (released 2006)
- Glenfiddich Vintage Reserve 1976 31YO @ 40% (released 2007)

RAW MATERIALS: Floor maltings until 1958, now unpeated malt from independents. Soft process water from the Robbie Dubh springs.

PLANT: Two full-Lauter mash tuns (10.2 tonnes per mash, eight mashes daily. Glenfiddich was the first distillery to employ continuous mashing). Twenty-four Oregon pine washbacks. Ten plain wash stills (charge 9,500 litres); 18 boil-ball spirit stills (charge 5,500 litres). All direct fired by gas. Shell-and-tube condensers.

MATURATION: On site, in a mix of American and European oak (15% European/85% American in Special Reserve).

STYLE: Light Speyside. Floral and fruity.

MATURE CHARACTER: Classic Speyside style – light, fresh, fragrant, fruity. The nose adds cereal notes and a pine-sap dimension, and sometimes I detect a very light scent of coal smoke. The taste is sweet throughout, with fresh citric notes. Supremely accessible. Light-bodied.

Glengarioch

REGION
Highland (East)
ADDRESS
Oldmeldrum,
Aberdeenshire
PHONE
01651 873450
WEBSITE
www.glengarioch.com
OWNER
Morrison Bowmore
Distillers
VISITORS
Visitor centre opened 2006,
with shop, V.I.P. tours and
small conference centre
CAPACITY
1.5m L.P.A.

HISTORICAL NOTES: The Garioch (pronounced 'Geery') is the tract of arable land, 150 square miles in size, beginning 18 miles north-west of Aberdeen. It used to be known as 'the granary of Aberdeenshire'. The market town of Oldmeldrum stands within it, and the current distillery was built here in 1797, possibly on the site of the earlier Meldrum Distillery which dates from before 1785.

It changed hands 40 years later, and again in 1884, when it was bought by J.G. Thomson & Company of Leith, an old established firm of wine and spirits merchants whose offices, The Vaults, now house the Scotch Malt Whisky Society. William Sanderson, creator of VAT 69, became 'proprietor' around 1908.

In 1933 William Sanderson & Son merged with Booth's Distilleries Ltd, owners of Royal Brackla, Millburn and Stromness Distilleries as well as their eponymous gin, and four years later the amalgamated company joined D.C.L. Management of Glengarioch was undertaken by S.M.D. in 1943; in 1968 they mothballed the old distillery – on account of 'chronic water shortages and limited production potential' – and two years later sold it to the Glasgow whisky broker (and owner of Bowmore Distillery), Stanley P. Morrison.

Having solved the water problem by digging a deep well in a nearby field, Morrison extended the plant from two to three stills in 1971, and to four in 1973, but retained the floor maltings. Peating levels were increased, the peat coming from New Pitsligo Moss nearby. The maltings were closed in the early 1990s, at which time the stills were converted to indirect firing by steam coils and pans. Morrison Bowmore Distillers were taken over by Suntory in 1994, and since then Glengarioch has endured periods of closure. It is currently in production, and the opening of a visitor centre in January 2006 signals confidence and has been a great success.

CURIOSITIES: Today the entire production is bottled as single malt; it was formerly a key filling for VAT 69.

The distillery is named Glengarioch, but its product Glen Garioch.

During the 1970s, fuel costs escalated (rising from 9% of production costs to 16% by 1980). Morrison's installed an innovative waste heat recovery system at Glengarioch which not only supplied heat for the kiln and pre-heated the wash, but provided heating to two acres of glasshouses, saving around £90,000 per annum. The distillery became famous for its tomatoes and hothouse plants, but the practice was discontinued in 1993. The system was repeated at Bowmore Distillery.

EXPRESSIONS:
- An 8YO was released in 2006 to replace the former 10YO.
- Glen Garioch 12YO @ 40% (duty-free only)
- Glen Garioch 15YO @ 40%
- Glen Garioch 21YO @ 40%

RAW MATERIALS: Floor maltings until 1993, supplying half the distillery's requirement; now unpeated malt from Simpson's of Berwick-upon-Tweed. Soft process water from Coutens Spring; cooling water from here and Meldrum Burn.

PLANT: Stainless steel full-Lauter tun with a peaked canopy (four tonnes per mash). Six stainless steel washbacks, one plain wash still (charge 21,500 litres), one plain spirit still (charge 9,500 litres). Both direct fired by gas until 1995, now indirect fired by steam. Shell-and-tube condensers, with after-coolers until 1993.

MATURATION: Bourbon and sherry casks. Four dunnage warehouses on site, with a capacity of 12,000 casks.

STYLE: Medium-bodied, slightly fruity/estery.

MATURE CHARACTER: Medium-rich in style, beefed up by the use of sherry-wood. A curious lavender note on the nose, alongside sherry and malt, and a distinct whiff of smoke. Sometimes also ginger snaps. The taste combines toffee-sweetness with some tannic dryness and again a hint of smoke in the finish.

Glenglassaugh

REGION
Speyside
ADDRESS
Portsoy, Aberdeenshire
OWNER
Glenglassaugh Distillery
Company Ltd (The Scaent
Group)
MOTHBALLED
1986
VISITORS
Visitor centre planned
CAPACITY
1m L.P.A.

HISTORICAL NOTES: Glenglassaugh was the distillery that its owners didn't talk about! It was built on the outskirts of the ancient burgh and harbour of Portsoy, on the Banffshire coast, in 1874 by an enterprising local businessman, James Moir, in partnership with two of his nephews and Thomas Wilson, coppersmith. Their intention was to sell most of their make as 'self' or single malt whisky, and they found a ready market for the surplus in Robertson & Baxter, brokers and blenders in Glasgow.

Moir died in 1887; his nephew refurbished the distillery, but when his brother died in 1892 he decided to sell Glenglassaugh to pay death duties. He offered it to Robertson & Baxter, who immediately sold it on to their sister company, Highland Distilleries (now part of the Edrington Group). Demand for Glenglassaugh dwindled after 1898; the distillery was silent from 1907 to 1960, when it was refurbished. It closed again in 1986, and, apart from a short period in production in 1998, it has remained silent. The warehouses on site were used by Edrington.

In February 2008, it was announced that Edrington had sold Glenglassaugh to a Dutch-based consortium, the Scaent Group, for £5 million. Stuart Nickerson, a former Distilleries Director with William Grant & Sons, who advised the consortium in their search for a distillery, was appointed Managing Director. The intention is to go back into production as soon as possible and to open a visitor centre once the distillery is operational.

CURIOSITIES: James Moir sold seeds, ironmongery, manure, wines and spirits. He was agent for the North of Scotland Bank, owner of a fishing boat and of salmon nets on the Deveron. He was also (after 1865) Colonel of the Local Volunteer Artillery Regiment.

In the mid 1980s Highland Distilleries wanted to increase the sweet, Speyside style of Glenglassaugh for use in The Famous Grouse. It was believed at

The charming village of Portsoy was considered to be the safest on the north-east coast in the sixteenth century, although a new harbour built in 1825 was swept away by a storm.

the time that soft water might help achieve this. Glenglassaugh's water was hard. After tankering some soft water in from Glen Rothes for tests, an experimental water softening plant was installed, and then a full plant. This proved too costly, and led to the decision to mothball Glenglassaugh and expand Glen Rothes.

EXPRESSIONS:

- Glenglassaugh 21YO @46% (non chill-filtered, released late 2008)
- Glenglassaugh 30YO @46% (non chill-filtered, released late 2008)
- Glenglassaugh 40YO @46% (non chill-filtered, released late 2008)

RAW MATERIALS: Medium-hard water from two deep wells in the vicinity of the Glassaugh Burn, which previously was softened on site prior to mashing. This softening process will not be used in future. Previously, malt supplied unpeated from Tamdhu malting; future supplies will be from commercial maltsters.

PLANT: Copper covered cast iron mash tun with traditional stirring gear and old-fashioned underback (5.25 tonnes mash), two stainless steel and four wooden washbacks. One boil-ball wash still (11,000 litres charge), one boil-ball spirit still (12,000 litres charge). Both indirect fired by steam pans. Shell-and-tube condensers.

MATURATION: Previously in a variety of ex-bourbon barrels, ex-sherry butts and refill hogsheads, matured on a variety of sites.

STYLE: Fruity, sweet, with traces of smoke, and spice, and an unusually dry and salty finish.

MATURE CHARACTER: The 1978 is sweet, with orange juice and pears, light oil and sea salt. The taste matches the aroma. The 1967 is more delicate and richer, but no trace of old wood. Sweet and salty. I have sometimes noted 'dried shellfish' in Glenglassaugh.

Glengoyne

G1

REGION
Highland (South)

ADDRESS
Dumgoyne, by Killearn,
Stirlingshire

PHONE
01360 550254

WEBSITE
www.glengoyne.com

OWNER
Ian Macleod Distillers

VISITORS
Visitor centre, blending
courses and its own helipad

CAPACITY
1.1m L.P.A.

HISTORICAL NOTES: Glengoyne straddles the Highland Line, with its warehouses below, and the distillery itself above. Until the 1970s it was classified as a Lowland malt. The land hereabouts is owned by the Edmonstones of Duntreath, and it was a representative of this family who obtained a licence to distill in 1833, under the name 'Burnfoot'.

The pretty site is indeed at the foot of the fast flowing Blairgar Burn, in a steep-sided wooded glen, covered in bluebells in spring.

The distillery was leased to George Connell, John McLelland (1851–67) and Archibald McLellan (1872–76), then to Lang Brothers, whisky blenders in Glasgow, at which time it was renamed Glen Guin. Alexander and Gavin Lang commenced trading in 1861 from the basement of the Argyll Free Church in Oswald Street (which they later took over as a bonded warehouse), giving rise to the jingle: 'The spirits below were the sprits of wine and the spirits above were the spirits Divine.'

Lang Brothers had long bought fillings from Robertson & Baxter, and in 1965 became wholly owned by R. & B. The distillery was refurbished and the stills increased from two to three. R. & B. was consolidated into the Edrington Group in 1999, and in 2003 Lang Brothers Ltd and Glengoyne Distillery were sold to Ian Macleod & Company, whisky blenders, of Broxburn.

CURIOSITIES: Air Marshall Sir Arthur Tedder, first Baron Tedder of Glenguin, was born at the distillery, where his father was the Excise officer from 1889 to 1893. Arthur (Senior) became Chief Inspector of Excise, and was knighted for his services to the Royal Commission of Enquiry into Whisky (1909).

EXPRESSIONS:
Shortly before they sold the distillery R. & B. released a 16YO Scottish Oak Finish, which had been re-racked into oak-wood grown in Glenisla, Angus. A large number of single cask bottlings have been released recently, including nine casks

'Glengoyne' derives from 'Glen Guin', 'the glen of the wild geese'. The present name was adopted in 1905.

selected by distillery operatives (in 2006 and 2007) and limited editions at 19, 32 and 37YO.

The core range comprises:

- Glengoyne 10YO @ 40% (relaunched 2006)
- Glengoyne 12YO @ cask strength (introduced 2004)
- Glengoyne 17YO @ 40% (repackaged 2006)
- Glengoyne 21YO @ 40% (repackaged 2007)

RAW MATERIALS: Soft water from Blairgar Burn which runs from the Campsie Hills. Floor maltings until 1910; now malt from Simpson's, Berwick-upon-Tweed.

PLANT: Traditional rake-and-plough mash tun with copper canopy (3.72 tonnes), six Oregon pine washbacks, one boil-ball wash still (charge 14,000 litres), two boil-ball spirit stills (charge 3,495 litres per still); all indirect fired. Shell-and-tube condensers.

MATURATION: Sherry (around 40%) and refill casks. Matured on site in three dunnage warehouses (6,700 casks), with plans to build a further two racked warehouses.

STYLE: Light fruity, hint of vegetables and nuts.

MATURE CHARACTER: Glengoyne gains weight with age. The core bottlings are a mix of ex-sherry and ex-bourbon casks. The nose is malty with sherry notes and a bruised-pear fruitiness. The taste is well-balanced: light sweetness, some acidity, drying in the finish. Medium-bodied.

Glen Grant

REGION
Speyside

ADDRESS
Elgin Road, Rothes, Moray

PHONE
01340 832118

WEBSITE
No

OWNER
Gruppo Campari

VISITORS
Visitor centre, with shop
and extensive woodland
garden

CAPACITY
5.9m L.P.A.

HISTORICAL NOTES: When their lease at Aberlour expired in 1839 the brothers John and James Grant moved down the road to Rothes and built a new distillery (originally named Drumbain), the first distillery in this village. From the outset it was described as 'one of the most extensive distilleries in the North', although goods had to be transported by road until the arrival of the railway in 1858 – a project in which James Grant (now Provost of Elgin) was closely involved. An early engine was named *Glen Grant.*

James Grant Junior, known as 'the Major', succeeded his father in 1872, at the beginning of the Whisky Boom. Glen Grant was already being sold as a single, described as 'pure, mild and agreeable ... peculiarly adapted for family use', in 'England, Scotland, and the Colonies'. It was sold by the cask, but the distillery provided customers with its distinctive label, featuring two kilted Highlanders seated beside a butt, with the motto 'From the Heath Covered Mountains of Scotia I Come'.

By 1887, the demand for Glen Grant was such that the Major built another distillery nearby, Glen Grant Number Two (see *Caperdonich*), and in 1898 installed the first pneumatic malting drums in the Highlands – electrically driven, and in operation until 1971, when on-site malting was discontinued.

The Major lived the life of a Victorian laird in Glen Grant House beside the distillery (now demolished), and laid out the splendid woodland garden that extends behind the distillery. In his day, it required 15 gardeners to keep it neat. It was restored and opened to the public in 1996, complete with the small safe in a summer house from which the Major would produce a bottle of Glen Grant for his guests! He died in 1931, aged 84, and was succeeded by his grandson, Douglas Mackessack.

In 1952, Glen Grant merged with George & J.G. Smith Ltd, to form The Glenlivet & Glen Grant Distilleries Ltd; in 1970 this concern amalgamated with the blending house, Hill, Thomson & Company,

Glen Grant was one of the very few single malts widely available pre-1970.

and with Longmorn Distilleries to become The Glenlivet Distillers Ltd, which was purchased by The Seagram Company in 1978. Douglas Mackessack announced this 'with regret, but as being inevitable if Glen Grant's economic survival was to be assured', handed a cash bonus to all employees and retired. In 2001, Pernod Ricard bought Seagram's Scotch whisky distilling interests and were obliged by E.U. monopolies regulations to sell Glen Grant. It was bought by Campari of Milan in 2006, who appointed Dennis Malcolm as Distillery Manager. He joined Glen Grant in 1961, becoming Manager in 1983 and later General Manager for all the Seagram's distilleries in 1992.

CURIOSITIES: The heating of the stills at Glen Grant is curious. The original four stills were direct fired by coal, the wash stills having rummagers driven by a water wheel (the last in the industry, used until 1979). Two more were added in 1973, direct fired by gas (L.P.G.), and a further four in 1977. In 1979 all ten were converted to gas. But this regime only lasted until 1983, when again the wash stills reverted to coal, using a waste heat boiler to heat steam for the (indirect fired) spirit stills. At this time the old stillhouse (containing the four original stills) was replaced by a new stillhouse, with two larger stills, so capacity was unaffected. All were converted to indirect firing in the late 1990s.

The so-called 'German helmet' wash still design, which has the appearance of a giant's hand-bell, is unique to Glen Grant. The four wash stills all have this peculiarity, and all are equipped with purifying drums on their necks to increase reflux.

The Glen Grant range was repackaged in 2007, the label stressing (twice!) 'Distilled in Tall Slender Stills'.

Thanks to the entrepreneurial flair of the distillery's Italian agent, Armando Giovinetti, Glen Grant became the first single malt to take off in an export market. Giovinetti realised that a young expression would have most appeal (he was challenging

> 'The character of whisky is determined not by the purity of the spirit manufactured, but by the impurities left in the spirit.'
>
> Douglas Mackessack

Grappa), and specified five years old. He promoted this vigorously from the mid 1960s, and by 1977 was selling around 200,000 cases a year.

Glen Grant is Italy's favourite malt (380,000 cases p.a.).

EXPRESSIONS:
- Glen Grant 5YO @ 40% (Italy only)
- Glen Grant (no age statement) @ 40%
- Glen Grant 10YO @ 40%
- Glen Grant 14YO @ cask strength

RAW MATERIALS: Unpeated malt from independent maltsters (own maltings removed 1962). Water from the Caperdonich Springs and the Glen Grant Burn (formerly named the Black Burn).

PLANT: Semi-Lauter mash tun (12.28 tonnes); ten Oregon pine washbacks. Four wash stills (15,100 litres charge each), of 'German helmet' design; four boil-pot spirit stills (7,800 litres charge each). Direct fired until late 1990s, now all indirect fired by steam; all fitted with purifiers. Worm tubs until 1980s, now all shell-and-tube condensers, with sub coolers and hot water recovery devices for pre-heating the charges to all eight stills.

MATURATION: Mainly refill U.S. hogsheads, mostly on Chivas sites (especially at Mulben, near Keith).

STYLE: Sweet, grassy and fruity (green apples).

MATURE CHARACTER: The house style favours refill wood to produce a light-coloured, fresh, fruity and summery whisky. The taste is sweet and lightly lemony, with cereals and nuts, apples and pears. Light-bodied.

Glengyle

REGION
Campbeltown
ADDRESS
Glengyle Road,
Campbeltown, Argyll
PHONE
01586 552009
WEBSITE
www.kilkerran.com
OWNER
Mitchell's Glengyle Ltd
VISITORS
No
CAPACITY
500,000 litres L.P.A.

The spirit from Glengyle is named 'Kilkerran' after St Kiaran, 'The Apostle of Kintyre'.

HISTORICAL NOTES: The original Glengyle Distillery operated from 1873 to 1925. It was built by William Mitchell & Company and remained in their ownership until 1919 when it was sold to West Highland Malt Distilleries Ltd. The distillery was closed in 1925; the stock and warehouses were sold – the latter became the Campbeltown Miniature Rifle Club, and was bought by Bloch Brothers in 1941 (see *Glen Scotia*). They announced that they were rebuilding and expanding, and even installing a grain distillery at Glengyle, but nothing happened and the site was sold to Argyll Farmers and used as a depot and sales office by Kintyre Farmers Co-operative.

It was bought by J. & A. Mitchell Ltd, owner of Springbank Distillery, in November 2000; a new distillery was built and production commenced in March 2004. Currently production is only 50,000 litres per annum, because of arrangements with Springbank.

CURIOSITIES: William Mitchell, the founder of the original Glengyle Distillery, was the son of Archibald Mitchell, one of the original partners in J. & A. Mitchell, who rebuilt the distillery. Hedley Wright, the Chairman of J. & A. Mitchell Ltd, is his great-great nephew.

Springbank and Glengyle produce all their malt requirements on site, in floor maltings. In this, they are unique.

EXPRESSIONS:
Not yet generally available. Bottles may be filled at the distillery, from a cask in the tasting room, which is continually topped up. A limited bottling at 5yo is planned from May 2009.

RAW MATERIALS: Water from Crosshills Loch. Lightly peated malt from Springbank Distillery maltings.

PLANT: Stainless steel semi-Lauter mash tun with a canopy (four tonnes). Four larch washbacks. One plain wash still (second-hand from Ben Wyvis Distillery; 11,000 litres charge), one plain spirit still (9,000 litres charge). Both indirect fired. Shell-and-tube condensers.

MATURATION: Bonded warehouses at Springbank Distillery.

STYLE: Heavier than Springbank, oily, meaty, sweet with cereal notes.

Glen Keith

REGION
Speyside
ADDRESS
Station Road, Keith,
Banffshire
PHONE
01542 783044
WEBSITE
No
OWNER
Chivas Brothers
CAPACITY
4m L.P.A.

In 1980 a 'micro-processor' was installed to control milling, mashing and later distilling – highly advanced for its time.

HISTORICAL NOTES: Glen Keith is situated on the opposite bank of the River Isla to Strathisla Distillery in the town of Keith. It was the first of Seagram's foundations, having been created out of a former meal mill in 1957/58, and was licensed to their subsidiary, Chivas Brothers. It was also the first distillery to have been built on Speyside since 1900, and as Philip Morrice writes 'an excellent job has been done in recreating the form and ambience of a turn-of-the-century Highland malt whisky distillery'. Although a modern unit, Glen Keith is traditional in design and partly built of dressed stone, including its pagoda-topped kiln.

It was originally designed for triple distillation, until 1970, when the number of stills increased from three to five (the sixth still was installed in 1983). These were the first stills in Scotland to be direct fired by gas, although they became indirect fired by steam pans and coils only three years later. The gradual expansion of capacity is reflected in the different shapes and sizes of stills, and a number of production trials have been run at Glen Keith over the years.

Seagram's mothballed Glen Keith in 1999, and the company's Scotch whisky interests were acquired by Pernod Ricard in 2001. There are currently no plans to bring Glen Keith back into production, although several of the distillery's facilities, for example the boiler, are used by Strathisla Distillery nearby.

CURIOSITIES: Seagram's laboratory, now the Chivas Technical Centre, is based at Glen Keith and services the needs of the entire group. The distillery was also formerly the 'brand home' of Passport blended whisky.

EXPRESSIONS:
All but a small amount goes to Chivas blends, especially Passport. One official bottling at 10YO (introduced 1994 as part of Seagram's Heritage Selection).

RAW MATERIALS: Own Saladin maltings until 1976; now

unpeated malt from independent maltsters. Soft process and cooling water from Balloch Spring, augmented when required from Newmill Spring.

PLANT: Traditional rake-and-plough mash tun with raised canopy (eight tonnes). Nine Oregon pine washbacks (one washback charges three wash stills). Three plain wash stills (15,300 litres charge each), two boil-ball spirit stills, one plain spirit still (11,100 litres charge each). Indirect fired by steam coils and pans.

MATURATION: Mainly refill casks, at various Chivas sites on Speyside and in the Central Belt.

STYLE: Light, sweet, grassy.

MATURE CHARACTER: Speyside style, with apples and bananas, hedgerow flowers, lemongrass and vanilla. Sweet to taste, with dried fruits (figs, dates) and light almonds. Medium-bodied.

Glenkinchie

G1

REGION
Lowland
ADDRESS
Pencaitland, East Lothian
PHONE
01875 324004
WEBSITE
www.malts.com
OWNER
Diageo plc
VISITORS
Visitor centre, with
museum and shop
CAPACITY
3m L.P.A.

HISTORICAL NOTES: The original distillery was called Milton, a typical farm distillery, established by the brothers John and George Rate in 1825 to make use of the surplus grains they produced after adopting the improved farming methods introduced by the Agricultural Revolution. Indeed, their landlord may have been John Cockburn of Ormiston, 'The Father of Scottish Husbandry' and one of the pioneers of agricultural improvements.

In 1837 they moved to the present site and built a new distillery, but by 1852 they were bankrupt. Their successor used part of the premises as a sawmill, but in 1880 the site was bought by a consortium of brewers and whisky merchants in Edinburgh, and production resumed. By 1890 the owner was Major James Grey who rebuilt the distillery and associated buildings as a model village. In 1914 he joined four other Lowland distillers to form Scottish Malt Distillers, a trade relationship designed to consolidate the interests of malt distillers in the Lowlands during a time of recession. This body joined D.C.L. in 1925, and Glenkinchie was licensed to John Haig & Company.

In 1988 Glenkinchie was adopted by the recently founded United Distillers plc as the Lowland representative in their Classic Malts series.

CURIOSITIES: The name comes from the Kinchie Burn, which supplies cooling water, and this name is a corruption of de Quincey, the family which owned the lands in medieval times.

In 1895 a fire started in the stables during an extremely cold night – so cold that the water froze in the hoses, and the staff were powerless. This so upset the distillery brewer that he went mad and was consigned to an asylum.

Glenkinchie had a substantial farm attached, and was long famous for its beef cattle, fattened on the residues of the process. The post-war Distillery Manager, Mr W.J. McPherson, won Supreme Champion at Smithfield show in 1949, 1952 and 1954.

For many years James Buchanan & Company's famous Clydesdale dray-horses spent their summer holidays at Glenkinchie.

With a capacity of nearly 21,000 litres, Glenkinchie's wash still is the largest pot still in Scotland. A large bronze bell bearing the date 1842 hangs in the mash-house. Until 'dramming' ceased at the distillery, the bell was sounded to mark the end of each shift – the time for drams to be dispensed!

The distillery's excellent visitor centre also houses what used to be called The Museum of Malt Whisky Production. This was begun by a former Manager, then taken up by S.M.D. It was redesigned and reopened in 1995. At its centre is a scale model (1:6) of a malt whisky distillery designed in 1924 for the British Empire Exhibition at Wembley by James Cruikshank, S.M.D.'s General Works Manager, and showing the whole process from malting to maturation. Adjacent to the distillery is a neat bowling green, installed about 1900 for the entertainment of distillery staff.

EXPRESSIONS:
Before its adoption as a Classic Malt, Glenkinchie was not bottled by its owners.
- Glenkinchie 10YO @ 43% (Classic Malts series, since 1989)
- Glenkinchie 12YO @ 43% (Classic Malts series, since 2007, to replace 10YO)
- Glenkinchie Distillers Edition 14YO @ 43% (Amontillado cask finished, since 1998)
- Glenkinchie 20YO @ 58.4% (limited edition, matured ten years in ex-Asbach brandy casks, released 2007)

RAW MATERIALS: Floor maltings until 1968; now lightly peated malt from Roseisle. Hard process water from a spring on site (formerly from Hopes Reservoir in the Lammermuir Hills); cooling water from the Kinchie Burn.

PLANT: Full-Lauter tun (9.4 tonnes). Five Oregon pine washbacks and one of Douglas fir. One lamp-glass wash still (20,000 litres charge); one lamp-glass spirit still (17,000 litres charge). Indirect fired since 1972. Worm tubs – uniquely, the worm on the spirit still is made from stainless steel (which increases the sulphury character required at Glenkinchie). The lye pipe connecting the worm to the still dips steeply, like an elephant's trunk, as it leaves the stillhouse. This also inhibits reflux and enhances heaviness.

MATURATION: Mainly ex-bourbon casks, matured on site and at Leven.

STYLE: Heavy and meaty as new-make, the mature whisky is grassy and lemony.

MATURE CHARACTER: During maturation, the heavy style of Glenkinchie's new-make becomes fresh and fragrant, and it loses all traces of sulphur. The nose is 'rural' – meadows, hedgerows, with lemon notes and a thread of smoke. The taste is fresh, starts lightly sweet and finishes dry, and very short. Light in character, but with medium body.

The Glenlivet

REGION
Speyside

ADDRESS
Minmore, Ballindalloch,
Moray

PHONE
01340 821720

WEBSITE
www.theglenlivet.com

OWNER
Chivas Brothers

VISITORS
Large visitor centre, with
museum, restaurant and
shop

CAPACITY
5.9m L.P.A.

HISTORICAL NOTES: George Smith of Upper Drummin farm, on the Duke of Gordon's Glenlivet Estate, was the first in the district to apply for a licence under the 1823 Spirits Act. Prior to this, like his neighbours, he distilled illegally: 'about a hogshead a week (250 litres) in the year following Waterloo (1815)'. When he 'went legal', his former colleagues saw this as an act of betrayal, and threatened to burn down his distillery – 'and him at the heart of it'. The pistols he carried for several years to ward off any such attempt are to be seen in the visitor centre today.

By the mid 1820s his whisky had won a reputation furth of the Highlands, and Andrew Usher of Edinburgh became his agent. During the 1840s he leased more farms, including Delnabo (where he took over a small distillery called Cairngorm from the previous tenant, John Gordon). By this time Usher's was offering the first recorded 'branded Scotch' – Usher's Old Vatted Glenlivet – which started as a blended malt and finished (after about 1860) as a blended whisky.

In 1858 George Smith leased Minmore Farm from the Duke and built a new distillery there. He was succeeded by his son, John Gordon Smith, in 1871.

The fame of Glenlivet whisky was such that many distilleries, some of them over 20 miles from the place itself (giving rise to Glenlivet being 'the longest glen in Scotland'), began to use the appellation, until J.G. Smith obtained a court order granting him sole rights to the definite article 'The', while others might use Glenlivet as a suffix only. By 1950 around 27 distilleries were doing this.

J.G. Smith died in 1901 and was succeeded by his nephew, George Smith Grant, who was in turn succeeded by his son, Bill, and grandson, Russell. Bill Smith Grant is the man who put malt whisky on the map of America. As soon as Prohibition ended in 1933 he began to look for business partners and shipped a few hundred cases; by 1939 shipments had increased ninefold, including stocks of 2-ozs miniatures for the famous Pullman Railway Company and Blue Ribbon inter-city express trains.

When George IV visited Edinburgh in October 1822, on his famous 'jaunt', arranged by Walter Scott, he drank nothing but (illicit) Glenlivet whisky.

In the post-war period it enjoyed cult status, although there was an acute shortage of mature stock. Some cases were reserved for the luxury transatlantic liners, SS *United States* and SS *America*.

In 1953 G. & J.G. Smith Ltd amalgamated with J. & J. Grant Ltd to form The Glenlivet & Glen Grant Distilleries Ltd, which again amalgamated in 1970 with Longmorn-Glenlivet and the blending house Hill Thomson & Company to form The Glenlivet Distilleries Ltd. In 1973, the distillery was expanded from four to six stills, and went over to direct firing by gas, rather than coal. A large and ugly dark-grains plant was built close by in 1975, which ruined whatever charm the distillery had retained. Chivas Brothers plan to remove the highest parts of this structure in the near future.

The Glenlivet Distilleries Ltd was purchased by the Seagram Company in 1978. The new owner installed a further two direct fired stills that year, but it was not until the mid 1980s that all eight were converted to indirect heating by steam coils and pans.

In 2001 Chivas Brothers (Pernod Ricard) acquired The Glenlivet Distillery along with most of Seagram's other whisky interests. In February 2008, building consent was sought for six new stills, eight new wash-backs and a new mash tun, nearly doubling capacity.

CURIOSITIES: Glenlivet was a wild and remote place in the old days. It bred a bold and self-reliant people who clung not only to Roman Catholicism, but to the tradition of whisky-making, long after private distilling was banned in the 1780s. By 1820 it was estimated that there were 200 illicit stills in the glen, and the whisky made there had the highest reputation of any in Scotland.

In August 2007 The Glenlivet launched its Smugglers' Trails, in conjunction with the Crown Estates (which owns the land hereabouts). Three way-marked walks of differing lengths into the surrounding countryside allow visitors to follow the trails once used by smugglers.

'Gie me the real Glenlivet, and I weel believe I could

mak' drinking toddy oot o' sea-water. The human mind
never tires o' Glenlivet, any mair than o' caller air.
If a body could just find oot the exac' proper proportion and quantity that ought to be drunk every day,
and keep to that, I verily trow that he might leeve
forever, without dying at a', and that doctors and kirk-
yards would go oot o' fashion.' – James Hogg, quoted by
Christopher North, 1826.

John Smith's Delnabo Distillery closed in 1858, owing
to poor water quality and consolidation at Minmore,
but he continued to lease the estate for stalking
and shooting – an indication of his prosperity! John
Gordon, the original distiller here, also had a distillery
at Croughly, near Tomintoul, the remains of which can
still be seen.

The Glenlivet was the first single malt whisky to be
promoted in the U.S.A. and remains the bestselling
malt in North America. It is the second bestselling
single malt in the world (500,000 nine-litre cases;
bested only by Glenfiddich).

'What makes The Glenlivet so special?', a *Time*
magazine journalist asked Bill Smith Grant in the
1950s. 'There's nothing secret about it,' he replied. 'It
just comes out like that ... I think it's 99 per cent the
water and a certain fiddle-faddle in the manufacture'.

Seagram's greatly expanded the visitor facilities in
1996/97, with a multi-media facility, restaurant etc. The
designers, who had earlier done an excellent job at
Strathisla Distillery (and elsewhere), were confronted
with a considerable challenge, which brings to mind
converting sows' ears into silk purses, but they have
succeeded admirably.

The site now welcomes around 40,000 people a year.

EXPRESSIONS:

A third of the make is bottled as a single; the rest goes into the
Chivas blends.

• Coronation Glenlivet, distilled on the day of King George VI's
coronation in 1937, and bottled to mark the coronation of his
daughter, Queen Elizabeth II in 1953, is probably the first-ever
commemorative bottling of any malt.

In 2004 Chivas Brothers embarked on a £6.5 million marketing campaign for The Glenlivet. The core expressions are:
- The Glenlivet 12YO @ 40% (Gold medal I.W.S.C. 2007, Gold Best in Class 2006)
- The Glenlivet 15YO French Oak Reserve @ 40%
- The Glenlivet 18YO @ 43%
- The Glenlivet 21YO Archive @ 43% (Gold Best in Class I.W.S.C. 2007)
- The Glenlivet XXV @ 43%
- The Glenlivet Cellar Collection (limited bottlings from 1959, 1964, 1967, 1969, American Oak Finish, 30YO (1971, 1972 and 1983)
The travel retail range adds:
- The Glenlivet 12YO First-fill @ 43% (from first-fill ex-bourbon casks, introduced 2005)
- The Glenlivet 15YO @ 43%
- The Glenlivet 16YO Nadurra @ 57.7% ('Nadurra' is Gaelic for 'natural', non chill-filtered from first-fill ex-bourbon casks, introduced 2005)

RAW MATERIALS: Mineral-rich, hard process water from Josie's Well; cooling water from bore-holes in the hills behind the distillery; reduction water from Blairfindy Spring. Own floor maltings until 1966, now unpeated malt from Crisp of Port Gordon, on the Moray Firth.

PLANT: Semi-Lauter mash tun (12.1 tonnes). Eight Oregon pine washbacks. Four lamp-glass wash stills (15,000 litres charge), four lamp-glass spirit stills (10,000 litres charge), indirect fired by steam coils and pans. Shell-and-tube condensers.

MATURATION: Ex-bourbon casks for the 12YO, ex-sherry casks for the 18YO; the rest are a mix of bourbon, sherry and refill casks.

STYLE: Medium-bodied, complex Speyside, with fruits (pineapple, pears, apples) and floral notes.

MATURE CHARACTER: The Glenlivet is a hugely complex malt, and develops depth and complexity with age. The younger expressions are soft, floral and fruity (apple, pineapple and peach). Some malty notes are apparent in both aroma and taste, and some vanilla from the American oak. The taste starts sweet, with a soft texture, and dries considerably in the finish. Medium-bodied.

Glenlochy Redeveloped

REGION
Highland (West)
ADDRESS
North Road, Inverlochy,
Fort William, Inverness-
shire
LAST OWNER
D.C.L./S.M.D.
CLOSED
1983

As well as buying distilleries for N.D.A. and for himself, in 1939 Joe Hobbs wisely bought a company in Norfolk which made fire extinguishers.

HISTORICAL NOTES: April 1900 was not the best time to open a distillery. Pattison's of Leith had just gone bust, bringing down a number of other companies; confidence in the industry had collapsed and maturing stocks were far greater than the market could cope with.

Three years before, when David McAndie bought the ground from Lord Abinger of Inverlochy Estate, the picture was brighter. Ben Nevis, Fort William's first distillery, was thriving and the West Highland Railway had reached the town in 1894. McAndie, who had recently built Glen Cawdor Distillery, Nairn, was joined by James Grant, owner of Highland Park Distillery and 13 local investors. The first manager came from Balblair Distillery.

In spite of an unpropitious start, Glenlochy remained in production until 1917, when all distilleries were closed by government order. In 1920 the shareholders sold to a consortium of Lancashire brewers; they resumed production in 1924 and closed again after two years. In 1934 the buildings and site were sold for £850 to a Lancashire car hirer, who sold them on three later to Joseph Hobbs, along with the Glenlochy Distillery Company (see *Ben Nevis*).

CURIOSITIES: The exterior of the distillery was built entirely of brick (unusually) and is decorated on the roof with ironwork; the pagoda has an unusually steep pitch. It has changed little.

Hobbs had a remit to buy distilleries from National Distillers of America, Inc., and sold Glenlochy to them in 1940 to raise money for his 'Great Glen Cattle Ranch'. D.C.L. took over National Distillers in 1953 and transferred management at Glenlochy to S.M.D., which modernised it in 1960 and 1976, then closed the distillery in 1983.

Joseph Hobbs was a colourful character. His parents emigrated to Canada when he was a child; as an adult he made a fortune in shipbuilding and property development (and in running whisky during Prohibition), then sustained heavy losses during the

Great Depression of 1930/31, and returned to England with less than £1,000, according to his obituary in *The Times.*

EXPRESSIONS:

Official bottlings have been released on two occasions only:

- Glenlochy 1969 25YO @ 62.2% (Rare Malts series, released 1995)
- Glenlochy 1969 26YO @ 59% (Rare Malts series, released 1996)

G1

Glenlossie

REGION
Speyside

ADDRESS
Thomshill, by Elgin, Moray

PHONE
01343 860331

WEBSITE
www.malts.com

OWNER
Diageo plc

VISITORS
By appointment

CAPACITY
2.6m L.P.A.

HISTORICAL NOTES: Glenlossie Distillery was built
by a publican and a few friends in 1876. John Duff,
tenant of the Fife Arms at Llanbryde and former
Manager of Glendronach Distillery, in partnership
with Alexander Grigor Allen (Procurator Fiscal of
Morayshire, and after 1880 part owner of Talisker
Distillery), H.M.S. Mackay (land agent and burgh
surveyor of Elgin) and John Hopkins (a London-based
blender, and owner from 1880 of Tobermory Distillery
and of a well-known blend, Old Mull). Hopkins was
agent for the new distillery's make. In 1896, when the
Glenlossie-Glenlivet Distillery Company was founded,
Mackay took over management. The company joined
D.C.L. in 1919 and was managed by S.M.D. (licensed to
John Haig & Company) from 1930.

In 1962 Glenlossie was expanded from four to six
stills, and ten years later a new distillery named
Mannochmore was built adjacent (see entry), to
operate in parallel with the original – part of S.M.D.'s
expansion plans in the early 1960s (see *Caol Ila* etc.).
A large dark-grains plant was built on the site (1968–
72), with a conspicuous white chimney which can be
seen from miles around. Each week it can process
2,600 tonnes of draff and eight million litres of pot ale
from 21 distilleries, to produce 1,000 tonnes of cattle
feed.

CURIOSITIES: 'With the exception of the Distilling
House (which is built of stone) the distillery is
constructed entirely of cement which, under the
sunlight as we descended the hill, looked beautifully
white and clean.' (Alfred Barnard, 1887)

A private railway siding on the Perth–Elgin line
gave direct access to southern market after 1896.
'Glenlossie-Glenlivet was efficiently managed ... New
Warehouses were built, and extension or improvements effected in almost every year up to 1917, when
all malt whisky distilleries were closed.' (Brian Spiller)

A horse-drawn fire engine, still preserved at Glenlossie, was little help in quelling a fire that destroyed part of the distillery in 1929.

EXPRESSIONS:
Glenlossie has always been a blending malt. It is ranked Top Class and was not available as a single until 1990:
• Glenlossie 10YO @ 43% (Flora & Fauna series)

RAW MATERIALS: Process water from the Bardon Burn, which sources in the Mannoch Hills; cooling water from the Gedloch Burn and the Burn of Foths. Floor maltings until 1962; now unpeated malt from Burghead.

PLANT: An unusual semi-Lauter mash tun, combining aspects of a Steiniker tun with the original Newmill Lauter knives (eight tonnes) – ensuring high efficiency. Eight larch washbacks. Three plain wash stills (15,500 litres charge); three plain spirit stills (17,500 litres charge); all with purifiers. All indirect fired. Shell-and-tube condensers.

MATURATION: On site in traditional and racked warehouses, and in the Central Belt.

STYLE: Grassy.

MATURE CHARACTER: A fresh, light, Speyside nose, with cut grass, faint flowers and hair lacquer. The taste is sweet and perfumed. Light-bodied.

G1

Glen Mhor Demolished

REGION
Highland (North)
ADDRESS
Telford Street, Muirtown,
Inverness, Inverness-shire
LAST OWNER
D.C.L. /S.M.D.
CLOSED
1983

Glen Mhor has been described as a classic example of 'The Highland Style'.

HISTORICAL NOTES: John Birnie, Manager of Glen Albyn Distillery and largely responsible for its success (output had trebled between 1887 and 1892), was frustrated in his ambition to buy shares in the distillery, so he formed a partnership with Charles Mackinlay & Company, wine and whisky merchants in Leith, bought the site across the road from Glen Albyn and alongside the Caledonian Canal, and built Glen Mhor Distillery. It went into production in 1894, designed by Charles Doig with power supplied by a 30-foot high turbine wheel, driven by water from the canal. Electric motors only replaced it in the early 1950s, and even then it continued to be used for driving the switchers on the washbacks until about 1960.

Mackinlay & Birnie became a limited company in 1906, with John Walker & Sons holding 40% of the shares, and bought Glen Albyn in 1920. A third still was added at Glen Mhor by 1925, and all stills went over to internal heating by steam in 1963. A Saladin box maltings was installed in 1949. Mackinlay & Birnie was acquired by D.C.L. in 1972 and transferred to S.M.D.

Glen Mhor closed in 1983 and the site is now a shopping centre.

CURIOSITIES: Supplies to both Glen Mhor and Glen Albyn were delivered by sea, including peat for the malt kiln, which came from Orkney.

Harper's Weekly, the trade gazette, commented: 'There is nothing decorative or grand about the appearance of the buildings; nevertheless they are most solidly constructed and well arranged for carrying on the work efficiently.'

EXPRESSIONS:
There are only two official bottlings of Glen Mhor and both are in the Rare Malts series:
- Glen Mhor 1979 22YO@ 61% (bottled 2001)
- Glen Mhor 1976 28YO @ 51.9% (bottled 2005)

Glenmorangie

REGION
Highland (North)
ADDRESS
Tain, Ross-shire
PHONE
01862 892043
WEBSITE
www.glenmorangie.com
OWNER
The Glenmorangie
Company
VISITORS
Visitor centre, with
museum (opened 1997)
and shop
CAPACITY
4m L.P.A.

There have been only seven distillery managers at Glenmorangie since its foundation.

HISTORICAL NOTES: Glenmorangie has been the best-selling single malt in Scotland for over 20 years, standing number two in the U.K. and number three in world sales. Creative advertising in the early 1980s may well have helped. In late 2007 the owners made radical alterations to their packaging, and it will be interesting to see how this goes down with consumers.

The distillery stands near the ancient Royal Burgh of Tain, in Ross-shire, overlooking the Dornoch Firth, on Morangie Farm, a spot well-known to illicit distillers. It was established in 1843 by William and John Matheson. The former was part-owner of Balblair Distillery and related to Alexander Matheson who founded Dalmore. By 1849 production had reached 20,000 gallons. A limited company was formed in 1887, and the distillery completely rebuilt the same year.

In 1918 the distillery was sold to Macdonald & Muir (40% share), the established Leith firm of blenders, and Durham & Company, a whisky broker (60%). By the late 1930s, M. & M. had acquired Durham's share and the malt was being used in their blends (notably Highland Queen and Martins V.V.O.); although it could be bought in bulk, Glenmorangie was not promoted as a single until the late 1970s. In 1979 capacity was doubled (to four stills), then doubled again in 1990.

By the late 1980s, M. & M. was experimenting with different wood types and with re-racking into wine barrels, in order to increase the range of expressions. The light style of Glenmorangie spirit does not lend itself to complete maturation in European oak, but can benefit from 'finishing' in such casks. A sherry-finished 18YO (introduced 1992) was soon followed by a port-wood and a Madeira-wood; these have been followed by more than a dozen other styles.

In 1996 Glenmorangie became a public limited company; in 2004 it bought the Scotch Malt Whisky Society, the Macdonald family sold its shares, and

So keen is Glenmorangie on its wood that the company owns forests in the Ozark Mountains of Kentucky.

both companies were acquired by the French luxury goods giant, Louis Vuitton Moët-Hennessey.

In October 2008, capacity will be increased to six million L.P.A., with the addition of four new stills, four new washbacks and a new mash tun.

CURIOSITIES: Glenmorangie was one of the first distilleries to heat its wash still indirectly, by steam coil (1883). The stills themselves, which are the tallest in Scotland, were originally used for distilling gin and the elegant shape has been retained.

Although there are records of Glenmorangie being shipped overseas (to the Vatican and San Francisco) in 1880, it was only in the late 1970s that its owners began to focus on their malt. In 1981 the 'Sixteen Men of Tain' print campaign was launched. This emphasised the high craft that went into making the malt, while humanising it – the ads featured woodcuts of the men themselves, from Distillery Manager to tractorman. Ahead of its time it ran for 20 years.

In 2007 Glenmorangie announced they were repackaging and renaming their key products. The familiar tan label with black and red lettering and a chequered border, introduced in the 1970s, has been replaced by cleaner, brighter, more sophisticated labelling, which nevertheless retains elements from the past. Bottle shapes have become more sensual, and the overall impression is more feminine.

Not far from the distillery, Glenmorangie owns a magnificently restored mansion, now named Glenmorangie House. Close to it is an important Pictish carved stone, the Cadboll Stone. The new packaging draws upon Celtic symbols from the stone to good effect.

EXPRESSIONS:

Glenmorangie has bottled a wide range of expressions over the past 20 years. Finishing has been done in Fino and Oloroso sherry-wood, port-wood, Madeira-wood, Claret, Côtes du Rhône, Malaga, Côte de Beaune, Côte de Nuits, Meursault, Sauternes, white rum and blond rum.

Glenmorangie's first stills came from a gin distillery, and are the tallest in Scotland. They worked so well that the shape and size have been copied ever since.

A number of limited edition vintages and wood finishes have also been released in recent years. These include most recently the Artisan Cask, 1993 Truffle Oak Reserve and a 30YO Oloroso finish; vintages from 1975, 1987 and 1988.

The new core range, launched in 2007, is only lightly chill-filtered:

- Glenmorangie Original (10YO @ 40%)
- Glenmorangie Nectar D'Or (around 12YO @ 46% finished in Sauternes barriques)
- Glenmorangie Lasanta (around 12YO @ 46% finished in ex-Oloroso casks)
- Glenmorangie Quinta Ruban (around 12YO @ 46% finished in ex-port pipes)
- Glenmorangie 18YO (a portion of this re-racked for three years into sherry-wood @ 40%)
- Glenmorangie Quarter Century (25YO @ 40% limited batches of 20 casks, some matured in ex-bourbon barrels, some ex-sherry and a portion ex-Burgundy barrels)
- Glenmorangie Signet (between 15–20YO @ 46%, launch autumn 2008)

RAW MATERIALS: The Tarlogie Spring – very hard, mineral-rich water. Floor maltings until 1977; now unpeated malt from independent maltsters.

PLANT: Stainless steel full-Lauter tun (9.8 tonnes per mash), six stainless steel washbacks. Four very tall (5.18m) boil-pot wash stills (11,300 litres charge); four very tall boil-pot spirit stills (7,500 litres charge). All indirect fired by steam. Shell-and-tube condensers.

MATURATION: First- and second-fill ex-bourbon American white oak casks; some other woods for finishing. Fourteen bonded warehouses on site; ten traditional dunnage, four racked to eleven casks high.

STYLE: Light, floral, citric (tangerine).

MATURE CHARACTER: Glenmorangie is light in style, but complex in character. Keynotes are vanilla, almonds, mandarins, apples, roses, spices and hay. The mouth feel is soft and fresh, the taste lightly sweet, with some cereal and fresh fruit. Medium-bodied.

Glen Moray

REGION
Speyside
ADDRESS
Bruceland Road, Elgin,
Moray
PHONE
01343 542577
WEBSITE
www.glenmoray.com
OWNER
The Glenmorangie
Company
VISITORS
Visitor centre, shop, café,
tasting area
CAPACITY
2m L.P.A.

HISTORICAL NOTES: Like several distilleries, Glen Moray was built on the site of an early nineteenth-century brewery to take advantage of a reliable water source. Unlike any other distillery, however, the grounds included the site of Elgin's gallows, on the edge of the town, beside the main road heading west; a grim warning to unruly Highlanders arriving in the city.

The distillery was built by a local consortium, the Glen Moray-Glenlivet Distillery Company Ltd, in 1897, making use of some of the old West Brewery buildings and 'being equipped with electric light throughout'. By 1910 it had closed, and it was acquired by Macdonald & Muir (see *Glenmorangie*) about 1923. They extended from two to four stills in 1958, making use of the make in their successful blends, notably Highland Queen.

Glen Moray single malt began to be released in 1976, but was only promoted from the early 1990s. Macdonald & Muir began their experiments with wood-finishing at Glen Moray – now a familiar feature of the Glenmorangie portfolio. Three wood finished expressions were released in 1999: Chardonnay (no age), Chenin Blanc (12 and 16YO).

Both distilleries were acquired by Louis Vuitton Moët Hennessy in 2004, and in September 2008 L.V.M.H. sold Glen Moray to the French spirits company, La Martiniquaise.

CURIOSITIES: Glen Moray has had only five managers in its 110-year lifetime. The last to retire (after 18 years, in 2005) was Ed Dodson, in whose honour a Manager's Choice from 1962 was released.

EXPRESSIONS:
Glen Moray is the third bestselling malt in the U.K. The core range comprises:
• Glen Moray Classic (no age statement)
• Glen Moray 12YO @ 40%
• Glen Moray 16YO @ 40%
• Distillery bottlings regularly available (around two a year).

Limited editions, 20- and 30-year-olds and several vintages have been released. A couple of new vintages were launched in 2006 – 1963 and 1964 – and a one-off limited edition, Mountain Oak, in 2007.

- Glen Moray Manager's Choice usually at around 15YO released annually.
- Glen Moray 1989 @ 57.6% (single bourbon cask bottled 2006, 240 bottles, only available at the distillery)

RAW MATERIALS: Hard water from the River Lossie. Floor maltings until 1958 then Saladin box maltings until 1977; unpeated malt from independent maltsters.

PLANT: Stainless steel semi-Lauter tun with peaked canopy (7.5 tonnes). Five stainless steel washbacks. Two plain wash stills (10,000 litres charge); two plain spirit stills (6,000 litres charge). Indirect fired. Shell-and-tube condensers.

MATURATION: Mainly first and refill ex-bourbon casks. Small amount of ex-sherry casks. Mix of dunnage and palletised warehouses on site, holding 65,000 casks in total.

STYLE: Fruity, floral, clean.

MATURE CHARACTER: Glen Moray is light in style, in its younger expressions, but elegantly balanced and 'well made'. The nose is floral and fruity, with butterscotch, vanilla and barley sugar. The taste is sweet, with nutty notes and a delicate fruitiness. Medium-bodied.

Glen Ord

REGION
Highland (North)

ADDRESS
Muir of Ord, Ross and
Cromarty

PHONE:
01887 822010

WEBSITE
www.malts.com

OWNER
Diageo plc

VISITORS
Spacious visitor centre,
with interesting artefacts

CAPACITY
3.4m L.P.A.

HISTORICAL NOTES: Like many others, the distillery at Muir of Ord was established on a site which had formerly been much used by smugglers (over 40 illicit stills), and which was famous for whisky production, being near Ferintosh and the Black Isle. The museum displays an illicit still which was dredged from a loch nearby.

In addition to this illicit activity, there were nine licensed distilleries in the district, all except one worked by farmers' co-operatives. The *New Statistical Account* (1840) states that 'distilling is the sole manufacture of the district'.

Ord Distillery was founded in 1838 by Thomas Mackenzie, the land-owner, and licensed to Robert Johnstone and Donald McLennan. Johnstone went bankrupt in 1843, as did his successor, Alexander McLennan. When he died in 1870 it passed to his widow, who prudently married Alex MacKenzie, a banker. In 1878 he built a new stillhouse, but this burnt down the same year, so he started again. He died in 1896 and ownership passed to James Watson & Company of Dundee, who extended the distillery and tripled production by 1901. When the last surviving Watson, John Jabez, died in 1923 Ord was sold to John Dewar & Sons, and thus passed to D.C.L. in 1925, and to S.M.D. in 1930.

Floor maltings were changed to Saladin boxes in 1961, and a large drum maltings built on an adjacent site in 1968. The distillery itself was rebuilt and expanded in 1966, in the 'Waterloo Street' design (see *Caol Ila*, *Glendullan* etc.), masterminded by Dr Charlie Potts, S.M.D.'s Chief Engineer. The visitor centre was opened in 1988, and today welcomes around 20,000 visitors a year.

CURIOSITIES: Glen Ord has its own sizeable maltings (Saladin boxes 1961–83, 18 drums added 1968), producing its own requirement and that of the seven other distilleries in the north of Scotland owned by S.M.D. at that time. Although of medium size, it is the third largest distillery owned by Diageo. Over the

Alfred Barnard, who visited in the mid 1880s, reported that whisky was being shipped to 'Singapore, South Africa and other colonies' under the brand name Glen Oran. He 'tasted some 1882 make and found it very agreeable to the palate'.

years the whisky has been branded as Glenordie, Ord, Glen Oran, Ordie and Muir of Ord.

The distillery was lit by paraffin lamps until 1949, with a water turbine as the main source of power (until 1961).

Ord was the main S.M.D. site for experiments in heating stills. Until 1958 all four stills were direct fired by coal; two were converted to direct oil firing that year, and in 1962 to indirect heating by steam. Each time the distillates were compared for consistency. In 1966, the two direct fired stills were converted, and two more stills installed. Hot water from the condensers is directed to the maltings, so they are run unusually hot, and condensation is completed by horizontally mounted 'after-coolers' (secondary condensers).

It used to be the custom to burn heather in the kilns during malting, to impart a 'rooty' flavour.

EXPRESSIONS:
- Glen Ord 12YO @ 40% (first bottled 1993, Gold Medals I.W.S.C. 1994, 1995)
- Glen Ord 12YO @ 43% (Hidden Malts series, introduced in 2002)
- Glen Ord 1975 28YO @ 58.3% (released 2003)
- Glen Ord 1978 25YO @ 58.3% (released 2004)
- Glen Ord 30YO Special Release @ 58.7% (6000 bottles, in 2005)
- The Singleton of Glen Ord 12YO @ 40% (mix of American and European oak, released 2006, for S.E. Asia)
- The Singleton of Glen Ord 18YO @ 40% (mix of American and European oak, released 2006, for S.E. Asia)

RAW MATERIALS: Lightly peated malt from own maltings. 85% of barley grown locally. Water via Alt Fionnadh (the White Burn) from two lochs (the 'Loch of the Peats', Loch nam Bonnach, and the 'Loch of the Birds', Loch nan Eun).

PLANT: Large cast iron semi-Lauter mash tun with copper dome (12.5 tonnes); eight Oregon pine washbacks. Three plain wash stills (18,000 litres charge); three plain spirit stills (16,000 litres charge). All steam fired. Shell-and-tube condensers, and after-coolers on all stills.

Excavations here in 1962, to make way for No. 1 warehouse, uncovered six skulls, one with a musket ball embedded in its jaw.

MATURATION: Approximately half first and refill sherry butts, and half refill hogsheads, for single malt bottlings. 12,500 casks matured on site in dunnage warehouse, the rest tankered to Cambus or to customers' own sites.

STYLE: Described as 'the best representative of the "Highland" style'. Sweet and heathery, with distinct waxiness.

MATURE CHARACTER: 'The Singleton of Glen Ord', which will replace other expressions, retains the malt's characteristic waxy texture and light smokiness, while adding depth and complexity. A big, rich nose with fruity (nectarines and dried orange peel) and floral (old-fashioned perfume) notes, flaked almonds and sandalwood. Very smooth and chewy texture; sweet, slightly mouth-cooling, with a long finish and a pleasant aftertaste of nougat. Medium-bodied.

G1

REGION
Speyside
ADDRESS
Burnside Street, Rothes,
Moray
PHONE
01340 872300
WEBSITE
www.glenrotheswhisky.
com
OWNER
The Edrington Group Ltd
VISITORS
Visitor centre, with replica
of Berry Brothers shop
CAPACITY
4.5m L.P.A.

Glenrothes

HISTORICAL NOTES: In 1868, James Stuart, a 'corn factor' in Rothes village on Speyside and proprietor of the Mills of Rothes, took over Macallan Distillery nearby, in partnership with Robert Dick and William Grant (agents for the Caledonian Bank), and John Cruikshank (solicitor). Macallan prospered and three years later they decided to build a second and larger distillery upstream from Mills of Rothes.

This was not a propitious time to be building a distillery; by midsummer 1878 Britain was involved in 'the worst economic crisis for over a century'; in October the City of Glasgow Bank collapsed and in December the Caledonian Bank closed its doors. James Stuart & Partners was dissolved, Stuart remaining at Macallan and the others taking over the half-built Glen Rothes-Glenlivet Distillery, trading as William Grant & Company. It opened on 28 December 1879, the night of the Tay Bridge Disaster (and see *Balmenach*), with Robertson & Baxter appointed as agents. On the suggestion of W.A. Robertson, Glen Rothes was merged with Bunnahabhain Distillery in 1887 to form the Highland Distilleries Company.

In 1896 the distillery was expanded to designs by Charles Doig of Elgin, with four stills and a second malt kiln, but a fire destroyed much of the distillery before the work was completed. In spite of installing Doig's patent appliances for preventing explosions in the new mill-room, this failed to avert another fire six years later.

Glen Rothes was enlarged to six stills in 1963 and to eight in 1980. In 1989 it was rebuilt with ten stills. In 1987 Highland licensed The Glenrothes brand to Berry Brothers & Rudd, the old established London wine merchants, which also owned 50% of Cutty Sark (the other 50% being owned by Robertson & Baxter), and they released the first 'official' bottling that year, at 12 years old.

CURIOSITIES: Twenty-seven Speyside distilleries adopted the suffix 'Glenlivet', owing to the fame of the original. In 1884 John Gordon Smith raised an action to limit this usage, but before it came to court the owners of Glen Rothes, Cragganmore, Mortlach, Glenfarclas, Linkwood, Glengrant (sic), Glenlossie and Benrinnes agreed to Smith's distillery being The Glenlivet, while they were 'permitted to add Glenlivet to their name and sell blends of their whiskies as Blended Glenlivet'. The remainder followed suit. Andrew Usher was allowed to continue selling Old Vatted Glenlivet.

The Ladies' Well, from which the distillery draws its process water, was the site of a murder in the thirteenth century. Mary Leslie, daughter of the Earl of Rothes, was killed by the notorious Wolf of Badenoch (Alexander Stewart, Earl of Buchan, and son of the King of Scots) while trying to protect her lover.

As well as relabelling in 1994 (see below) Glenrothes adopted a unique dumpy bottle shape, known affectionately as La Bomba. In 2005 they introduced La Bombette, a hand-grenade-sized 10cl mini bottle, which holds two large measures.

EXPRESSIONS:
Glenrothes was repackaged in 1994, the design inspired by labels found on duty-paid samples in a blending room. Each 'vintage' is a parcel of casks from the declared year and has its own personality, although the core character of the malt remains constant – very much a wine merchant's approach.

So far 'The Glenrothes Vintages' (all at 43%) have comprised: 1971, 1972, 1973, 1974, 1975, 1978, 1979, 1981, 1982, 1984, 1985, 1989, 1991, 1992, 1994. In addition, The Glenrothes is released in very occasional single casks (at natural strength). Only ten of these have been released to date, and they are highly sought after.

RAW MATERIALS: Water from the Ladies' Well and Ardcanny Spring. Lightly peated malt from Tamdhu

A fire in 1922 engulfed No. 1 warehouse, pitching large amounts of mature whisky into the Rothes Burn, to the pleasure of locals and, it is said, even passing cows.

Distillery maltings and from Simpson's.

PLANT: Stainless steel semi-Lauter mash tun (4.92 tonnes). Twelve Oregon pine washbacks and eight of stainless steel washbacks (latter not currently in use). Five boil-pot wash stills (12,750 litres charge); five boil-pot spirit stills (15,000 litres charge), all indirect fired by steam. Shell-and-tube condensers.

MATURATION: American oak casks (ex-sherry and ex-bourbon), European oak ex-sherry. Four racked and 12 dunnage warehouses are on site.

STYLE: Sweet and fruity, but also heavy and rich.

MATURE CHARACTER: Glenrothes is a heavy style of malt, and takes sherry-wood maturation well, and advanced age. The 'Select Reserve' best displays the distillery character: on the nose, nougat, dried fruits and nuts, caramel, vanilla sponge. Sweet to taste, with a soft texture, drying towards the end, with a nutty aftertaste and hints of chocolate. A useful combination of freshness and depth. Medium-bodied.

Glen Scotia

REGION
Campbeltown

ADDRESS
High Street, Campbeltown,
Argyll

PHONE
01586 552288

WEBSITE
www.lochlomonddistillery.
com

OWNER
Loch Lomond Distillery
Company

VISITORS
By appointment

CAPACITY
750,000 L.P.A.

HISTORICAL NOTES: Glen Scotia has had a patchy existence, but, unlike 30 other distilleries that once operated in Campbeltown, it has survived.

The distillery was established in 1832, named simply Scotia, by Stewart, Galbraith & Company, which became a limited company in 1895 and sold to West Highland Malt Distilleries in 1919. Duncan MacCallum, a well-known local distiller, bought Scotia in 1924, just before the Great Depression. It was closed from 1928 to 1930, then sold to Bloch Brothers after MacCallum's suicide in 1930; Sir Maurice Bloch sold it and Scapa Distillery to Hiram Walker in 1954.

A. Gillies & Company bought Glen Scotia next year and operated it until 1984. They sold to Gibson International in 1989 (owner of Littlemill Distillery), which went into receivership in 1994, when the distillery was bought by Glen Catrine Bonded Warehouse Ltd (sister company to the present owner), who mothballed it. From 1999 Glen Scotia has been in production for only a few weeks a year, operated by a team from Springbank Distillery, but since 2007 it has been in part-time production, day shifts only, making around 100,000 L.P.A. per annum.

CURIOSITIES: As David Stirk writes in his book *The Distilleries of Campbeltown*, 'the nadir of [the decline in Campbeltown distilling] is perhaps most poignantly represented with the suicide on 23 December 1930 of Duncan MacCallum, aged 83, once a leading distiller in the town, when he drowned himself in Crosshill Loch'.

Bloch Brothers changed the name from Scotia to Glen Scotia in 1934/35. In a press release dated October 1940, they state that much of the make is exported to America 'after blending'.

EXPRESSIONS:
- Glen Scotia 12YO @ 40% (introduced 2005)
- Glen Scotia 17YO @ 40% (introduced 2006)
- Glen Scotia 6YO @ 40% (lightly peated, introduced 2006)

MacCallum's ghost has been seen at Glen Scotia, and his death supposedly inspired the well-known song which starts 'Oh, Campbeltown Loch, I wish ye were whisky'.

RAW MATERIALS: Soft water from Crosshill Loch. Unpeated and lightly peated (four to five weeks per annum) from Greencore maltings, Buckie.

PLANT: Corten steel rake-and-plough mash tun with a canopy (2.72 and 1.92 tonnes per mash at the moment). Six Corten steel washbacks. One plain wash still (7,500 litres charge), one plain spirit still (8,400 litres charge), both indirect fired. Shell-and-tube condensers.

MATURATION: Bourbon barrels mostly, with some sherry hogsheads and butts. Single racked warehouse on site holding 6,500 casks, all matured on site.

STYLE: Maritime and oily.

MATURE CHARACTER: Glen Scotia has a 'maritime character': seaweed, docks, briny, lightly peaty. The taste is somewhat oily and smooth, with cereal notes, nuts, light sweetness, distinct saltiness and some shoreline seaweed notes. Dry overall and medium-bodied. Variable.

Glen Spey

G1

REGION
Speyside
ADDRESS
Rothes, Moray
PHONE
01340 832000
WEBSITE
www.malts.com
OWNER
Diageo plc
VISITOR
By appointment
CAPACITY
1.5m L.P.A.

HISTORICAL NOTES: James Stuart, grain merchant in Rothes, licensee (1868–86) then owner (1886–92) of Macallan Distillery (see also *Glen Rothes* Distillery), built Glen Spey (originally a corn mill, and named Mill of Rothes Distillery). He sold it the year after he bought Macallan to W. & A. Gilbey, the London wine and spirits merchant, for £11,000. This was the first time an English company had bought a Scotch whisky distillery. They went on to build Knockando Distillery in 1904.

In 1962, Gilbey's merged with Justerini & Brooks, another long established London wine and spirits merchant, enjoying considerable success in America with its blend, J. & B. Rare. The new company was named Independent Distillers & Vintners (I.D.V.); Glen Spey was doubled in capacity in 1970, sold to Watney Mann (brewers) two years later, and acquired by Grand Metropolitan the same year. Grand Metropolitan merged with Guinness in 1997 to form U.D.V., now called Diageo.

Glen Spey has long been a key filling for the J. & B. blends. For a time it was the own-label malt in Unwin's off-licences, but it was not bottled as a single by its owners until 2001.

CURIOSITIES: Glen Spey is discreetly tucked in off the main street in Rothes, below a fragment of the outer wall of the once formidable Rothes Castle. The castle dates from the twelfth century, and King Edward I of England lodged there in 1296. By 1309 it was owned by the powerful Leslie family, created Earls of 'Rothays' in the sixteenth century, and Dukes of Rothes in 1680 (this only lasted one year). The castle and adjoining buildings were burned by the locals 'to prevent thieves from harbouring in it' in 1662.

In the days of direct firing by coal and lighting by naked flames, distilleries were plagued by fire (see *Talisker, Glenrothes, Glenlossie* etc.). Glen Spey was badly damaged by a fire in 1920.

During World War II troops were billeted at Glen Spey. One soldier was electrocuted, and it is said that his ghost still haunts the distillery.

EXPRESSIONS:
• Glen Spey 12YO @ 43% (Flora & Fauna series, 2001)

RAW MATERIALS: Floor maltings until 1969, now unpeated malt from Burghead. Soft process water from the Doonie Spring; cooling water from the River Rothes.

PLANT: Semi-Lauter mash tun (4.4 tonnes). Eight stainless steel washbacks. Two lamp-glass wash stills (10,600 litres charge); two lamp-glass spirit stills (7,000 litres charge), with purifiers. All indirect fired. Shell-and-tube condensers.

MATURATION: Refill ex-bourbon hogsheads. Mainly in the Central Belt.

STYLE: Nutty-spicy, light.

MATURE CHARACTER: A light style of malt, made for blending. The nutty, cereal character comes through on the nose, with a Speyside floral element. The taste is sweet, with a malty, grassy character. Some have identified roast chestnuts. Shortish finish. Innocuous. Medium- to light-bodied, all by design.

G1   Glentauchers

REGION
Speyside
ADDRESS
Mulben, Keith, Banffshire
PHONE
01542 860272
WEBSITE
No
OWNER
Chivas Brothers
VISITORS
No
CAPACITY
3.4m L.P.A.

HISTORICAL NOTES: Glentauchers was founded in 1897 by James Buchanan & Company (of Black & White fame) in partnership with their spirit supplier, W.P. Lowrie: the former bought out the latter in 1906. The attractive buildings three miles outside Keith were designed by John Alcock, under the supervision of the legendary Charles Doig. Like many other distilleries of the period, the site was chosen for its water supply and communications: a railway siding was constructed at the back of the site. It went into production in May 1898.

Curiously, experiments in the continuous distillation of malt whisky were conducted here around 1910. The plans for the 'continuous pot still' form part of the Doig Collection in Moray District Library, Elgin. There is also an example from Convalmore Distillery in the Whisky Museum, Dufftown.

Buchanan's joined D.C.L. in the Big Amalgamation of 1925, and Glentauchers was managed by S.M.D. from 1930, but licensed to James Buchanan & Company until 1949.

During the general refurbishment of distilleries in the mid 1960s, Glentauchers was expanded from two to six stills (1966), with a new stillhouse built alongside its maltings. These were closed in 1968, although the two pagoda-topped Doig kilns remain and the building still houses a single drum malting dating from about 1925.

By the mid 1980s the pendulum had swung the other way. Glentauchers was mothballed in 1985, and then sold to Allied Distillers in 1989. Production recommenced in August that year.

Ownership changed again in 2005, when Pernod Ricard bought most of Allied's Scotch whisky interests. Cast iron tanks in the stillhouse were replaced in 2006 (some of them dated from the 1930s), although the wooden Intermediate Spirit Receiver was retained. The mashhouse was upgraded in 2007. At that time it was determined that Glentauchers would remain a manual operation (unlike most of Chivas Brothers' other distilleries), to provide a practical training facility for all staff, including management.

CURIOSITIES: James Buchanan went to London as an agent for Chas MacKinlay & Company in 1879, aged 30.

By the time of his death, aged 86, Buchanan was a peer (Lord Woolavington), owned estates in four continents, had twice won the Derby and had given enormous sums to charitable causes and hospitals. He left over seven million pounds – a huge fortune in 1935.

EXPRESSIONS:
Glentauchers has always been a blending whisky, particularly for Buchanan's blends, now a key component in Ballantine's.
• Glentauchers 15YO was issued by Allied (in their Special Distillery Bottling range) in 2000. Not currently bottled as a single.

RAW MATERIALS: Production water from two reservoirs fed by the Rosarie and Tauchers Burns; the former supplies process water and the latter cooling water. Maltings closed 1968, now unpeated malt from independent maltsters.

PLANT: Full-Lauter mash tun (12 tonnes) since 2007. Six larch washbacks. Three plain wash stills (10,000 litres charge), three plain spirit stills (6,300 litres charge). Indirect fired by steam pans and coils. Shell-and-tube condensers.

MATURATION: Refill American oak casks.

STYLE: Medium-bodied Speyside – sweet and fruity.

MATURE CHARACTER: Another malt which is principally made for blending. Broadly Speyside in style – sweet, fragrant, fruity, estery – Glentauchers adds a dash of coconut, almonds and cereal to the profile. Sweet to taste, with little body but a pleasant, summery impression. Light-bodied.

Glenturret

REGION
Highland (South)

ADDRESS
The Hosh, Crieff, Perthshire

PHONE
01764 656565

WEBSITE
www.thefamousgrouse.
co.uk

OWNER
The Edrington Group Ltd

VISITORS
Popular visitor centre for all the family – The Famous Grouse Experience – with restaurant, shop, tours and tastings

CAPACITY
340,000 L.P.A.

HISTORICAL NOTES: There was an illicit farm distillery at The Hosh from 1775, and based on this, Glenturret claims to be the oldest distillery in Scotland. The first licence was granted to John Drummond in 1818. He continued until he went bankrupt in 1842. John McCallum followed him (1852–74) but also went bust; then it was taken over by Thomas Stewart, who changed its name from 'Hosh' to 'Glenturret' in 1875. (There had been another Glenturret Distillery nearby, but this folded in the 1850s).

Again it changed hands in 1903, to those of Mitchell Brothers Ltd; production ceased in 1921, and in 1929 Mitchells went into liquidation and the distillery was dismantled.

Glenturret's revival was owing to James Fairlie, who bought the site in 1957 and reinstated the equipment 1959–60 – often using second-hand plant and integrating new buildings with the old – with a view to 'preserving the craft traditions of malt whisky distilling and developing its appreciation'. To the latter end, he opened to the public and arranged tours and tastings – if Glenfiddich was the first distillery to do this, Glenturret was a close second. The British Prime Minister, Sir Alec Douglas-Home, visited in 1964.

In 1981, James Fairlie sold the distillery to Rémy Cointreau, who greatly expanded the visitor facilities. At that time, Rémy had a trading relationship with Highland Distilleries, and in 1993 Glenturret joined Highland Distilleries (now Edrington). In 2002 Edrington invested £2.2 million in further upgrading the visitor facilities, now named 'The Famous Grouse Experience', although the distillery had no previous connection to The Famous Grouse.

CURIOSITIES: Illicit distilling may have been carried on at The Hosh from before 1775: parish records reveal there were once many stills in the district, going back to 1717. Maybe this was due to the two hills which encompass it providing good vantage points from which to observe hostile militia or excisemen.

Glenturret was long famous for its cat, Towser, who is commemorated by a bronze statue. She died in 1987, aged 24, having dispatched 28,899 mice – a fact which is recorded in The Guinness Book of Records!

Alfred Barnard found Glenturret to be antiquated in the 1880s; it remains so today, by design. The Famous Grouse Experience welcomes around 100,000 visitors a year. The restaurant is well-known for its excellent haggis, neeps and tatties!

EXPRESSIONS:
Glenturret has a very small range (downsized from a wider range), including only one official bottling, the 10YO, and occasional limited or single cask releases.
- Glenturret 10YO @ 40% (introduced 2003, to replace a 12YO)
- Glenturret 8YO @ 40% (introduced 2006)
- Glenturret 1991 14YO @ CS (single cask released 2007)
- Glenturret 1992 15YO @ CS (single cask released 2007)
- Glenturret 1977 29YO @ CS (single cask released 2007)

RAW MATERIALS: Soft water from Loch Turret. Lightly peated malt from Simpson's.

PLANT: Open stainless mash tun (one tonne per mash), stirred by hand with a wooden paddle (this is unique). Eight Douglas fir washbacks (unusually, two washbacks charge the wash still). One boil-ball wash still (12,600 litres charge), one plain spirit still (6,800 litres charge; pre 1972, the spirit still was the wash still). Both indirect fired by steam. Shell-and-tube condenser s.

MATURATION: Refill American and Spanish oak, six bonded warehouses on site. Some goes to Buckley Bond, Bishopbriggs.

STYLE: Fruity (orange), floral, slightly medicinal, with cereal notes.

MATURE CHARACTER: The younger expressions retain the distillery character well: floral, nutty, malty, with a hint of smoke. The taste is sweetish, with honey traces, nuts and cereal, and a thread of smoke. Medium-bodied.

Glenugie Demolished

REGION
Highland (East)
ADDRESS
Invernettie, by Peterhead,
Aberdeenshire
LAST OWNER
Whitbread & Company Ltd
CLOSED
1983

Glenugie takes its name from the river that meets the sea at Inverugie, on the northern edge of Peterhead, the leading fishing port in the 1980s.

HISTORICAL NOTES: The distillery was established in the early 1830s on the site of an old windmill (the stump of which still survives) and was named Invernettie until 1837, when it was converted into a brewery. It was converted back in 1875 by the Scottish Highland Distillers Company Ltd, a company which was wound up only six years later. It passed through several hands, with periods of silence, including from 1925 to 1937.

In 1937 it was bought by Seager Evans, gin distillers in London, who had built Strathclyde Grain Spirit Distillery in 1927 (see entry) and acquired the blended whisky Long John in 1936. Seager Evans sold out to Schenley Industries Inc., of New York, in 1956, and this provided a welcome injection of capital at a time when blended Scotch was taking off worldwide. Ownership of the Scottish distilleries was transferred to Long John Distillers Ltd, and Glenugie was completely refurbished with new plant and equipment, two new stills and shell-and-tube condensers. Output was doubled. The company also built new distilleries at Tormore on Speyside and within Strathclyde, named Kinclaith.

In 1962 the company bought Laphroaig Distillery (see entry), and in 1970 changed its name to Long John International; in 1975, it was sold to Whitbread & Company Ltd, the brewers, whose spirits interests were bought by Allied-Lyons plc in January 1990 for £454 million. But by this time Glenugie had been closed for seven years. Not long after 1983 the property was divided and acquired by two North Sea oil engineering firms. The original buildings have since been demolished.

CURIOSITIES: The main distillery building had unusual cast iron framing. The distillery only ever had one pair of stills.

EXPRESSIONS:
• Glenugie was never bottled as a single by its proprietor.

Glenury Royal *Demolished*

REGION
Highland (East)

ADDRESS
Glenury Road, Stonehaven,
Aberdeenshire

LAST OWNER
D.C.L./S.M.D.

CLOSED
1983

*Joseph Hobbs
landscaped the
site and planted
flowering shrubs
and trees. He also
installed a small
laboratory at
Glenury, with a pair
of miniature stills
for experimental
distillations.*

HISTORICAL NOTES: There was a distillery on the Ury estate before 1825, when the *Aberdeen Journal* reported that fire had destroyed its maltings, and in 1838 another Aberdeen newspaper states: 'The Glenury Distillery was originally established by the late Duke of Gordon, with a view to put down smuggling', but it does not say when.

It first appears in Excise records for 1833, owned by Captain Robert Barclay (1779–1854), Laird of Ury (his forbear had bought the estate in 1648) and sometime M.P. for Kincardine. Barclay was a Quaker and a progressive farmer, and built (or rebuilt) the distillery to provide a market for local barley. He also had a friend at Court, whom he referred to as 'Mrs Windsor', who persuaded King William IV to allow him to use the 'Royal' suffix from 1835.

On his death in 1847 the distillery was sold to William Ritchie of Dunottar and remained in his family until 1936 when it was sold to Joseph Hobbs for £7,500. It had been closed since 1925, but resumed the following year, and in 1938 Hobbs sold it on to the Associated Scottish Distilleries Ltd for £18,500. This company was a subsidiary of National Distillers of America, which had made an arrangement with Hobbs to acquire distilleries: between 1934 and 1938 they bought Bruichladdich, Glenesk, Fettercairn, Glenlochy, Benromach and Strathdee Distilleries, as well as Glenury Royal, which became the company's head office. (See *Ben Nevis*.) National Distillers withdrew from Scotland in 1953 and sold A.S.D. and its distilleries to the D.C.L. (Bruichladdich and Fettercairn had already been sold, and Strathdee closed).

In 1965/66 Glenury Royal was expanded to four stills and much rebuilt.

It was terminally closed in 1985 and the site sold for residential development eight years later.

CURIOSITIES: Captain Barcay was an exceptionally strong man, and a considerable athlete. In 1799 he walked from London via Cambridge to Birmingham

– a distance of 150 miles – in two days; two years later
he walked from Ury to Boroughbridge in Yorkshire
in five days. He was a popular man. Two hundred
of his neighbours entertained him to dinner in the
distillery's maltings in 1838.

EXPRESSIONS:
Three times bottled in the Rare Malts series, at 28YO (1970),
29YO (1970) and 23YO (1971).
Won Most Outstanding Single Malt and Best Single Malt Over
12 Years at the 1996 I.W.S.C.
• Glenury Royal 1968 36YO @ 51.2% (released 2005)
• Glenury Royal 1953 50YO @ 42.8% (released 2003)

Highland Park

REGION
Highland (Island)
ADDRESS
Holm Road, Kirkwall,
Orkney
PHONE
01856 874619/885632
WEBSITE
www.highlandpark.com
OWNER
Edrington Group Ltd
VISITORS
Visitor centre and shop
CAPACITY
2.5m L.P.A.

HISTORICAL NOTES: Highland Park Distillery stands on a hill overlooking Kirkwall, Orkney's main town – on an area of common land long known as Parks of Rosebank. It proudly describes itself as 'The Northernmost Scotch Whisky Distillery in the World'.

From 1798, illicit whisky had been made here by a local brewer named Mansie (i.e. Magnus) Eunson, described as 'the greatest and most accomplished smuggler in Orkney', and also as a 'thug and small-time hood'. He enjoyed he protection of the Provost (i.e. mayor) of Kirkwall, whose son took over the running of the enterprise until 1814, when he was forced to close.

In 1813 Rosebank had been enclosed, divided into lots and its name changed to Highland Park (although the distillery itself was known as Kirkwall Distillery until 1876). Ironically, the lots which contained the distillery were taken up by the local Collector of Excise, John Robertson, who had long pursued Mansie Eunson (and who finished up as Supervisor of Excise in London). Another lot was taken by Robert Borwick, his son-in-law, and in 1826 Borwick acquired the whole ground, including the distillery, and immediately took out a licence.

Borwick ran the distillery until his death in 1840, when it passed to his son George. By 1860 George was 'tired of the trade' and leased the plant to a local firm; on his death in 1869, ownership passed to his son, the Reverend James Borwick, who put it on the market for £450, believing that owning a distillery was incompatible with his calling. It was sold to a local farmer, who sold it on in 1876 to William Stuart, owner of Miltonduff Distillery.

Stuart went into partnership with his cousin, James Mackay, and they set about improving Highland Park. During their first season they produced 19,300 gallons of whisky; this had more than doubled by 1882/83. Robertson & Baxter, brokers in Glasgow, became their main customer. James Mackay died in 1885, and Stuart now went into partnership with James Grant, who became sole partner ten years later.

Upon receiving samples in 1914, Sir Alexander Walker wrote: 'I am in the process of conversion to the idea that Highland Park is the only whisky worth drinking and Johnnie Walker only fit for selling to deluded Sassenachs.'

He immediately replaced the two stills with larger ones, and installed two further pairs in 1897. But the boom of the 1890s was about to turn to bust. Orders from R. & B. dropped from 60,000 to a mere 107 gallons in 1904/05. But the distillery remained in production throughout the First World War.

James Grant had brought his son and son-in-law into the business in 1908. His son Walter Grant turned the firm into a limited company and offered it to Robertson & Baxter's sister company, Highland Distilleries. The deal was concluded in 1937.

Highland Distilleries began to promote Highland Park as a single malt in 1979 and installed a visitor centre in 1986, which was awarded five stars by VisitScotland in 2000. The owning company's name was changed to Edrington in 1999.

CURIOSITIES: The *Pembroke Castle* called at Kirkwall on her maiden voyage in September 1883. Sir Donald Currie, the ship's owner, and his guests were entertained by the town's leading councillor '... who produced his well-known big bottle of Old Highland Park whisky. No sooner had this famous brand been tasted than they one and all agreed they had never met with any whisky like it before, that what was called Scotch in England was a different from this as chalk from cheese'. Twelve gallons of Highland Park were taken aboard, and the cruise continued to Copenhagen where '... the King of Denmark, the Emperor of Russia and a very distinguished party were entertained on board. The Highland Park whisky was procured and pronounced by all the finest they had ever tasted'.

A hogshead of Highland Park, distilled in 1877, set a record price at auction in Edinburgh in 1892.

Immediately after acquiring Highland Park, Highland Distilleries were obliged to buy 'a quarter acre of supposedly valueless and unworked blue stone quarry – Cattie Maggie's Quarry', in order to secure their water supply. The pool in the quarry feeds the springs that 'give Highland Park its unique flavour'.

EXPRESSIONS:

The core range comprises the 12, 18 and 25YO (the last two being introduced in 1997). A number of special and limited bottlings have been released in recent years. The bottle was redressed and repackaged in 2006.

- Highland Park The Saint Magnus Festival 2006
- Highland Park 25YO @ 48.1% (released 2005)
- Highland Park 30YO @ 48.1% (released 2005)
- Highland Park 21YO Ambassador Cask 1 @ 56.1% (single cask released 2005)
- Highland Park 10YO Ambassador Cask 2 @ 58.8% (single cask released 2006)
- Highland Park 33YO Ambassador Cask 3 @ 44.8% (single cask released 2007)
- Highland Park 20YO Rebus @ 44.7% (single cask released 2007)
- Highland Park 40YO @ 48.3% (single cask released 2008)

RAW MATERIALS: Hard water pumped up to the distillery from the Crantit Lagoons and one spring. Own floor maltings produce 20% of requirements, peated at around 20ppm phenols; the rest is unpeated from Tamdhu maltings. Local peat from Hobbister Hill.

PLANT: Stainless steel full-Lauter tun with a peaked canopy (5.5 tonnes per mash), 12 Oregon pine washbacks and two of Siberian larch. Two plain wash stills (14, 600 litres charge each), two plain spirit stills (9,000 litres charge each) both indirect fired by steam. Shell-and-tube condensers.

MATURATION: Ex-sherry and refill casks. Nineteen dunnage and four racked warehouses on site with over 45,000 casks.

STYLE: Malty, slightly smoky.

MATURE CHARACTER: The nose presents heather pollen and liquid honey, with caramelised oranges, sweet malt, a hint of oak and a drift of smouldering heather. The mouth feel is smooth, the taste sweet, slightly salty then dry, with toffee, traces of spice (cinnamon, ginger) and a twist of smoke. Medium-bodied.

Huntly

REGION
Highland (East)

ADDRESS
Old Toll Road, Huntly,
Aberdeenshire

PHONE
01466 794055

WEBSITE
www.huntlydistillers.com

OWNER
Huntly Distillers Ltd

VISITORS
Welcome

CAPACITY
1.1m L.P.A.

The site of the distillery is known as 'Battlehill', on account of past skirmishes.

HISTORICAL NOTES: A new distillery at Huntly will open in the summer of 2009 (D.V.). Its completion will realise the life-long ambition of Euan Shand, owner of the respected independent bottler, Duncan Taylor & Company (see *Leading Independent Bottlers*), who himself was raised at Glendronach Distillery, close by.

Huntly was once a centre of distilling – in 1798/99 there were 14 small licensed distillers in the district. The site chosen for the new distillery – which was a former granary (the old granary buildings will house the new stillhouse) – is adjacent to that of a former 'Huntly Distillery', also known as Pirries Mill (established 1824; defunct by 1867).

It is also ten minutes from Ardmore, Glendronach and An Cnoc Distilleries.

It is the company's intention to produce gin and vodka on site as well as malt and grain whisky, and to this end an extra pot still (for gin) and two column stills will be installed.

Huntly will be the first distillery in modern times to do this (but see also *Loch Lomond*).

CURIOSITIES: Duncan Taylor & Company began as whisky brokers and blenders in Glasgow in 1938, with a focus on exporting their own blended whiskies to the U.S.A. When Euan Shand bought the company and its stocks in 2001 he acquired 'one of the largest privately held collections of rare Scotch whisky casks in the world'. He moved the operation to Huntly, where the company also bottles its whiskies.

Huntly's ambition is to be the first entirely 'green' distillery. To this end, the roofs of new buildings will be covered with grass, the rainfall from them and other roofs being 'harvested' for assorted uses. The process will be run from a boiler fired by local wood chip and wood pulp, and in due course split staves. The owners are also looking at ways to dry and use draff in the boiler. Scottish oak has been already sourced (as fallen timber) and is currently being coopered. It is planned to use this for complete maturations, not just as finishing casks.

RAW MATERIALS: Malt from independent maltsters. Locally sourced grain. Considering establishing own maltings. Water from springs on site.

PLANT: Semi-Lauter mash tun (2.5 tonnes per mash). Nine stainless steel washbacks. One plain, short wash stills (11,000 litres charge), one short-neck plain spirit still (6,500 litres charge). Both indirect-fired; steam production from wood chip boiler. Both stills with shell-and-tube condensers. Two continuous stills (four 48-feet high columns); a copper pot gin still, with variable neck (3,500 litres charge).

MATURATION: American ex-bourbon, European ex-sherry and port and new Scottish oak. Five thousand casks matured in Huntly.

STYLE: Looking for a robust Highland style.

Imperial Mothballed

REGION
Speyside
ADDRESS
Carron, Moray
OWNER
Chivas Brothers
CAPACITY
1.6m L.P.A.

A local journalist reported of Imperial's crown that 'once gilded it would flash and glitter in the sunlight like the crescent on a Turkish minaret … among the dark pine woods of Carron and the brown hills which encircle the rushing Spey'.

HISTORICAL NOTES: Built in 1897 by Thomas Mackenzie, owner of nearby Dailuaine Distillery and distant Talisker on the Isle of Skye, Imperial's construction (an iron framework supporting thick red-brick walls, to resist fire) was a novelty in Scotland. The distillery was named in honour of Queen Victoria's Diamond Jubilee, celebrated that year, and the original maltings (designed by Charles Doig) was surmounted by an enormous cast iron crown.

This was not a good time to open a distillery, since the Whisky Boom of the 1890s burst in 1899. Imperial closed after one season. Production restarted ten years later (1919), but difficulties with effluent disposal caused it to be closed again in 1925, by which time it was owned by D.C.L. The maltings continued to operate, but it was not for 30 years that improvements in waste treatment combined with demand to allow it to re-open, and this year (1955) the mashhouse and stillhouse were modernised. A second pair of stills and Saladin maltings were added in 1964.

S.M.D. closed Imperial in 1985 and sold the distillery to Allied four years later. They refurbished and went back into production in 1991, but it was mothballed again seven years later. In truth, the distillery has been closed for 60% of its existence.

When Allied was broken up and sold in 2005, Imperial Distillery went to Chivas Brothers. Although the plant is still in situ, it is not certain whether Imperial will operate again, and it is currently for sale as a development site.

CURIOSITIES: It is said that one of the problems with Imperial is the size of its four stills – so large they cannot be run flexibly. The problem of effluent disposal was solved in the 1950s when it was discovered that nutritious elements in draff and pot ale could be recovered by drying, to make a high-protein animal feed.

In December 2007, the distillery was raided by copper thieves.

EXPRESSIONS:
An Imperial 15YO was issued by Allied in 2000 (in their Special Distillery Bottling range). Not currently bottled by its owner; more familiar in Gordon & Macphail bottlings, including a range of five different finishes to a 10YO Imperial issued in 2000.

RAW MATERIALS: Production water from the Balintomb Burn. Unpeated malt from Burghead.

PLANT: Stainless steel rake-and-plough mash tun (11.56 tonnes). Six larch washbacks. Two lamp-glass wash stills (36,000 litres), two plain spirit stills (36,500 litres). Indirect fired by steam pans and coils.

MATURATION: Refill American oak casks. Its own dunnage warehouses are now empty.

STYLE: Speyside.

Inchgower

REGION
Speyside

ADDRESS
Buckie, Moray

PHONE
01542 836700

WEBSITE
www.malts.com

OWNER
Diageo plc

VISITORS
By appointment

CAPACITY
1.9m L.P.A.

HISTORICAL NOTES: Inchgower stands outside the fishing port of Buckie. The distillery was built in 1871 by Alexander Wilson & Company to replace their distillery at Tochineal nearby, which had become too small – and where the landlord had doubled the rent. Tochineal's plant was moved over to the new distillery. Wilson & Company operated Inchgower until 1936, when the firm went bankrupt and both the distillery and the family house was bought by Buckie Town Council for £1,600; two years later the distillery was sold for £3,000 to Arthur Bell & Sons.

Bell's was acquired by Guinness in 1985, Guinness bought the D.C.L. in 1987, and thus Inchgower came to be owned by Diageo.

CURIOSITIES: Inchgower was Bell's second distillery (the first was Dufftown). It was bought by Arthur Kinmond Bell, Chairman of the company and oldest son of Arthur Bell. A.K. was a notable philanthropist, and during the 1930s had built 150 high-quality houses and offered them at low rent to needy and unemployed people in Perth. He died two years after acquiring Inchgower, in 1942. The *Perthshire Advertiser* referred to him as Perth's 'greatest benefactor of all time'.

The distillery supplied fillings for Bell's blends, and as the brand's popularity increased, it was expanded (to four stills in 1966) and worked harder and faster, which did not help the quality of the make. From 1979 Bell's was the No. 1 bestselling Scotch in the U.K. (a position it holds to this day).

EXPRESSIONS:
Bell's bottled small amounts of Inchgower as a single from the early 1980s.
• Inchgower 14YO @ 43% (Flora & Fauna series, from 1991)
• Inchgower 27YO @ 55.6% (Rare Malts series, distilled 1976, released 2003)

RAW MATERIALS: Unpeated malt from Burghead. Water from springs in the Minduff Hills.

Like all distilleries, Inchgower operated a farm as part of its business. In 1885 the residues from the distillery (draff and pot ale) fed 100 head of cattle, 200 sheep and pigs.

PLANT: Mash tun (8.2 tonnes). Six Oregon pine washbacks. Two plain wash stills and two plain spirit stills. All indirect fired. Shell-and-tube condensers, with after-coolers.

MATURATION: Mainly refill American oak.

STYLE: Nutty-spicy, malty.

MATURE CHARACTER: The nose is malty, caramelised and lightly sherried, yet the overall impression is dry. There are some coffee and chocolate notes, and sometimes a whiff of smoke. The taste is sweet then dry, with a hint of salt; bruised apples and hazelnuts. Medium-bodied.

Invergordon Grain Distillery

ADDRESS
Invergordon, Ross-shire
OWNER
Whyte & Mackay/U.B.G.
CAPACITY
40m L.P.A.

HISTORICAL NOTES: By 1958 all government restrictions on whisky distilling were relaxed. There was an acute shortage of capacity, in both malt and grain spirit, to meet the burgeoning post-war demand. The grain whisky distilleries at Lochside, Girvan, Moffat and Invergordon are examples of the industry's response to this demand.

Invergordon stands on the north shore of the Cromarty Firth, 'a place of considerable mark', according to the *Imperial Gazetteer* (1854), 'substantially built, well-situated for traffic and of growing importance for the shipment of farm produce from the surrounding country'. At that time it had a population of nearly 1,000. The port was named for Sir William Gordon, its owner in the late eighteenth century.

Since World War II, several attempts had been made to bring industrial activity to the Highlands north of Inverness. One such was Invergordon Distillery, promoted strongly by James Grigor, Provost of Inverness, in the late 1950s. With good reason: communications by sea and road were excellent; it was on the edge of a notable barley-growing region, and the water was first-rate.

The Invergordon Distillers Ltd was incorporated in March 1959 to build the first and only grain whisky distillery in the Highlands. Production commenced in July 1961, with one Coffey still producing 10,000 GPA per week; Stanley P. Morrison was appointed agent. Two further Coffey stills were added in 1963, and another in 1978, with extra columns on the Dumbarton model (see entry) to produce neutral spirit. These were designed in-house by the distillery's engineer.

In 1985 Invergordon bought the long established whisky company, Charles Mackinlay & Company (see *Jura*, *Glenallachie* etc.), for £7.8 million, and three years later four of the directors led a management buy-out. Their independence did not last long: Whyte & Mackay (which had a 41% shareholding in the company), having failed to take over in 1991, acquired

In 1916, under the Defence of the Realm Act, Lloyd George established the state management of all pubs and off-licences in Invergordon and Carlisle as an experiment. This remained in Carlisle until the 1970s.

a sufficient majority in October 1993.

The subsequent history of Invergordon Distillery is linked to the ups and downs of Whyte & Mackay (see *Jura* and *Who Owns Whom?*), but will hopefully stabilise under the new ownership of United Distillers Group of India, part of the giant United Breweries Group, which bought Whyte & Mackay in 2007.

CURIOSITIES: In 1965 a pot still malt distillery named Ben Wyvis was built within the Invergordon complex. It ceased production in 1977 (see *Ben Wyvis*).

EXPRESSIONS:
Invergordon Single Grain 10YO @ 40% (launched 1990)

RAW MATERIALS: Water from Loch Glass.

PLANT: Four Coffey stills.

MATURATION: American oak. On site.

STYLE: Light and sweet.

MATURE CHARACTER: Fresh and sweet, with pear drops and acetone. Clean and light-bodied, but somewhat one-dimensional compared to malt whisky.

In

Inverleven Demolished

REGION
Lowland
ADDRESS
Glasgow Road, Dumbarton
LAST OWNER
Allied Distillers
CLOSED
1991

HISTORICAL NOTES: Inverleven was installed within Hiram Walker's Dumbarton grain whisky distillery in 1938, the same year that the distillery opened. Both were licensed to Walker's subsidiary, George Ballantine & Sons, designed to make fillings for the Ballantine's blends.

Inverleven had two conventional stills and (after 1959) a Lomond still; the latter has disappeared, but the former two were bought by Bruichladdich Distillery in 2007 and will be used in their proposed Port Charlotte Distillery on Islay.

The stills were originally direct fired, but were changed to steam heating in the early 1960s. Inverleven closed in 1991. It had a capacity of 1.3m L.P.A.

CURIOSITIES: The distillery's site, in the shadow of Dumbarton Rock and at the mouth of the River Leven, was formerly a shipyard (derelict since 1933) and the high red-brick building itself was designed in America. It is 'very much what one would expect to find in the Midwest of the United States rather than Lowland Scotland' (Philip Morrice). The building was demolished in 2006.

'It was said that the plant might not have been built had not Sir Henry Ross, Chairman of D.C.L., not kept Harry Hatch of Hiram Walker waiting over-long, whereupon Hatch, who had come to buy grain whisky, announced that he would build his own grain distillery.' (Charles Craig).

EXPRESSIONS:
Never bottled by its owner. Occasionally bottled by independents.

Jura

REGION
Highland (Island)
ADDRESS
Craighouse, Isle of Jura,
Argyll
PHONE
01496 820240
WEBSITE
www.isleofjura.com
OWNER
Whyte & Mackay
VISITORS
Visitor centre, and
apartments
CAPACITY
2.2m L.P.A.

HISTORICAL NOTES: Perhaps surprisingly for a place so remote from the Excise, Jura had a licensed distillery by 1810 – at Craighouse, the site of the present distillery and also of a previous, unlicensed still – the Small Isles Distillery. The licensee was Archibald Campbell, the laird of Jura.

Several tenants ran the distillery with little success. The first was William Abercrombie (to 1831), then Archibald Fletcher (until 1851). When Fletcher gave up the lease, there were a mere 5,450 litres of whisky under bond. Campbell's son thought of selling the stills for scrap (value £400), but was soon approached by Norman Buchanan of Glasgow (who acquired Caol Ila Distillery at the same time), but he went bankrupt ten years later. After a gap of some years, in 1876 the laird signed a 34-year lease of the distillery with James Ferguson of Glasgow, but he abandoned the site in 1901 (taking with him all the equipment, which he had paid for), when the tenancy still had 17 years to run. The laird removed the roof to avoid paying rates and the original distillery fell into ruin.

It was revived in 1963 by two local landowners, Robin Fletcher and Tony Riley-Smith (uncle of the founder of *Whisky Magazine*), who wanted to bring employment to the island. With backing from Mackinlay Macpherson & Company (soon taken over by Scottish & Newcastle Brewers), they recruited the services of William Delmé-Evans, who had designed and built Tullibardine Distillery in the late 1940s. 'It was our intention to produce a Highland-type malt, differing from the typically peaty stuff last produced in 1900', he wrote. The first single malt bottling was released in 1974.

The distillery was expanded by Dr Alan Rutherford (who went on to become Head of Production at U.D.) from 1976 to 1978 (from two to four stills). Invergordon Distillers acquired Mackinlay's and its distilleries in 1985, and were themselves bought by Whyte & Mackay ten years later.

George Orwell lived in a remote cottage on Jura in the late 1940s, and finished Nineteen Eighty-Four here.

CURIOSITIES: The stills here, designed by Delmé-Evans, are unusually tall (7.7m), to produce a lighter style of malt.

Apartments in the former manager's house were refurbished in 2006 and are available to let. Jura has long been packaged in an unusual waisted bottle, elegant and even voluptuous. This bottle shape was first adopted by MacKinlay & Birnie for their Glen Mhor malt, and has been used by Jura from the start.

EXPRESSIONS:
First bottled as a single by its owners in 1974. Key expressions repackaged in 2006.
- Isle of Jura 10YO @ 40%
- Isle of Jura 16YO @ 40%
- Isle of Jura Superstition @ 45% (peated, a mix of 13YO and 21YO whiskies, released December 2002)
- Isle of Jura Legacy @ 40% (travel retail only, a mix of 10YO and older whiskies)
- Isle of Jura 21YO @ 40%
- Isle of Jura 30YO CS (single cask, 468 bottles, released December 2004)
- Isle of Jura 36YO @ 44% (single cask, 449 bottles, released 2001)
- Isle of Jura Vintage 1973 @ 55.6% (released Februrary 2003)
- Isle of Jura 1975 @ 60.9% (single cask, 192 bottles)
- Isle of Jura 1984 19YO @ 42% (800 cases, George Orwell edition, drawn from two different styles of sherry-wood)
- Isle of Jura 40YO @ 46% (released 2007)

RAW MATERIALS: Unpeated malt from Port Ellen Maltings (also occasionally heavy peated malt for Superstition), Inverness, Aberdeen and Pencaitland. Water from the Market Loch.

PLANT: Semi-Lauter mash tun (4.75 tonnes); six stainless steel washbacks. Two wash stills (25,000 litres capacity each, 24,150 litres charge) of lamp-glass design; two lamp-glass spirit stills (22,000 litres capacity each, 15,500 litres charge). Indirect fired. Shell-and-tube condensers.

MATURATION: 27,000 casks matured on site in high racked warehouses (for single malt bottlings). 50% first-fill bourbon,

50% second- and third-fill; 5% sherry butts used in some expressions. 33% of the make bottled is as single malt.

STYLE: Oily, earthy-piney, with lemon notes.

MATURE CHARACTER: The oiliness apparent in the new-make comes through in the mature whisky, along with pine sap, orange zest and dry nuts. The taste is oily, with some maltiness; sweetish to start, becoming dry, with a dash of salt. Medium- to light-bodied.

Kilchoman

REGION
Islay

ADDRESS
Rockside Farm, Isle of Islay, Argyll

PHONE
01496 850011

WEBSITE
www.kilchomandistillery. com

OWNER
Kilchoman Distillery Company Ltd

CAPACITY
100,000 L.P.A.

HISTORICAL NOTES: Kilchoman's situation on the wild west coast of Islay, tucked in behind the sea cliffs and close to the wide white strand of Machir Bay, is striking. It is also historic. These lands were gifted by the Lords of the Isles to their physicians, the Beaton or MacBeatha family, who arrived in Scotland from Ireland in 1300, and may well have brought the secrets of distilling with them. Fergus McVey was confirmed in possession by James VI in 1609: the fine carved cross in Kilchoman Kirkyard, dating from even earlier, commemorates another member of the family.

The distillery was the brain-child of Anthony Wills, wine and spirits merchant, who moved to Islay in 2000, having married Cathy Wilks, an Illeach, some years earlier. A year later he leased and renovated some semi-derelict buildings at Rockside Farm, Kilchoman, from its owner, Mark French, who grew malting quality barley and had a fine herd of cows to consume the residues of distilling. The distillery was officially opened by the present writer on 3 June 2005, and went into production in December that year.

CURIOSITIES: Kilchoman's slogan is 'Taking whisky back to its roots', based on the fact that it is a veritable farm distillery, as many were in days gone by – on Islay alone there were 13 farm distilleries in the early nineteenth century. It is not unique in this regard (see *Daftmill*), however, it can make the proud claim to do everything on site – from growing the barley to bottling the whisky – and this is unique.

The distillery has a charming café and shop run by Cathy Wills. The whole enterprise has a family feel about it.

EXPRESSIONS:
Miniatures of new-make spirit are available at the distillery. The first Kilchoman single malt whisky will be bottled in July 2009.

RAW MATERIALS: Soft peaty water from the Allt Glean Osmail

It might be argued that Kilchoman was the cradle of distilling in Scotland.

Burn. Floor maltings on site, using barley grown on the farm and peat from Duich Moss (30ppm phenols) and the balance from Port Ellen Maltings (heavily peated at 50ppm phenols). Own grown malt accounts for 30–40% of production – spirit made from this is casked separately from that made from Port Ellen malt.

PLANT: Semi-Lauter mash tun (one tonne). Four stainless steel washbacks. One plain wash still (2,700 litres charge), one boil-pot spirit still (1,500 litres charge), both indirect fired by steam coils. Shell-and-tube condensers.

MATURATION: 85% in fresh (currently from Buffalo Trace) and refill ex-bourbon barrels, and 15% in ex-Oloroso butts. All matured on site.

STYLE: Unusually sweet, fruity and smoky.

Kinclaith Demolished

REGION
Lowland

ADDRESS
40 Moffat Street, Glasgow

LAST OWNER
Allied Distillers

CLOSED
1975

HISTORICAL NOTES: Kinclaith was built in 1956/57 within Strathclyde Distillery to provide fillings for Long John (see *Strathclyde*). It was dismantled in 1976/77, after Long John International had been sold to Whitbread, to allow for expansion at Strathclyde.

A miniature bottle (5cl) of Kinclaith 1966 achieved £107 at auction in 2002.

EXPRESSIONS:
Never bottled by its owner, a handful of bottlings have been released by G. & M., Cadenhead's and Signatory – all of which achieve high prices at auction.

Ki

Kininvie

REGION
Speyside
ADDRESS
Dufftown, Moray
PHONE
01340 882000
WEBSITE
No
OWNER
William Grant & Sons Ltd
VISITORS
No
CAPACITY
4.4m L.P.A.

A limited bottling (500 bottles) was released in February 2008 to mark the opening of Heathrow Terminal 5.

HISTORICAL NOTES: Kininvie Distillery was built from scratch in 1990 next door to William Grant's Glenfiddich/Balvenie distilleries. It went into production on 4 July.

CURIOSITIES: It was opened by Janet Sheed Roberts, William Grant's grand-daughter (see below).

In order to prevent independent bottlers using their brand-names, Kininvie, Balvenie and Glenfiddoch, William Grant 'tea-spoon' (i.e. add small amounts of one make into another) before selling casks, and give them different names. Aldunie (Kininvie), Burnside (Balvenie) and Wardhead (Glenfiddich).

EXPRESSIONS:
Kininvie was built to supply Grant's Family Reserve and Monkey Shoulder (blended malt, released 2005), however, a very limited amount was bottled in August 2006 at 15YO – 'Bottled for Janet Roberts' 105th Birthday'.
Hazelwood Reserve 17YO @ 52.5% (sherry-wood matured. The name is that of Janet Roberts' home since 1933, Hazelwood House, close to the distillery.)

RAW MATERIALS: Water from springs in the Conval Hills. Unpeated malt from independent maltsters.

PLANT: Semi-Lauter mash tun located within Balvenie Distillery, but dedicated to Kininvie's needs (11.25 tonnes). Nine Douglas fir washbacks. Three plain wash stills (14,600 litres charge), six boil-pot spirit stills (8,600 litres charge) all indirect fired by steam coils. Shell-and-tube condensers.

MATURATION: Refill ex-bourbon and ex-sherry casks.

STYLE: Floral.

Knockando

REGION
Speyside

ADDRESS
Knockando, Aberlour,
Moray

PHONE
01340 810205

WEBSITE
www.malts.com

OWNER
Diageo plc

VISITORS
Visitor centre

CAPACITY
1.3m L.P.A.

HISTORICAL NOTES: The distillery was designed by
Charles Doig for John Tyler Thomson, chartered
accountant and spirits broker in Elgin, who traded
as the Knockando-Glenlivet Distillery Company. It
is situated on the north bank of the Spey, and the
Strathspey railway runs through the distillery; a
dedicated siding was installed in 1905. The name is
that of the parish, and comes from Cnoc-an-Dubh,
'the dark hillock'.

Production started in 1899, the year of the collapse
of Pattison's of Leith, a leading blender and buyer of
fillings. With the whisky industry in recession as a
result, Knockando closed next year, and was sold in
1904 to W. & A. Gilbey, the London wine and spirits
merchant, for £3,500.

Gilbey's merged with United Wine Traders (part
of which was Justerini & Brooks) in 1962, to become
Independent Distillers & Vintners, and Knockando
became the key constituent of J. & B. Rare, and later
the 'brand home' (which it remains). In 1969 it was
doubled in size (to four stills).

I.D.V. was taken over by Watney Mann in 1972, who
sold to Grand Metropolitan the same year. Grand
Metropolitan/I.D.V. and Guinness/U.D. merged in
1997 to form U.D.V., which in turn became Diageo.

CURIOSITIES: I.D.V. were offering Knockando as a
single malt by 1977/78. As wine merchants, they also
bottled by 'vintage' rather than age, although the
'vintages' declared were usually around 12 years. This
practice is now discontinued.

From 1978 until 2006, Knockando was managed by
Innes Shaw, who had worked there man and boy. His
great-grandfather was employed as a joiner when the
distillery was built, and the visitor centre exhibits
invoices from him. He later became Manager at
Cragganmore and an exciseman.

Knockando was the first distillery on Speyside to install electricity.

EXPRESSIONS:
Until 2002, Knockando was bottled by 'vintage', displaying the year of distillation, not the age – although this was usually around 12YO and at either 43% or 40% volume. 'Vintages' were declared in 1963 (bottled 1976), 1964, 1968 (bottled 1992), 1972, every year from 1975 to 1982, 1986, Master Reserve 21YO. Currently bottlings are released at 12 and 18YO:
- Knockando 12YO @ 40%
- Knockando 18YO @ 40%

RAW MATERIALS: Soft process water from the Cardnach Spring; cooling water from the River Spey. Floor maltings until 1968; now lightly peated malt from Burghead.

PLANT: Full-Lauter mash tun (9.5 tonnes). Four Oregon pine washbacks. Two lamp-glass wash stills (16,000 litres charge); two boil-ball spirit stills (16,000 litres charge). All indirect fired. Shell-and-tube condensers.

MATURATION: Refill ex-bourbon hogsheads.

STYLE: Malty, cereal-like.

MATURE CHARACTER: The keynote breakfast cereal-style comes through in the standard 12YO expression, Sugar Puffs to be exact, with honey, walnuts and a trace of olive oil. The taste is sweet and simple, with cereal and nuts. Medium- to light-bodied. A good breakfast malt.

Knockdhu

REGION
Highland (East)

ADDRESS
Knock, by Keith, Moray

PHONE
01466 771223

WEBSITE
www.ancnoc.com

OWNER
Inverhouse Distillers Ltd

VISITORS
By appointment

CAPACITY
1.4m L.P.A.

HISTORICAL NOTES: The distillery is situated beneath the dark, rounded hump of Knock Hill: 'Knockdhu' means 'the dark hillock'. It was the first malt whisky distillery to be commissioned by D.C.L., which until then, 1893/94, had confined its interests to grain whisky production. The site was chosen on account of the water quality from springs on the hill, close to 'good barley country' and near 'an inexhaustible supply of excellent peats'; it also helped that the Great North of Scotland Railway line between Aberdeen and Elgin ran adjacent to the site. The make was used primarily in the Haig blends.

A visitor remarked in 1925 how 'remarkably well kept' the site was, with a 'handsome avenue' leading up to the 'severe buildings', and a nicely laid-out orchard of apple, cherry and plum trees. Even at that time it was equipped with 'a powerful electric light plant'. In 1930 management was transferred to S.M.D.

Knockdhu was a casualty of the world recession of the early 1980s. It was closed in 1983, but was sold to Inver House five years later. They released the first single malt bottling in 1990, then changed the brand name to an Cnoc (see below). Inver House became part of the leading Far Eastern spirits company, ThaiBev plc, in 2001.

CURIOSITIES: When it was built, Knockdhu was a very modern distillery. Its refrigeration plant was the first of its kind in the north of Scotland; the Manager and Excise Officer's houses were provided with 'handsome villas' and 'private lavatories'. Situated three miles east of Keith, it is on the very edge of Speyside, and some classify the make as such.

In 1960 a tractor replaced the horse and cart that moved goods between the distillery and the railway station. 'A sad day for everybody,' wrote an employee. 'And particularly for the man who worked with the horse, because it was a dear friend.'

The distillery is Knockdhu, the malt is an Cnoc, following a gentleman's agreement not long after Inver House took over, in order to avoid any possible

Between 1940 and 1945 the distillery was occupied by a unit of the Indian army, billeted in the malt barns, with stabling for their horses and mules.

confusion with Knockando. Its positioning is young-ish and artistic, with sponsorship focused on the arts: 'an Cnoc is at home in an arts-based, quirky, style bar'.

EXPRESSIONS:
Since 2004 the core range has comprised the 12YO with occasional limited editions and annual vintage bottlings, usually around 14YO.
• an Cnoc 1991 @ 46% (limited edition, released 2005)
• an Cnoc 30YO @ 50% (limited edition from 1975, released 2006)
• an Cnoc 1993 @ 46% (limited edition, released 2007)
• an Cnoc 16YO @ 46% (introduced 2007)
• an Cnoc 1994 @ 46% (limited edition, released 2008)

RAW MATERIALS: Process water from springs on Knock Hill; cooling water from the Ternemny Burn. Malt from independent maltsters.

PLANT: Traditional deep bed, cast iron mash tun but with semi-Lauter stirring gear (4.15 tonnes). Six Douglas fir washbacks. One tall boil-ball wash still (10,500 litres charge); one tall boil-ball spirit still (11,000 litres charge). Both indirect fired. Worm tub shared by both stills.

MATURATION: Mainly U.S. ex-bourbon casks. Matured on site in four dunnage warehouses and one racked warehouse for single malt bottlings, holding some 7,600 casks.

STYLE: Speyside style – fruity-floral, estery, with lemon notes, but with added body from the worm tubs.

MATURE CHARACTER: A light Speyside style; sweet, floral (buttercups), cereal, lemony, with a suggestion of vanilla cream. The texture is light, the taste sweet, with cooked apples and lemon meringue pie.

Ladyburn Dismantled

REGION
Lowland
ADDRESS
Girvan, Ayrshire
LAST OWNER
William Grant & Sons Ltd
CLOSED
1975

HISTORICAL NOTES: William Grant & Sons, owners of the phenomenally successful Grant's Standfast blended whisky (now *Grant's Family Reserve*) built a large grain distillery at Girvan in 1963/64, with a small malt whisky distillery within it, installed 1966, to supply fillings for their blend (see *Girvan*).

The distillery had two pairs of stills. The venture was abandoned in 1975 and the distillery dismantled.

CURIOSITIES: According to Mrs Udo, Grant's still possess 30 casks of Ladyburn and may be bottling it as a single in the near future.

EXPRESSIONS:
There are only two known proprietary bottlings of Ladyburn (to date): a 12yo and a 27yo (from 1973 @ 50.4%). In addition, a couple of casks have been bottled by Cadenhead's (@ 12 and 14yo) and G. & M. from 1970.

Lagavulin

REGION
Islay

ADDRESS
Port Ellen, Isle of Islay,
Argyll

PHONE
01496 302400

WEBSITE
www.malts.com

OWNER
Diageo plc

VISITORS
Visitor centre

CAPACITY
2.3m L.P.A.

HISTORICAL NOTES: Guarding the opening to Lagavulin Bay stand the crumbling remains of Dunyveg Castle, power-base of the Lords of the Isles and where the lords kept their galleys.

There were illicit stills in this sheltered 'hollow of the mill' in the eighteenth century, but the first licensed operation was established in 1815 by John Johnston. In the 1820s he acquired a neighbouring distillery, Ardmore, and his son combined the two in 1837.

John Crawford Graham, brother of the Glasgow wine merchant Alexander Graham and in partnership with James Logan Mackie, bought the distillery in 1852. Another brother, Walter Graham, had the lease of Laphroaig Distillery, next door, and ran the two together for four years. J.L. Mackie took over the business in 1860 and sent his nephew Peter to serve an apprenticeship at Lagavulin.

Peter Mackie joined his uncle in the business and in 1890 became Managing Partner. The same year, he created the blend White Horse; so successful was this that by 1908 Mackie & Company was named among the Big Five (with Walker's, Dewar's, Buchanan and Haig). In 1924, the year of Peter Mackie's death, the company became White Horse Distillers. This merged with D.C.L. in 1927.

CURIOSITIES: Peter Mackie was an authority on shooting, and wrote *The Gamekeeper's Handbook*; he insisted his distillery workers ate a proper diet (see *Craigellachie*); he was a tireless spokesman for the whisky industry, and was made a baronet in 1920.

In 1908, Peter Mackie built a second distillery within Lagavulin, which he named Malt Mill. Until the previous year he had been the agent for Laphroaig, but he fell out with the owners in considerable acrimony, and resolved to make a whisky which was very similar and which would damage Laphroaig's market. The plan was a failure, but Malt Mill operated until 1962; its make went into blends.

'There are only a few of the Scotch distillers that can turn out spirit for use as single whiskies, and that made at Lagavulin can claim to be one of the most prominent.'

Alfred Barnard, 1887

I know of only three bottles of single Malt Mill, and some others which I suspect are fakes.

The building which housed Malt Mill is now Lagavulin's visitor centre.

EXPRESSIONS:
Lagavulin was bottled by D.C.L. at 12YO, but when it became the Islay representative of the Classic Malts in 1989 it was decided to bottle at 16YO. This advanced age combined with under-production during the 1980s and the phenomenal global success of the whisky made it difficult to buy in some markets.
- Lagavulin 16YO @ 43% (Classic Malts series, from 1989)
- Lagavulin Distillers Edition @ 43% (Pedro Ximinez finish, introduced 1998)
- Lagavulin 12YO @ Cask Strength (introduced 2002)
- Lagavulin 25YO @ 57.2% (limited to 9,000 bottles from 1978, released 2002)

RAW MATERIALS: Floor maltings until 1974; now heavily peated malt (30–35ppm phenols) from Port Ellen. Dark, soft water from the Solum lochs.

PLANT: Full-Lauter mash tun (4.32 tonnes). Ten Oregon pine washbacks. Two plain wash stills (10,500 litres charge), two plain spirit stills (12,200 litres charge). All indirect fired. Shell-and-tube condensers.

MATURATION: Mainly refill American, with some refill European. Some matured on site and at Port Ellen and Caol Ila Distilleries; mostly in the Central Belt.

STYLE: Rich, sweet, peaty.

MATURE CHARACTER: Lagavulin is the richest and most complex of the Islay malts. The nose has berries, Lapsang Souchong tea, sherry, sweet seaweed, wax polish, camphor, carbolic and scented smoke. A big, rich mouth feel; very sweet to start, then a big blast of peat smoke in the finish and a long aftertaste. Full-bodied.

Laphroaig

REGION
Islay
ADDRESS
Port Ellen, Isle of Islay,
Argyll
PHONE
01496 302418
WEBSITE
www.laphroaig.com
OWNER
Beam Global Spirits & Wine
VISITORS
Yes, and a well-organised
Friends of Laphroaig group
CAPACITY
2.6m L.P.A.

HISTORICAL NOTES: Alexander and Donald Johnston, who were tenant farmers in Tallant and Kildalton by 1810, established the distillery at Laphroaig in 1815. Their forbears were MacIains from Glencoe ('Mac-Iain' Anglicises to 'John-son'), who came to Islay in the early fifteenth century.

Their landlord was Walter Frederick Campbell, an enlightened improver; he founded both Port Ellen, named after his wife, and Port Charlotte, named for his mother, and supported the ventures enthusiastically.

Donald Johnston bought his brother out in 1836, but died in 1847 after falling into a vat of pot ale and was succeeded by his 11-year-old son, Dugald; Laphroaig was looked after by his uncle and managed by Walter Graham from neighbouring Lagavulin Distillery until he came of age in 1857. Laphroaig labels still recall 'D. Johnston & Company', and the distillery remained in the family until the 1960s.

Perhaps the most remarkable scion of the family was Ian Hunter, great-grandson of Donald, who became Manager of Laphroaig in 1908 and sole owner of the business 20 years later. One of his first tasks was to change the distillery's agents, Mackie & Company of Glasgow. Unusually, Laphroaig was being sold as a single malt even in those days. Peter Mackie (later Sir Peter), owner of Lagavulin Distillery, was furious; Mackie's had, after all, 'built the brand'. (See *Lagavulin*.)

In the 1920s, Ian Hunter set about selling his whisky in the United States. While he was abroad, the distillery was managed by his secretary, Bessie Williamson, and when he died in 1954 he bequeathed Laphroaig to her.

By the mid 1950s the distillery was badly in need of repair. In order to raise the funds to do this, Bessie Williamson sold a third of her shares to an American distiller, the Schenley Corporation, and by 1970 Schenley had complete ownership. The days of privately owned distilleries were over and, like many other distilleries, Laphroaig became an item on a

Laphroaig was possibly the first single malt Scotch to be promoted in the U.S. Prohibition was still in place, but a loophole in the law allowed whisky to be sold 'for medicinal purposes'.

multi-national corporation's balance sheet: Long John International, Whitbread, Allied Lyons, Allied Domecq and since 2005, Fortune Brands, owners of Jim Beam Bourbon.

The new owners are very proud of the distillery's heritage, however, and can be relied upon to consolidate Laphroaig's position as a global brand. They have even appointed an Illeach as Manager: John Campbell is Islay born and bred, and at 35 is the island's youngest Distillery Manager.

CURIOSITIES: Bessie Williamson was the first woman in modern times to manage a distillery (earlier, there had been others, notably Elizabeth Cumming of Cardow).

Whitbread sold to Allied Lyons (in 1989), but not before appointing a Manager at Laphroaig who would become a legend in the whisky trade – Iain Henderson. The new owners wanted to promote the brand vigorously, and Iain introduced the novel 'Friends of Laphroaig' concept (there are currently over 230,000 'Friends'), travelling the world as Brand Ambassador and increasing sales from 20,000 cases in 1989 to 170,000 cases in 2002, when he retired.

Prince Charles granted his Royal Warrant to Laphroaig in 1994.

EXPRESSIONS:
The core range comprises:
• Laphroaig 10YO @ 40%
• Laphroaig 10YO @ CS (different strengths each batch)
• Laphroaig 15YO @ 43%
• Laphroaig 25YO @ 40% (released 2007)
• Laphroaig 25YO @ CS (released 2008)
• Laphroaig Quarter Cask (re-racked into 100-litre American oak casks for seven months, introduced 2004)
• Annual limited editions at older ages are released for the Friends of Laphroaig.

RAW MATERIALS: Soft peaty water from Kilbride Reservoir, with support from Loch na Beinne Brice. Own floor maltings supply around 15% of requirement; the rest from Port Ellen and mainland maltings (at 35–40ppm phenols). Peat from Machrie Moss, owned by the distillery and still cut by hand.

PLANT: Stainless steel full-Lauter tun (8.5 tonnes per mash). Six stainless steel washbacks. Wash charger since 2001. Three plain wash stills (10,500 litres charge per still); four lamp-glass spirit stills (one charge at 9,400 litres and three at 4,700 litres). All indirect fired by steam. All shell-and-tube condensers.

MATURATION: Primarily first-fill ex-bourbon barrels from Maker's Mark Distillery; in the past a mix of American and European casks, and in recent years regular bottlings from quarter casks. Eight dunnage and racked warehouses on site with 55,000 casks in total. Five thousand casks at Ardbeg; 40% of production tankered to be matured in Glasgow; 65–70% of the current output of 2.6m L.P.A. is bottled as single malt.

STYLE: Sweet, spicy and peaty.

MATURE CHARACTER: Laphroaig positions itself as 'the definitive Islay malt' because it epitomises the classic Islay character. It also claims on the label to be 'the most richly flavoured of all Scotch whiskies'. This may once have been the case; modern expressions are less extreme. The nose is pungent and smoky (coal smoke), with coal tar soap and iodine. The taste is surprisingly sweet to start, then salty and dry, with billows of tarry smoke and medicinal, seaweed-like flavours. Full-bodied.

Linkwood

REGION
Speyside

ADDRESS
Elgin, Moray

PHONE
01343 547004

WEBSITE
www.malts.com

OWNER
Diageo plc

VISITORS
No

CAPACITY
2.24m L.P.A.

HISTORICAL NOTES: Linkwood was founded in 1821 by Peter Brown, factor of Linkwood Estate and agricultural improver, and commenced operation three years later. After 1842 it was managed for him by James Walker (later James Walker & Company), who had come from Aberlour Distillery. On Peter Brown's death in 1868, the distillery passed to his son, William, who demolished and rebuilt it in 1874. The family business became a limited company as Linkwood-Glenlivet Distillery Company Ltd in 1897, and Innes Cameron, a whisky broker in Elgin, joined the board five years later. He would rise to control the company until his death in 1932, when the distillery was acquired by D.C.L.

Major refurbishment took place in 1963, and in 1971. A new distillery was built next door, with four stills (in the 'Waterloo Street' style) – an indication of the excellence of the make, which is ranked Top Class and is used as a 'top dressing' malt in several famous blends. The new distillery was referred to as Linkwood B and operated in parallel with the original (Linkwood A) until 1985, when the old Linkwood closed. The spirits from A and B were vatted together prior to filling into cask. The two stills in Linkwood A are still in place and might be brought back into production if required. The washbacks in the old distillery are sometimes used.

CURIOSITIES: In 1936 a new Manager was appointed to Linkwood, Roderick Mackenzie – 'a Gaelic-speaking native of Wester Ross, who for many years supervised its making with unremitting vigilance. No equipment was replaced unless it was essential. Even the spiders' webs were not removed for fear of changing its character.' (Professor R.J.S. McDowell)

Professor McDowell is referring to the refurbishment of 1962/63, where the new stills were exact replicas of the ones they replaced, as was the S.M.D. custom.

The founder's brother was General Sir George Brown, commander of the Light Brigade during the Crimean War.

EXPRESSIONS:

Such is the usefulness of Linkwood that for many years it was available as a single only through Gordon & Macphail.

- Linkwood 12YO @ 43% (Flora & Fauna series, from 1990)
- Linkwood 26YO @ 56.1% (Rare Malts series, 1975, released 2002)
- Linkwood 30YO @ 54.9% (Rare Malts series, 1974, released 2005)

RAW MATERIALS: Floor maltings until 1963, now unpeated malt from Burghead. Process water from springs near Millbuies Loch; cooling water from the Burn of Linkwood and the Burn of Bogs.

PLANT: Full-Lauter mash tun (12 tonnes). Eleven larch washbacks. Three plain wash stills (14,500 litres charge), three plain spirit stills (16,000 litres charge). All indirect fired. Shell-and-tube condensers.

MATURATION: Mainly refill American hogshead, some refill European butts. Two thousand casks matured on site, mainly in the Central Belt.

STYLE: Floral.

MATURE CHARACTER: A light Speyside style. Estery, with bubblegum, acetone, lemon sherbet, tea roses – clean, fresh and sweet. The taste also is sweet, with traces of white wine (Gewürztraminer grapes), lemon zest and sherbet. Light-bodied.

Littlemill Demolished

REGION
Lowland
ADDRESS
Dumbarton Road, Bowling,
Dunbartonshire
LAST OWNER
Loch Lomond Distillery
Company
CLOSED
1984

HISTORICAL NOTES: Littlemill claimed to have been founded at least by 1772 (when accommodation for Excise officers was built), but before that there was a brewery on the site, attached to Dunglass Castle nearby, which may date from the fourteenth century.

Having passed through several hands, it was improved and enlarged in 1875 by one William Hay, but continued to change hands, until it was bought in 1931 by Duncan Thomas, an American gentleman, who lived in the former exciseman's house. He would go on to build Loch Lomond Distillery in 1965 (see entry), in partnership with Barton Brands of Chicago, agents in the U.S.A. for The Glenlivet until 1971 when the company bought out Duncan Thomas' interests in both Littlemill and Loch Lomond.

Both distilleries were mothballed in 1984, and Loch Lomond was sold to Glen Catrine Bonded Warehouse Ltd the following year.

Barton Distilling (Scotland) Ltd, as the company was now named, came under the control of Amalgamated Distilled Products of Glasgow (part of the Argyll Group), which sold its whisky interests in 1987 to Gibson International. Littlemill resumed production in 1989, when the company also acquired Glen Scotia Distillery in Campbeltown. Two years later, Gibson International and its distilleries were acquired by the company's Managing Director, Ian Lockwood, and Finance Director, Bob Murdoch, in a 'multi-million pound' management buy-out. The restructured company went into receivership in 1994 and its assets were bought by Glen Catrine Bonded Warehouse, who dismantled Littlemill two years later.

Over the following years, the buildings deteriorated, then there was a fire, and the site has now largely been cleared.

CURIOSITIES: The first thorough government survey of whisky in 1821 showed that Littlemill was then producing 20,000 proof gallons (over 90,000 litres) per annum. By the time Alfred Barnard visited in the

Littlemill was a contender for the 'oldest distillery in Scotland' award.

mid 1880s it was producing 150,000 gallons, and being sent to 'England, Ireland, India and the Colonies'.

'The locality abounds in charming landscapes not unlike Richmond upon the River Thames. The quiet beauty of the hill slopes and wooded plantations, the hedges covered with summer roses, and the numerous mountain rills, has made this place the favourite resort of artists.'

EXPRESSIONS:

Recently Littlemill has been put on the market primarily as a 12YO, breaking a long stretch of 8YOs launched by proprietors of the now closed distillery. In the past, heavily peated (Dumbuck) and lightly peated (Dunglass) styles were produced for blending.

Loch Lomond Malt and Grain Distillery

REGION
Highland (West)

ADDRESS
Alexandria, Dunbartonshire

PHONE
01389 752781

WEBSITE
www.lochlomonddistillery.
com

OWNER
Loch Lomond Distillery
Company Ltd

VISITORS
No

CAPACITY
4m L.P.A. malt, 17m L.P.A.
grain

HISTORICAL NOTES: Loch Lomond Distillery is a large and practical site, a production unit whose design owes little to aesthetics, without arrangements for visitors. It is situated in an industrial estate on the edge of Alexandria, about a mile and a half from Loch Lomond itself.

The distillery was constructed in 1965/66 by converting a former dye works belonging to the once famous United Turkey Red Company. The job was done by American-born Duncan Thomas (owner of Littlemill Distillery), in partnership with Barton Brands of Chicago, agents in the U.S.A. for The Glenlivet until 1971 when the company bought out Duncan Thomas's interests in both Littlemill and Loch Lomond.

At this time Loch Lomond was producing two styles, Rossdhu and Inchmurrin, from a single pair of stills with rectifying heads (see below). The first dark grains plant in any malt distillery was also installed here when the buildings were converted.

Like many distilleries, Loch Lomond was mothballed in 1984, then sold in 1985 to Inver House Distilleries, who sold it on the following year to Glen Catrine Bonded Warehouse Company Ltd. This company was the bottling subsidiary of A. Bulloch & Company, a family-owned drinks wholesaler (and at that time retailer as well), in order to secure supplies of malt whisky. In 1992 a second pair of pot stills, copying the first pair, was added, fitted with rectifying heads; in 1994, a Coffey still, to make grain whisky; a third pair of traditional pot stills, with narrow necks, was installed in 1998; and a fourth pair in 2007/08, at which time a unique modified Coffey still, to make malt whisky, was also added.

CURIOSITIES: The range of stills at Loch Lomond, combined with different peating levels, allows it to produce eight different styles of malt whisky and a grain whisky, and makes it almost self-sufficient as a blender. Most of the whisky made here goes for blending. Currently, only the new distilleries at

'Loch Lomond' was Captain Haddock's favourite whisky (see Hergé's Adventures of Tintin), but since these books were written between 1929 and 1958, his dram would not have been this Loch Lomond! The owners of the distillery have painted a tanker in the same style as that of Hergé's book – bright yellow with bold black lettering!

Huntly and Girvan (Ailsa Bay) produce both malt and grain whiskies on the same site.

Loch Lomond's unusual stills with rectifying heads were inspired by similar plant at Littlemill Distillery. The heads are fitted with perforated plates (as in a patent still), and spirit may be made at different strengths, and different degrees of lightness, up to around 85% A.B.V. (rather than the 70% in traditional pot still distillation).

Spirit from the new modified Coffey still may be drawn off at different strengths from plates all the way down the column. It is much more controllable and consistent than the modified pot stills.

Loch Lomond is the largest loch in the U.K. It is 24 miles long, five miles wide, up to 600 feet deep and has 38 islands. It has been a world-famous beauty spot since the eighteenth century.

The famous song about the Bonnie Banks of Loch Lomond, whose refrain is

Oh ye'll tak' the high road and I'll tak' the low road,
An' I'll be in Scotland before ye',
But wae is my heart until we meet again
On the bonnie, bonnie banks o' Loch Lomond

commemorates two Jacobite prisoners, held at Carlisle after the Jacobite Rising of 1745, one of whom was to be hanged and the other released to take the low road home.

EXPRESSIONS:

The distillery's website states: 'We produce a full range of malts from heavily peated (typical of Islay), to complex fruity (typical of Speyside), to full-bodied fruity (typical of Highland), and also soft and fruity (typical of Lowland).' They are generically bottled under the 'Distillery Select' label, and under the brand names Loch Lomond, Inchmurrin (designed to mature early), Croftengea, Inchmoan, Inchfad, Craiglodge and Glen Douglas. Confusingly, the brand names do not follow the style, 'peated', 'heavily peated' etc. or wood finishes.

Core expressions are:

• Loch Lomond Blue Label @ 40% (introduced 1999)
• Loch Lomond Black Label 21YO @ 40%

- Loch Lomond Single Blended @ 40% (both malt and grain fillings made on site)
  Current Distillery Select bottlings include single batches and single casks from Croftengea, Inchmoan, Craiglodge, Glen Douglas and Inchmurrin.

RAW MATERIALS: Wheat from independent merchants. Water from bore-holes and Loch Lomond

PLANT: Single Coffey still.

MATURATION: Mainly American oak ex-bourbon casks.

STYLE: Light and estery.

MATURE CHARACTER: Loch Lomond Blue Label: a light-bodied whisky which might be mistaken for a Lowland. The nose is sweet and fruity/malty, with floral notes, and slightly minty. The taste is sweet then dry, with cereal and herbal flavours.

Lochside Demolished

REGION
Highland (East)
ADDRESS
Montrose, Angus
LAST OWNER
Allied Distillers
CLOSED
1992

In November 1973, ownership passed to Destilerias y Crainza del Whisky S.A. of Madrid (D.Y.C. – pronounced 'Deek'), the first time a European company had bought into the Scotch whisky industry.

HISTORICAL NOTES: Lochside Distillery was established within a former Deuchar's brewery in 1957 in the pretty Angus port of Montrose. The brewery dated from 1781, but was rebuilt in the late nineteenth century and was 'far too big for a malt distillery'. Nevertheless, the bold Joseph Hobbs, owner of Ben Nevis Distillery, trading as MacNab Distilleries Ltd, was behind the conversion (see *Ben Nevis*).

His first intention was to make grain whisky, but when other larger grain distilleries were built (notably Invergordon in 1959) he installed four pot stills as well (in 1961), as he had done at Ben Nevis. As at Ben Nevis, he also experimented with the idea of 'blending at birth' – mixing grain and malt new make prior to filling casks. This experiment was discontinued after his death in 1964, but blending and bottling continued to be done on site, and at one time the blend Sandy MacNab's commanded a loyal following.

The new owner ceased grain production soon after, but continued to produce malt whisky until 1992, originally at the rate of 2.5 million L.P.A. (later cut back by 60%), and exported it in bulk to Spain. In its heyday 35 staff were employed. When D.Y.C. was taken over by Allied Domecq in 1992, production ceased immediately and when mature stocks were depleted by 1996 Lochside was closed and dismantled the following year. The bonded warehouse was demolished in 1999 and the rest demolished in March 2005, following a fire earlier that year which brought down part of the roof. Planning permission for residential housing was immediately applied for.

CURIOSITIES: Deuchar's acquired the site in 1830 and employed Charles Doig to rebuild it in a 'Continental' style with a tall tower resembling a castle keep, but with a pitched roof.

EXPRESSIONS:
Lochside was bottled by its owners from 1987 to 1991 at 10YO.
Older bottlings have occasionally been done by independents.

Longmorn

REGION
Speyside
ADDRESS
Longmorn, by Elgin,
Moray
PHONE
01542 783400
WEBSITE
No
OWNER
Chivas Brothers
VISITORS
By appointment
CAPACITY
3.5m L.P.A.

HISTORICAL NOTES: John Duff (who built Glenlossie Distillery in 1876, a quarter of a mile away), whose family owned the lands of Miltonduff, directly to the west, over the River Spey, and who would found Benriach Distillery right next door, two years later) founded Longmorn Distillery in 1893, in partnership with a couple of local businessmen. The location was close to both a good water source and the railway; it had previously been the site of a meal mill founded in the sixteenth century, and long before that of an ancient chapel.

It lasted a mere five years. With the collapse of Pattison's of Leith and a dramatic down-turn in the industry, John Duff was obliged to relinquish control of both Longmorn and Benriach, and by 1901 the Board of Directors included J.A. Dewar (of John Dewar & Sons), Arthur Sanderson (of VAT 69) and James Anderson (of J.G. Thompson, Leith).

In 1899 management passed to James R. Grant, and later his two sons, who became known as 'The Longmorn Grants'; in 1970 they amalgamated with The Glenlivet Grants and the Grants of Glen Grant, and with Hill Thompson & Company, to form The Glenlivet Distilleries Ltd, which was bought by Seagram's in 1977.

The distillery was extended to six stills in 1972 and to eight in 1974, but its appearance has changed little over the years. Seagram was bought by Groupe Pernod Ricard in 2001, and Longmorn is now operated by its subsidiary, Chivas Brothers Ltd.

CURIOSITIES: Until 1980 a railway line connected Longmorn with BenRiach, and latterly a 'puggie' diesel locomotive carried malt from the latter to the former. This engine is now preserved at Aviemore.

The name derives from a seventh-century British saint, Eran, to whom Longmorn church is dedicated. The church was named Lannmoeran, meaning 'the enclosure of beloved (St) Eran'. Another account derives the name from Saint Marnoch (or Maernog), who died in 625 and whose feast day was celebrated

The local newspaper began its report on the opening: 'Still another distillery! Evidently the latest one announced for Longmorn is not the last that this district will see... When is all this going to end?' However, The National Guardian reported in 1897 that the make had 'jumped into favour with buyers from the earliest day on which it was offered'.

in many Scottish towns, including, presumably, Kilmarnock. A third source claims that the name comes from the Llann Morgan (the place of the holy man) – no doubt an ancestor of Diageo's current Marketing Director (Malts), Dr Nicholas Morgan.

Longmorn has been described as 'the master blender's second choice' (the first being his own creation!), and I certainly know one master blender (retired) who would agree with this!

EXPRESSIONS:
Prior to 1993 when a 15YO was introduced (Seagram's Heritage Selection series; it won I.W.S.C. gold medals that year and in 1994) only occasional bottlings were released by Longmorn's owners, since it is a key filling for Chivas Regal 18YO and other blends.

• Longmorn 16YO @ 48% (introduced 2007 with stylish packaging to replace the 15YO)

RAW MATERIALS: Production water from springs on Mannoch Hill. Own floor maltings until 1970, now unpeated malt from independent maltsters.

PLANT: Traditional rake-and-plough mash tun (eight tonnes). Eight stainless steel washbacks. Four plain wash stills (10,000 litres charge), four plain spirit stills (6,600 litres charge). All direct fired until 1970; wash stills direct fired until 1990s; now all indirect fired by steam pans and coils. All shell-and-tube condensers.

MATURATION: Refill American oak hogsheads and barrels, some European oak butts.

STYLE: Fruity, with body.

MATURE CHARACTER: Longmorn is a rich whisky and benefits from long maturation in ex-sherry casks. Both the 15YO and the 16YO have discernible traces of sherry on the nose, backed with fruit (oranges, also dried figs) and some malt, and an interesting spicy note – cinnamon? nutmeg? The mouth feel is big and rounded, the taste sweet (fruit, caramel, malt) then drying slightly towards the finish, which is long and somewhat tannic. Medium-bodied.

Macallan

REGION
Speyside

ADDRESS
Easter Elchies, Craigellachie, Moray

PHONE
01340 871471

WEBSITE
www.themacallan.com

OWNER
The Edrington Group Ltd

VISITORS
Visitor centre opened 2001

CAPACITY
8m L.P.A.

HISTORICAL NOTES: Originally named Elchies Distillery, Macallan took out a licence in 1824 – one of the first on Speyside to do so. It is likely that there was a farm distillery here before this, since the site is close to one of the few crossing points on the Spey used by cattle drovers. Easter Elchies House, which commands the site, dates from 1700. It has been well-restored by the owners of the distillery.

The founder was Alexander Reid. On his death in 1847, the lease passed through a couple of hands until in 1868 it was taken by James Stuart, a corn merchant in Rothes and owner of Mills of Rothes (see *Glenrothes* and *Glen Spey*). He bought the distillery from the Earl of Seafield in 1886, rebuilt it in stone the same year (the earlier distillery was made of wood) and sold it to Roderick Kemp in 1892. Kemp owned Talisker Distillery from 1879 to 1892, and when he fell out with his partner, attempted to buy Glenfiddich, Cardow and Mortlach before he acquired Elchies Distillery, which he rebuilt, changed its name to Macallan-Glenlivet and greatly improved the quality of the make.

On his death in 1909, ownership passed into a family trust for Kemp's descendants, members of the Harbinson and Shiach families, and they managed it until the present owner bought them out in 1996. A new stillhouse was built in 1954/56 with two wash and three spirit stills, all with shell-and-tube condensers (until now they had worm tubs) and in 1965/66 seven further stills were added in a separate, purpose-built stillhouse, doubling capacity to 90,000 gallons per annum. In 1967 Macallan-Glenlivet became a publicly quoted company, with Kemp's descendants holding 62.5% of the shares, in order to finance the building programme and lay down stock.

The second stillhouse closed in 1990, but has been recommissioned and resumed operation in September 2008.

Macallan produced one million gallons for the first time in 1970, but 93% of that went for blending. Two years later sales of bottled Macallan doubled;

Allan Shiach, Chairman of Macallan-Glenlivet (1979–96), was also a renowned Hollywood script writer, with films like Don't Look Now *and* Castaway *to his credit.*

the board decided to conserve mature stocks and increased production by 24%. The number of stills were again increased in 1974 (to 18) and 1975 (to 21), but that year there was a dramatic drop in orders from blenders – 'the worst downturn in the distillery's history' – encouraging the Directors to allocate further stock for bottling as a single malt.

In 1996 Highland Distilleries (now Edrington) combined its shareholding with that of Suntory to successfully mount a hostile takeover of the company. Edrington took Macallan out of public ownership in 2001.

CURIOSITIES: In the late nineteenth century, Easter Elchies House was rented by the Earl of Elgin as a shooting lodge. It was while on holiday here that the ninth Earl received word that he had been created Governor of India.

In late 2008 a further two large warehouses were opened, and there are plans to build an additional four in the coming years.

Promotion of The Macallan as a single malt began in 1980 and immediately resulted in increased sales: by 1984 it was number three in Scotland and number five in the world, winning Queen Awards for Export Achievement in 1983 and 1988.

EXPRESSIONS:

The Macallan went to market with proprietary bottlings in 1980, beginning with the 10yo for the U.K. and 12yo for export markets, followed by the 18yo in 1983, the 25yo in 1987 and the 30yo in 1998. Prior to this, only limited amounts were bottled each year, primarily by Campbell, Hope & King and Gordon & Macphail, both in Elgin.

Since then there have been numerous expressions. Traditional Macallan (branded 'Sherry Oak', matured in sherry seasoned Spanish oak casks) is bottled at 10, 12, 18, 25 and 30 years old. In 2004 a parallel range using a combination of Spanish and American oak sherry casks, and bourbon casks, branded 'Fine Oak', was launched with bottlings at 8, 10, 12, 15, 17, 18, 21, 25 and 30 years.

• Special Releases are often only found in Global Duty Free. Recent expressions include 1851 'Inspiration' and 'Elegancia' 12yo. In domestic markets, premium releases have included 'Gran Reserva' (now Taiwan only) and periodic limited editions of Lalique decanters filled with 50–60 years old Macallan.

Macallan has the smallest spirit stills on Speyside (illustrated on Bank of Scotland £10 notes), and the largest single-roofed warehouse in Europe.

From April 2009 , the range in Global Travel Retail will be replaced by 'The 1824 Collection': Select Oak, Whisky Maker's Edition, Estate Reserve @ 45.7% vol and 1824 Limited Release (limited to 1,824 bottles per annum, the first release being solely matured in sherry seasoned Spanish oak casks), @ 48%. The Fine and Rare Collection is a range of vintage Macallan currently dating from 1926 to 1976. Exceptional single cask bottlings are available at the distillery.

RAW MATERIALS: Soft water from bore-hole aquifers on site. Floor maltings closed late 1950s. Unpeated malt mainly from Simpson's of Berwick-upon-Tweed.

PLANT: *Stillhouse 1:* Full-Lauter stainless steel mash tun with a peaked canopy (7.5 tonnes per mash), 16 stainless steel washbacks. Five plain wash stills (12,750 litres charge), ten plain spirit stills (3,900 litres charge; each wash still charges two spirit stills). Wash stills direct fired by gas; spirit stills indirect fired by steam coils. Shell-and-tube condensers.
 Stillhouse 2: New full-Lauter mash tun, with a deep bed (six tonnes per mash), six new Douglas fir washbacks. Two plain wash stills (12,000 litres charge; bases replaced, heads and lyne arms original), four plain spirit stills (3,900 litres charge, all original). All indirect fired. Shell-and-tube condensers (five original, one replaced).

MATURATION: Dry-Oloroso sherry, European and American oak first and refill butts and hogsheads for traditional Macallan. Mainly refill bourbon barrels and American oak sherry-seasoned casks for the Fine Oak range.

STYLE: Rich, robust, oily, and fruity.

MATURE CHARACTER: The Macallan is the benchmark 'sherried' style of malt (although it is now bottled in a parallel range of non-sherried whiskies). The nose is rich and chocolatey, with dried orange peel, dried fruits, sherry, nuts and a trace of sulphur. The mouth feel is smooth and voluptuous; the taste sweetish to start, but tannic-dry overall, with sherry, Christmas cake (burnt edges), caramel. Full-bodied.

Macduff

REGION
Highland (East)
ADDRESS
Macduff, Moray
PHONE
01261 812612
WEBSITE
No
OWNER
John Dewar & Sons
VISITORS
By appointment
CAPACITY
3.2m L.P.A.

Stills generally work in pairs, and so an even number of stills is the norm. Only two distilleries have five stills, Macduff and Talisker.

HISTORICAL NOTES: Macduff Distillery was a child of the Sixties. It was built in 1962 by a consortium, which included Brodie Hepburn (whisky blenders in Glasgow, with interests in the recently built Tullibardine and Deanston Distilleries), trading as Glen Deveron Distillers Ltd. It was designed by William Delmé-Evans (see *Tullibardine, Jura*) and incorporated several novelties which have now become commonplace, such as indirect firing by steam coils, shell-and-tube condensers and a stainless steel mash tun.

Glen Deveron Distillers sold to Block, Grey & Block in 1966, who added one still that year and another in 1968, and sold to William Lawson Distillers in 1972, a subsidiary of the Italian company, Martini & Rossi. The tun room and stillhouse was rebuilt in 1990, and a fifth still installed. Bacardi bought Martini & Rossi, including William Lawson Ltd, Macduff Distillery and the Glen Deveron brand in 1992, and ownership was transferred to John Dewar & Sons when they acquired that company from Diageo in 1998.

CURIOSITIES: The model village of Macduff was laid out by James Duff, second Earl of Fife, in 1783, planned around one of the best harbours on the Moray Firth, which became a leading herring port during the nineteenth century, curing and exporting fish direct to the Baltic. There was great rivalry between Macduff and the older and more gracious Royal Burgh of Banff, a mile away across the Deveron Estuary.

William Lawson was Manager of the Irish wine & spirits merchants, E. & J. Burke of Dublin, in 1889, who sold their Scotch under the Lawson's label. This trademark was bought by Martini & Rossi in 1963 and amended to avoid any confusion with the D.C.L. brand, Peter Dawson. In 1969 all Martini & Rossi's whisky interests were placed under the newly created William Lawson Distillers Ltd.

Unknown in the U.K., William Lawson's blended Scotch sells around 15 million bottles annually, especially in Southern Europe and Mexico. Almost all the make from Macduff goes into this and other blends.

EXPRESSIONS:
Proprietary bottling is always Glen Deveron; independent bottlings Macduff. William Lawson introduced an 8YO and a 12YO in the mid 1980s.
- Glen Deveron 10YO @ 40%
- Glen Deveron 5YO @ 40% (Italy only)

RAW MATERIALS: Unpeated malt from independent maltsters. Soft process water from bore-holes on site and springs. Cooling water from the Gelly Burn.

PLANT: Semi-Lauter mash tun (6.6 tonnes). Nine stainless steel washbacks. Two plain wash stills (16,100 litres each charge), three plain spirit stills (16,000 litres each charge). All indirect fired by steam pans and coils. Shell-and-tube condensers; spirit stills mounted horizontally, with after coolers.

MATURATION: No filling on site since 2002; tankered to Coatbridge, matured in Central Belt. Mix of first-fill and refill hogsheads and butts.

STYLE: Malty, nutty-spicy.

MATURE CHARACTER: Medium-rich and sweet on the nose, with malty and sherry notes. The taste is sweet, with apples and pears, and perhaps mangos and papayas, then drying into nuts and cereals. Medium length; medium-bodied.

Mannochmore

REGION
Speyside

ADDRESS
Birnie, Elgin, Moray

PHONE
01343 860331

WEBSITE
www.malts.com

OWNER
Diageo plc

VISITORS
No

CAPACITY
3.3m L.P.A.

Bottles of Loch Dhu now fetch around £300 at auction.

HISTORICAL NOTES: Mannochmore is another example of Scottish Malt Distillers' building frenzy during the 1960s and early 1970s. The new distillery was raised in 1971 adjacent to the company's Glenlossie Distillery, which itself had been tripled in capacity ten years previously. Like several of the distilleries built during this period, in what became known as the 'Waterloo Street' style, efficiency was everything (see *Caol Ila*). Its original purpose was to provide fillings for the Haig blends, which had been market leaders in the U.K. during the 1950s and 1960s, but which were now in decline.

In 1996 a famous expression of Mannochmore was released under the name 'Loch Dhu – the Black Whisky'. It was heavily tinted with spirit caramel (so much so as to have a bitter taste), and was designed to be mixed with Coca-Cola or Ginger Ale. It enjoyed popularity in Denmark but nowhere else and was soon discontinued.

EXPRESSIONS:
- Mannochmore 12YO @ 43% (Flora & Fauna series, from 1990)
- Mannochmore 22YO @ 60.1% (Rare Malts series, released 1997)

RAW MATERIALS: Lightly peated malt from Burghead. Water from the Mannoch Hills via the Barden Burn.

PLANT: Cast iron full-Lauter mash tun (11.5 tonnes). Eight larch washbacks. Three plain wash stills (14,400 litres charge); three plain spirit stills (17,000 litres charge). All indirect fired. Shell-and-tube condensers.

MATURATION: Refill American hogsheads. Matured mainly in the Central Belt.

STYLE: Grassy.

MATURE CHARACTER: The nose is light and floral, fresh and bright, with breakfast cereals. The taste is Speyside-sweet, with a creamy mouth feel, fresh fruits and a woody dryness in the short finish. Light-bodied.

Millburn Redeveloped

REGION
Highland (North)
ADDRESS
Millburn Road, Inverness
LAST OWNER
D.C.L./S.M.D.
CLOSED
1985

The distillery ceased production in 1985 and by 1989 was a Beefeater steak house.

HISTORICAL NOTES: It is not known for certain when Millburn was established, possibly in 1807, though the first written record was in 1825. The site is about a mile east of the centre of Inverness, adjacent to the former Cameron Highlanders barracks.

Production ceased in 1837. In 1853 the feu was taken by a local corn merchant, David Rose, who used the building as a flour mill – there were five mills drawing water from the Mill Burn at that time. In 1876 he applied to use the town water supply and commissioned a new and larger distillery on the site.

The property went to David Rose's son, George, in 1883 and he sold to Alexander Price Haig and his brother David, of the famous distilling dynasty, in 1892. They refurbished: 'the whole of the internal arrangements have been remodelled and the plant and machinery are entirely new'. But the depression in the industry following World War I persuaded them to sell to Booth's Distillery Ltd, the famous gin distillers, in 1921, for £25,000. In April the following year fire destroyed most of the distillery buildings and large stocks of barley and malt, the cost estimated at £40,000. The fire brigade was 'greatly assisted' by men of the Cameron Highlanders in controlling the fire: Lt Col. David Price Haig had been a territorial officer in the regiment for 30 years.

Reconstruction was entrusted to Charles Doig of Elgin, and the new distillery, which opened in 1887, was capable of producing 150,000 gallons a year – nearly twice the former output.

Booth's bought Wm Sanderson & Son Ltd (blenders of VAT 69) in 1935, and was itself taken over by D.C.L. in 1937, and managed by S.M.D. from 1943. Production ceased during World War II. In 1958 mechanical stoking was installed, and the two stills were converted to indirect firing by steam coils in 1966. Saladin box maltings had been installed two years before, when electric power was also introduced.

CURIOSITIES: Booth's Distillery Ltd, the famous gin distillers, used the make for their house whisky,

Cabinet, and later for VAT 69. Under S.M.D., Millburn was licensed to Macleay Duff, and went into their blends, including a blended malt at 12YO.

The buildings that once housed the distillery now house the Auld Distillery Restaurant and Pub.

EXPRESSIONS:

- Millburn 1969 35YO @ 51.2% (Rare Malts series, released 2005)
- Millburn 1975 25YO @ 61.9% (Rare Malts series, released 2001)
- Millburn 1975 18YO @ 58.5% (Rare Malts series, released 1995)

Mi

Miltonduff

REGION
Speyside
ADDRESS
Miltonduff, Elgin, Moray
PHONE
01343 547433
WEBSITE
No
OWNER
Chivas Brothers
VISITORS
By appointment
CAPACITY
5.24m L.P.A.

HISTORICAL NOTES: The distillery was built six miles south-west of Elgin, in the grounds of Pluscarden Abbey.

Not surprisingly, many illicit distillers used the vicinity in the late eighteenth century – around 50, it is claimed – and the present distillery, founded in 1824, is on the site of one of them, Milton, where once stood the abbey's meal mill. The name was changed when the Duff family bought the land, hence Milton of Duff. It retains an old water wheel.

It was acquired by William Stuart (a co-proprietor of Highland Park Distillery) in 1866; he was joined by Thomas Yool in 1890 and the distillery was extended in the mid 1890s, at which time it was producing over one million litres of alcohol.

In 1936 Yool sold to Hiram Walker, who had bought George Ballantine & Company the year before. In 1974/75 'modernisation visited Miltonduff with a vengeance', raising capacity to 5.24 million litres per annum – one of the largest distilleries in Scotland. A reception centre was also installed at this time, but it soon closed.

In 1986 Allied Distillers acquired 51% of Hiram Walker, and the rest the following year. In 2005, the majority of Allied Distillers' whisky interests were bought by Pernod Ricard, including Ballantine's and Miltonduff Distillery, which is now operated by their subsidiary Chivas Brothers.

CURIOSITIES: Pluscarden was originally a priory, endowed by King Alexander II in 1230. In 1454 it absorbed the old Benedictine Priory of Urquhart, only to fall into disuse at the Reformation. Nearly 400 years later it was gifted to the Benedictine Community of Prinknash by Lord Colum Chrichton Stuart; monks again took up residence in 1948, while the buildings were being restored. In 1974 it was elevated to the status of Abbey.

Between 1964 and 1981, two Lomond stills were in operation at Miltonduff, producing Mosstowie single malt (see *Dumbarton*, *Inverleven*). The Lomond style

Pluscarden Abbey was once famous for its ale – so good that 'it filled the abbey with unutterable bliss'. The excellence of this brew was attributed to the Black Burn, which had been blessed by a saintly abbot in the fifteenth century, and which supplies the distillery today.

of still was invented in 1955 by Hiram Walker's leading chemical engineer, Alistair Cunningham. It had an unusually wide, drum-like neck, which housed three rectifying plates, similar to those found in a column still. The purpose of the plates was to vary the amount of reflux, and thus the styles of whisky produced. They could be rotated – the horizontal position would maximise reflux, and the vertical position minimise it. They could be used dry or filled with water, which, again, increased reflux. Mosstowie was lighter in character than Miltonduff.

Miltonduff also housed Allied Distillers' Malt Distilleries Technical Centre, with laboratory, engineering department and warehouse management offices. It now houses Chivas Brothers' Northern Operations Headquarters. The laboratory was moved into Glen Keith Technical Centre. CO_2 extraction from the washbacks was pioneered here.

In the 1960s a novel method of heating the wash stills was pioneered at Miltonduff. The wash passed through a series of heat exchangers (using hot water from the condensers), which would heat it to 75–80° prior to charging the still. Once the still was charged, the wash was drawn through another heat exchanger where steam heated it to boiling point. It was returned to the still as vapour via a diffuser, and would in turn heat the residual wash in the still. This continued until distillation was complete.

EXPRESSIONS:
An official 15YO @ 46% was released in 2002 and Chivas Brothers released a few bottles in the summer of 2006. Otherwise Gordon and MacPhail have bottled under licence. Not currently bottled by its owner as a single, the make goes into the Ballantine's and Chivas Regal blends.

RAW MATERIALS: Unpeated malt from Kilgours, Kirkcaldy; own floor maltings removed in the 1970s. Process water from a spring on site; cooling water from the Black Burn.

PLANT: Full-Lauter mash tun, with copper dome (14.5 tonnes); 16 stainless steel washbacks. Three plain wash stills (18,100 litres charge); three plain spirit stills (18,400 litres charge), all dumpy, with broad necks and sharply descending lye arms. All indirect fired. Shell-and-tube condensers.

MATURATION: Mainly refill U.S. hogsheads, some first-fill.

STYLE: Sweet, grassy and fragrant, with some spice.

MATURE CHARACTER: Miltonduff has always been a blending malt, and the few expressions that have appeared as singles reflect this. The nose is grainy and malty, with some honey notes and light floral scents. The taste is sweet, with some fruit and nuts. Medium-bodied.

Mo

ADDRESS
Airdrie, Lanarkshire
OWNER
Inver House Distillers
CAPACITY
30m L.P.A.
CLOSED
1986

It is said that the name Killyloch should have been Lillyloch (from where the site draws its process water), but the stencil had been wrongly cut.

Moffat Malt & Grain Distillery (Dismantled)

HISTORICAL NOTES: The distillery complex, which was also known as Moffat after the mills which stood there, formerly stood on the outskirts of Airdrie, a spread of 30 high-racked maturation warehouses, holding around 480,000 casks, a bottling plant and offices. The distillery itself has been removed.

The location was chosen on account of its excellent water supply, the ready availability of labour and its geographical centrality, with good road links. There had been a paper mill here, which had been closed for about three years when Inver House acquired the somewhat derelict site.

Inver House was at this time a subsidiary of Publicker Industries Inc. of Philadelphia, and the intention was to produce both malt and grain whisky on the same site, principally to meet the demand for Inver House Green Plaid, a blended Scotch, in the U.S.A. Conversion of the old mill began in the spring of 1964; the first malt whisky was distilled here in February 1965, and the first grain whisky a month later. Three different styles of malt whisky were made in three pairs of stills, named Killyloch, Glenflagler and Islebrae, with varying degrees of peating (Killyloch unpeated, Glenflagler lightly peated, Islebrae heavily peated). Islebrae was originally named Glen Moffat. The grain whisky from Moffat was named Garnheath.

Malt whisky distilling ceased in 1982; grain distilling in 1986. In 1988 Inver House was bought from its American owners by its management (led by Bill Robison) for £8.2 million. The company had made a loss of £2.12 million the year before, taking accumulated losses to £9.7 million. It has since been a resounding success, the directors selling to Pacific Spirits, a Thai company, for £56 million in 2001.

CURIOSITIES: The size of the Moffat complex at the time of its construction dictated that it have its own maltings, so the Wanderhaufen system of box maltings (known as the 'moving street') was installed, soon after the distillery itself had gone into production – first one 'street' and ultimately seven, steeping up to 700 tonnes of barley a day, with four kilns. At this time it was the largest maltings in Europe. The maltings closed in 1978.

At its peak in the 1970s a thousand people were employed in the Moffat distillery complex.

EXPRESSIONS:

The grain whisky was never bottled. The four malts have appeared but only very occasionally, from independent bottlers. Glenflagler was bottled by Inver House in the mid 1980s, at five and eight years old.

Mortlach

REGION
Speyside
ADDRESS
Dufftown, Moray
PHONE
01340 820318
WEBSITE
www.malts.com
OWNER
Diageo plc
VISITORS
By appointment
CAPACITY
2.91m L.P.A.

Mortlach was the first distillery to be built in Dufftown, which would in time become a major distilling centre with nine distilleries, six of which are still in operation.

HISTORICAL NOTES: Mortlach was first licensed in 1823 to James Findlater, who used a site that had been formerly used by smugglers on account of the excellent water from Highlander John's Well. He ran it in partnership with two local men, Alexander Gordon and Donald McIntosh, but in 1831 it was sold for £270 to John Robertson. By 1842 it was owned by J. & J. Grant, who were building Glen Grant Distillery at the time and removed the distillery plant to their new site in Rothes. The granary at Mortlach was used as a Free Church, until one was built in Dufftown.

In the late 1840s the buildings were bought by John Gordon, who initially installed a brewery there before resuming distilling, after 'enlarging and improving the works'. He sold his whisky 'mostly in Leith and Glasgow, but [it has] attained some celebrity in the district under the name of *The Real John Gordon*'. (*Elgin Courant*, 1862)

He resumed distilling in 1851 and two years later took George Cowie into partnership. Cowie had been a railway surveyor, and would become Provost of Dufftown, and by 1869 was outright owner of Mortlach Distillery. His son Dr Alexander Mitchell Cowie, who was a senior medical officer in Hong Kong, returned to join his father in 1895. He became a leading figure in the whisky industry and Deputy Lieutenant of Banffshire: over the next 30 years he built a high reputation for Mortlach (it is ranked Top Class by blenders), doubling the distillery's capacity (to six stills) in 1897, when a private railway spur, shared with Glendullan, was installed.

Dr Cowie's only son was killed in World War I, and in 1923 he sold the distillery to John Walker & Sons, a key customer for fillings, and thus joined the D.C.L. in 1925. The distillery was managed by S.M.D. from 1936. Unlike most malt distilleries, Mortlach stayed open during World War II, except in 1944.

Most of the distillery buildings were demolished and rebuilt in the early 1960s (completed 1964), introducing mechanical coal-stoking to the stills (they were converted to indirect firing in 1971).

Mortlach is a key filling for the Johnnie Walker blends.

CURIOSITIES: Mortlach has possibly the strangest set of stills in the business, and the most complex distilling regime. There are six stills, but all different sizes and shapes, and the regime is not quite triple distillation; actually it's 2.7! It takes six months of training for a new stillman to work it out! There is no space here to describe the regime, but crucial to the equation is No. 1 spirit still, known as the 'Wee Witchie', which is charged three times in each run.

Over the 20 years from 1866 to 1886 William Grant of Glenfiddich learned his trade at Mortlach, working in all parts of the business and finishing as Manager, before starting his own enterprises down the road.

EXPRESSIONS:
- Mortlach 16YO @ 43% (Flora & Fauna series, since 1990)
- Mortlach 22YO @ CS% (Rare Malts series, 1972, released 1995)
- Mortlach 23YO @ 59.4% (Rare Malts series, 1972, released 1996)
- Mortlach 20YO @ 62.2% (Rare Malts series, 1978, released 1998)
- Mortlach 32YO @ 50.1% (Special Releases series, 1971, released 2004)

RAW MATERIALS: Floor maltings until 1968, now unpeated malt from Burghead. Soft process water from Guidman's Knowe springs; cooling water from springs in the Conval Hills.

PLANT: Full-Lauter tun (12 tonnes). Six larch washbacks. Three boil-ball wash stills (two 7,500 litres charge, one 16,000 litres charge); three boil-ball spirit stills (one 7,000 litres charge [the 'Wee Witchie'], one 9,300 litres charge). Direct-fired until 1971, now all indirect-fired. Worm tubs.

MATURATION: For proprietary bottlings refill European casks are used. Some matured on site, the rest in the Central Belt.

STYLE: Heavy, meaty.

MATURE CHARACTER: A big, rich whisky. Dry fruitcake, with burnt edges, moistened with Madeira. Soft, full-bodied texture; hint of allspice in the taste. Long finish.

North British Grain Distillery

ADDRESS
Gorgie, Edinburgh
PHONE
0131 337 3363
OWNER
Lothian Distillers Ltd
CAPACITY
64m L.P.A.

HISTORICAL NOTES: In 1885 a group of independent blenders and spirits merchants banded together to build a distillery in Edinburgh for the supply of grain whisky, in response to the monopoly of D.C.L., with its 'varying qualities and fluctuating prices'. Their goal was 'to check a great monopoly and maintain a uniformly low price'. Andrew Usher was the first Chairman, John Crabbie Vice-Chairman and William Sanderson Managing Director.

A greenfield site was chosen, to the north of Gorgie Road and west of Dalry (and the Caledonian Distillery). It was well-connected with railway lines (notably the Wester Dalry branch of the Caledonian Railway, connecting to Glasgow, and the Granton & Leith branch of the same railway, running to Leith, principal grain port in Scotland), and with ample water from the Union Canal, which passed close by.

Production commenced in September 1887, with one Coffey still, and in the first year 1.5 million gallons were made and sold; within four years capacity was doubled, so by 1897 production had risen to three million gallons, and the whole of the next year's production had been sold in advance. The Chairman announced, 'there is no whisky more popular in Scotland'.

Difficult trading during the 1920s led to an arrangement with D.C.L. to ration their annual production to the amounts ordered for the ensuing year. Since D.C.L. usually sold about four times as much spirit as the North British, production was divided four-fifths/one-fifth, reducing North British output to 2/2.5m gallons a year. This arrangement lasted until 1934, by which time Prohibition had been repealed in the U.S. and sales rose sharply. Then came World War II and such a shortage of grain that the North British had to cease distilling in 1939.

Although distilling resumed at the end of hostilities, grains were rationed until 1949. The 1950s were years of expansion and modernisation. An extensive site – a former tram depot – was acquired to the west of the distillery, and the former Scottish Brewers site on

The North British is the sole remaining distillery in Edinburgh, which once had many, among them Canonmills, Lochrin, Bonnington, Leith, Sunbury, Abbeyhill and Edinburgh Distilleries. It is currently the second largest distillery in Scotland.

During World War I the North British was required to make spirits for munitions, and was then closed altogether as grain supplies dwindled.

Slateford Road, to the south of the distillery. A new site was developed at Muirhall, 18 miles away, beyond West Calder, capable of holding 40m proof gallons in 26 warehouses. Production capacity increased even more rapidly to meet orders which were climbing year on year. In 1955, output stood at 3m gallons; by 1961 it was 6m gallons, and by 1972, 12m gallons. At this time the company was employing around 400 people.

In 1968 an evaporation plant for dregg was installed, and a dark-grains plant producing pelletised cattle feed. This was extended in 1976 to process draff and dreg from Caledonian Distillery nearby. CO_2 was pumped to Caledonian for recovery.

In 1993, management of the North British was assumed by Lothian Distillers Ltd, a partnership between I.D.V. and Robertson & Baxter. I.D.V. merged with U.D. in 1998 to become U.D.V. and later Diageo. R. & B. changed its name to Edrington in 1999 .

CURIOSITIES: In 1947 the North British's transport fleet consisted of a horse and cart; in 1967 it boasted six Commer motor lorries (which delivered casks as far away as Aberdeen) and four bulk tankers. It also owned two diesel locomotives to pull the 'grain train' to and from the Port of Leith.

In 1959 W.G. Farquharson, Chairman of North British and of Arthur Bell & Sons, proposed building a Lowland malt distillery within the complex (as other distillers had done), but this came to nothing.

The 250 millionth cask of North British proof grain whisky was distilled on 12 November 1970. It was sealed in a commemorative keg and is displayed at the distillery.

EXPRESSIONS:
- The N.B. Centenary Blend was released for staff in 1985.
- North British 1980 12YO @ 61.5% (released 1992)
- North British 18YO @ 60.3% (released 1998)

RAW MATERIALS: Maize mainly from the South of France. Water from reservoirs in the Pentland Hills. Drum maltings until 1948, then Saladin boxes until 2007, now green malt from independent maltsters. Note: it is the only remaining distillery to use green malt. Mixed in proportion 1:4 – the highest malt content of any grain whisky.

PLANT: Two mash tuns. Three Coffey stills. Patent still with three columns decommissioned in 2007, but still in situ.

MATURATION: Mainly U.S. ex-bourbon first-fill and refill casks; filled and matured at Muirhall, West Calder.

STYLE: Robust.

North Port Demolished

REGION
Highland (East)
ADDRESS
Brechin, Angus
LAST OWNER
D.C.L./S.M.D.
CLOSED
1983

North Port was closed in May 1983 due to the world recession at that time and as part of S.M.D.'s policy to reduce output to bring the level of maturing stock in line with anticipated future sales.

HISTORICAL NOTES: A 'port' is the old Scots word for a town gate, but by the time the distillery was built in 1820, the medieval North Port had long disappeared. The town itself is of ancient foundation, the cathedral here having been endowed by King David I in 1150. It stands in the midst of excellent corn country and local farmers carted their crop into the malting barns: the founder's family had farmed in the district for two generations.

The distillery was built by a local worthy, David Guthrie, who had established the town's first bank in 1809 and served as Provost. Its original name was the Townhead Distillery Company, but in 1823 this was changed to Brechin Distillery Company.

Ownership passed to the founder's sons, and a limited company was established in 1893. In 1922 it was bought by D.C.L. in partnership with W.H. Holt & Company (wine and spirits merchants in Manchester) and wound up. The distillery and stocks were sold to S.M.D. The make was used for blending, except a small amount in the early 1980s, which was bottled as a single by D.C.L. subsidiary, John Hopkins & Company, for sale in Italy.

CURIOSITIES: The *History of Brechin* (1839) reports: 'Formerly the neighbourhood of Brechin was much infested with bands of smugglers, carrying whisky from the Grampian Highlands to the low country, and Brechin itself depended upon these *merchants* for the supply of *mountain dew*. Now the matter is reversed. There is an extensive distillery in the town, called the North Port Distillery (supplying) a far purer spirit than was formerly drunk under the name of smuggled whisky ... (and whisky was) the chief potation of all classes (in Brechin).'

EXPRESSIONS:
- North Port 1971 23YO @ 54.7% (Rare Malts series, released 1994)
- North Port 1979 20YO @ 61.2% (Rare Malts series, released 1999)

North of Scotland

Grain Distillery (Demolished)

ADDRESS
Cambus, Alloa,
Clackmannanshire
OWNER
North of Scotland Distilling
Company Ltd
CAPACITY
3m proof gallons P.A.

The distillery's name changed in 1964 to North of Scotland Distillery, although Clackmannanshire is a long way from the 'north of Scotland'.

HISTORICAL NOTES: Strathmore Distillery was established as a private venture by George Christie (see *Strathspey*) in 1957, on a 1.5-acre site, formerly used by Robert Knox's Forth Brewery (established 1786) at Cambus, close to the distillery of that name in Alloa. Originally, it produced malt whisky in three modified Coffey stills, but by 1960 had switched to grain whisky production – the smallest grain whisky distillery in Scotland.

The distillery was closed in 1980, sold to D.C.L. in 1982 and dismantled by 1993. The buildings were demolished soon after.

CURIOSITIES: The distillery was said to be haunted by a former brewer, whose apparition was repeatedly 'sighted by both employees and Excise officers'. (Phillip Morrice)

'The North of Scotland Distillery keeps a higher than usual proportion of feints and foreshots [congeners] when distilling its whisky in order to give it more character, so that it can be recognised as North of Scotland grain.' (Phillip Morrice)

EXPRESSIONS:
The make was bottled in limited amounts as Alloa Single Grain and North of Scotland. The latter brand was once registered by George Strachan, a well-known wine and spirits merchant in Aboyne, Aberdeenshire.

Oban

REGION

Highland (West)

ADDRESS

Stafford Street, Oban, Argyll

PHONE

01631 572004

WEBSITE

www.malts.com

OWNER

Diageo plc

VISITORS

Visitor centre and shop

CAPACITY

700,000 L.P.A.

HISTORICAL NOTES: Founded in 1794, Oban is among the earliest surviving malt whisky distilleries. Its founders were John and Hugh Stevenson, local worthies with interests in slate quarrying, house building and shipbuilding in and around Oban since 1778. The town of Oban grew up around the distillery, which is squashed between the main street and a high cliff. The brothers had originally equipped the site as a brewery in 1793, and continued to trade under the name the Oban Brewery Company.

The distillery remained in their family until 1866, and after one other owner it was acquired in 1883 by J. Walter Higgin, who refurbished and modernised it. Three years previously the West Highland railway line, connecting Oban to Glasgow, was opened. The town became a popular tourist resort, and Higgin could send his whisky direct to market in Glasgow.

In 1898 the distillery was bought by a consortium led by the redoubtable Alexander Edward, a well-known figure in the whisky trade (see *Aultmore*) with the support of Buchanan's, Dewar's and Mackie's (White Horse). In 1923 Buchanan-Dewar took over Oban Distillery, and thus it joined D.C.L. in 1925.

The make was chosen by U.D. to represent the West Highland style in their Classic Malts series (1988).

CURIOSITIES: The building which houses the Manager's office was formerly the dwelling of the Stevenson Brothers who founded the distillery. By the time Alfred Barnard visited in 1885, Higgin had converted it into offices, but retained the peephole door in the former sitting room, which the Stevensons had installed to keep an eye on operations in the stillhouse.

EXPRESSIONS:

- Oban 14YO @ 43% (Classic Malts series, from 1989)
- Oban Distillers' Edition 14YO @ 43% (re-racked into Montilla fino casks, from 1998)
- Oban 32YO @ 55.1% (Special Release limited to 6,000 bottles, 2002)

In the 1890s, when the cliff behind the distillery was being dynamited to make room for a new warehouse, caves were discovered containing human remains and artefacts dating from the Mesolithic era (4,500–3,000 BC).

- Oban 20YO @ 57.9% (Special Release limited to 1,020 bottles, 2004)
- Oban 18YO @ 43% (limited to U.S. only, released late 2008)

RAW MATERIALS: Floor maltings until 1968; now lightly peated malt from Roseisle. Soft water from Lochs Gleann a' Bearraidh.

PLANT: Traditional mash tun (6.5 tonnes), using a sparge ring. Four European larch washbacks. One lamp-glass wash still (11,600 litres charge); one lamp-glass spirit still (7,000 litres charge). Both indirect fired. Rectangular worm tubs, both worms in same tub (as at Cragganmore).

MATURATION: Refill American hogsheads. Matured mainly in the Central Belt. Around 4,000 casks on site.

STYLE: Fruity, lightly maritime.

MATURE CHARACTER: The seaside location of the distillery somehow communicates itself to the flavour of the whisky, in spite of it being matured inland. The nose is fresh and maritime, with seaweed and salt behind fresh fruits and a hint of smoke behind that. The mouth feel is soft and slightly oily; the taste is sweet, with dried figs and light spiciness, a trace of salt and a thread of smoke. Medium-bodied.

Parkmore Dismantled

REGION
Speyside
ADDRESS
Dufftown, Moray
OWNER
The Edrington Group
CLOSED
1931

'Externally the most perfect survivor of the late 1890s boom in distilleries.'

Charles Craig

HISTORICAL NOTES: Parkmore is an elegant small distillery, typical in style to others of the 1890s, designed by Charles Doig, and the fifth distillery to be built in Dufftown. James Watson & Company, a well-known Dundee blending house (established in 1815 and owners of Ord and Pulteney Distilleries, and of the blend Baxter's Barley Bree) was behind the scheme, and took whole ownership in 1900.

In 1923, Watson's was acquired by Buchanan-Dewar's and John Walker & Sons; Dewar's took the distilleries and eight million gallons of mature stock was shared between them. It was described as 'one of the most important stocks of old whisky in the country'. All three (including Watson's) joined D.C.L. in 1925.

Parkmore was managed by S.M.D. from 1930 and was closed in 1931. The site was licensed to Daniel Crawford & Son Ltd, a very minor D.C.L. subsidiary, and used for warehousing and stores. It was sold for the same purpose to Highland Distilleries (now the Edrington Group) in 1988.

EXPRESSIONS:
Never bottled as a single by its owner. Two bottles purporting to come from Parkmore Distillery (16YO from 1911 and 7YO 'late nineteenth century') were sold at auction in 2001.

Pittyvaich Demolished

REGION
Speyside
ADDRESS
Dufftown, Moray
LAST OWNER
United Distillers
CLOSED
1993

HISTORICAL NOTES: Pittyvaich-Glenlivet was built by Arthur Bell & Sons Ltd in 1975, next door to their Dufftown-Glenlivet Distillery, and operated in parallel with it. A dark-grains plant to look after the needs of both distilleries was built at the same time.

They were raised on the site of Pittyvaich House, which was probably built in the 1850s and was demolished to make way for the distillery. The new buildings were described as 'ultra-modern, so they bear little resemblance, if any, to the kind of distillery you see along Speyside' by Bell's historian, Jack House (1976). 'They started with the plant and built the outside of the distillery around it.'

Dufftown had been extended to four stills in 1967 (and a further pair would be installed in 1979). Pittyvaich had two pairs of stills – such was the demand for Bell's Extra Special at the time. The new distillery had a capacity of a million proof gallons.

U.K. sales of Bell's rose from £8.8 million in 1970 to £159 million in 1980, by which time the brand was the most popular Scotch in the U.K., commanding 25% of the market.

By the early 1990s Pittyvaich's buildings had deteriorated, and its asbestos roofs had to be replaced. It was decided to close the site in 1993 and the distillery was demolished in 2002.

CURIOSITIES: The prefix 'Pit-' is one of the very few words that have come down to us from Pictish, in which times it signified a farmstead, place or land-holding. The prefix is common, especially in the Eastern counties, the former kingdoms of the Picts. 'Vaich' is Gaelic and may mean either 'byre' (cattle-shed), possibly 'cattle-field' or perhaps 'birchwood'.

EXPRESSIONS:
The only official bottling is the 12YO (Flora & Fauna series, 1991).

Port Dundas Grain Distillery

ADDRESS
North Canal, Borron Street,
Glasgow
PHONE
0141 332 2253
OWNER
Diageo plc
CAPACITY
39m L.P.A.

Alfred Barnard was impressed by the piggery at Port Dundas which accommodated 400 pigs, including some 'highly-bred animals of great size' housed in pens decorated with their prize cards. Swine fever wiped them out around 1900, and they were not replaced.

HISTORICAL NOTES: There have been three Port Dundas Distilleries at the Glasgow end of the Forth and Clyde Canal. The first was founded in 1811, the second in 1813 and the third in 1838. The last only operated for two years; the first two amalgamated in 1845, when Coffey stills were installed in parallel with their pot stills – Port Dundas continued to make grain whisky in pot stills until at least the late 1880s.

The owner, M. Macfarlane & Company, successor to Daniel Macfarlane, the founder of one of the distilleries, joined D.C.L. on its foundation in 1877 (see *Cameronbridge*, *Carsebridge*), at which time the distillery had three Coffey and five pot stills – one of them the largest in the industry. At the time of Alfred Barnard's visit ten years later it was the largest distillery in the British Isles, producing 12 million L.P.A. on a nine-acre site. It was badly damaged by fire in 1903, rebuilt by 1914, with a new drum maltings and situated within one of the first reinforced concrete buildings in Europe (closed and gutted 1983), and was again badly damaged in 1916 when No. 6 warehouse went up in flames, along with 12,000 hogsheads of whisky.

The distillery was transferred to Scottish Grain Distillers in 1966 and extensively modernised during the 1970s, to double output at a cost of £10 million. With the site increasing to 25 acres, following the acquisition of neighbouring maltings and fertiliser plant, a super-efficient dark-grains plant replaced the original in 1977 and a CO_2 recovery plant was also installed (this is a by-product of fermentation). At this time Port Dundas was D.C.L.'s flagship distillery. In 1992 the licence was taken by U.D.'s subsidiary, United Malt and Grain Distillers.

CURIOSITIES: Port Dundas was part of the Forth and Clyde Canal project (completed 1790), and took its name from Sir Lawrence Dundas of Kerse, President of the Canal Company. The distillery was built on the north bank of the canal and made good use of both it and the nearby railway line to carry goods in and out. The canal closed in the 1960s (stretches of it have been reopened in recent years for recreation), and today all materials come by road.

EXPRESSIONS:
Bottled once, in the early 1990s by U.D., no age statement @ 40%.

RAW MATERIALS: Wheat and maize (since 1955). Process water from Loch Katrine (the distillery was licensed to draw water from the canal, but it was found to be neither cold enough nor clean enough).

PLANT: Three Coffey stills, one stainless steel.

MATURATION: Mainly American oak, first-fill and refill ex-bourbon hogsheads and barrels.

STYLE: Traditionally full-bodied, and having a poor reputation in the 1960s (Morrice), Port Dundas make has become lighter and cleaner since the improvements of the 1970s.

Po

Port Ellen Dismantled

REGION
Islay

ADDRESS
Port Ellen, Isle of Islay

OWNER
Diageo

CLOSED
1983

HISTORICAL NOTES: Port Ellen single malt enjoys cult status among collectors who favour the smoky style. They mourn its passing, although many of the distillery buildings still stand, including the two pagoda-topped kilns (the third was demolished in 2004, as it was unsafe); the dunnage warehouses, among the oldest in Scotland, are still used for maturing Lagavulin, and other buildings have been converted into small business units.

The distillery began as a malt mill, established before 1824 by Alexander Kerr Mackay with the support of the laird of Islay, Walter Frederick Campbell. By 1825 John Morrison was making whisky here, as a sub-tenant, and possibly as a representative of his uncle, Ebenezer Ramsay, Procurator Fiscal of Clackmannan, a relation of the Stein distilling dynasty, with extensive distilling interests around Alloa. The business did not prosper, and in 1833 Uncle Ebenezer sent first his son then his nephew to Islay to investigate. His son reported that the distillery was unworkable; however, the nephew, John Ramsay, reported the contrary.

John Ramsay (1815–92) was 18 years old. After some training as a distiller in Alloa, he was installed as Manager. Within only a few years he was also managing the laird's affairs and became his business partner in some enterprises, including the introduction of the first bi-weekly steamship service between Islay and Glasgow. Ramsay became a leading agriculturalist on the island, Chairman of the Glasgow Chamber of Commerce, Liberal MP for Stirling (1868) and for Falkirk (1874–86). When he died he owned the entire parish of Kildalton, had built numerous farmhouses, estate houses and steadings, and done much to improve the standard of farming on the island.

Port Ellen was continued by his widow and then their son, Captain Iain Ramsay of Kildalton. Keeping the business going after World War I (in which he was wounded) was a struggle, and he was obliged to sell the distillery to his former agent, James Buchanan & Company, in partnership with John

Port Ellen was the first distillery to export whisky direct to the United States.

Dewar & Sons. When these companies joined D.C.L. in 1925, Port Ellen went with them.

It was put under the management of S.M.D. from 1930 and was immediately closed (for 37 years), although the maltings continued to operate. In 1967 it was rebuilt within the shell of the original distillery, with four mechanically stoked stills (converted to steam heating in 1970) and worm tubs. In 1973 a drum maltings was built adjacent to the distillery, first to supply S.M.D.'s requirement at its three Islay distilleries, and then in terms of a concordat signed by all the Islay and Jura distillers in 1987, to supply at least a portion of their malt requirement so as to keep the maltings in full production.

Port Ellen Distillery closed in 1983.

CURIOSITIES: All the Islay distilleries (except the new-comer Kilchoman) were built on the sea's edge, to facilitate deliveries of barley and coal and the export of whisky. A pier was built at Port Ellen in 1826 and the village grew up around it, named after Eleanor, wife of J.F. Campbell of Islay.

From 1869 the sales side of the business was handled by W.P. Lowrie in Glasgow, the pioneer of cask seasoning with sherry and the original supplier of James Buchanan, whose Black & White brand became so successful he bought Lowrie's in 1906.

EXPRESSIONS:

Like many others, Port Ellen was a blending malt, and the first 'official' bottling was to celebrate the 25th anniversary of the Port Ellen Maltings in 1998 (a 21YO @ 58.4%).

- Port Ellen 1978 20YO @ 60.90% (Rare Malts series, released 1998)
- Port Ellen 1978 22YO @ 60.50% (Rare Malts series, released 2000
- Port Ellen 1979 22YO first release @ 56.20% (bottled 2001)
- Port Ellen 1978 24YO second release @ 59.35% (bottled 2002)
- Port Ellen 1979 24YO third release @ 57.3% (bottled 2003)
- Port Ellen 1978 25YO fourth release @ 56.2% (bottled 2004)
- Port Ellen 1979 25YO fifth release @ 57.4% (bottled 2005)

Pulteney

REGION
Highland (North)

ADDRESS
Pulteneytown, Wick,
Caithness

PHONE
01955 602371

WEBSITE
www.oldpulteney.com

OWNER
Inver House Distillers

VISITORS
Visitor centre since 2004
in a converted dunnage
warehouse with facility to
fill your own bottle

CAPACITY
1.6m L.P.A.

HISTORICAL NOTES: The awkwardly named Pulteneytown is the fishing port of Wick. It was built as a model village in 1810 and was named after Sir William Pulteney, Director of the British Fisheries Society.

Pulteneytown was designed by the leading civil engineer, Thomas Telford, who was also responsible for Craigellachie Bridge. By the mid nineteenth century it was the largest herring port in Europe (and in the world, by weight of catch), used as a base by over 1,000 boats and attracting 7,000 migrant workers during the season.

The distillery was built in 1826 by James Henderson, whose family continued to own it until 1920, when it was sold to James Watson & Company of Dundee, passing to Dewar's three years later, and thence to the D.C.L., who mothballed it in 1930. In 1951 it was sold to a solicitor, Robert Cumming (who also bought Balblair) but he soon sold to J. & G. Stodart, a subsidiary of Hiram Walker & Sons, who rebuilt it in 1958. It passed to Allied in 1961, and they sold to Inver House in 1995.

CURIOSITIES: Sir William Pulteney was born in Dumfriesshire as Sir William Johnstone. He changed his name when he married the niece of the Earl of Bath. When she inherited her uncle's fortune, Sir William became one of the richest men in England.

In his youth in Dumfries he had met a young and impoverished stonemason, Thomas Telford, and when he became rich, Pulteney became Telford's main sponsor – under which patronage he became the leading civil engineer of the day. Indeed Thomas Telford is often described as 'The Father of Civil Engineering'. In 1801 Telford devised a master plan to improve communications in the Highlands, a massive project that was to last 20 years. It included the building of the Caledonian Canal along the Great Glen and redesigning sections of the Crinan Canal, nearly a thousand miles of new roads, over a thousand new bridges (including the famous bridge

Pulteney is the most northerly distillery on mainland Scotland, and is one of only two named after people (the other being Glen Grant).

over the Spey at Craigellachie), numerous harbour improvements and 32 churches.

It is claimed that the unusual flat-topped stills were truncated because they were too tall to fit in the stillhouse (see also Cragganmore).

Under the influence of the American evangelist Aimee Semple Macpherson in the 1920s, Wick went 'dry' until 1947. To mark the 50th anniversary of repeal, a 12YO Old Pulteney was released, and in 2007 the 60th anniversary was celebrated with a charity ball in aid of the R.N.L.I. It is planned that this should become an annual event.

Old Pulteney used to be described as the 'Manzanilla of the North': it was pale and distinctly briny. The contemporary malt is gentler. Today it is positioned as 'the genuine maritime malt', and its bottle and tube are illustrated with steam trawlers. In 2006 it was the main sponsor of the I.R.C. Scottish (Yacht Racing) Championships. The brand also sponsored Sir Robin Knox-Johnson, who successfully completed his second solo round-the-world race in 2007.

EXPRESSIONS:
The single malt coming from the distillery has long been named Old Pulteney.
- Old Pulteney 12YO @ 40% (introduced 1997)
- Old Pulteney Millennium 15YO @ 60.9% (released 2000)
- Old Pulteney 17YO @ 46% (introduced 2004)
- Old Pulteney 21YO @ 46% (introduced 2005, I.W.S.C. Gold 2007)
- Old Pulteney 15YO @ 54.9% (released 2006, for France)
- Old Pulteney 23YO @ 46% (ex-bourbon, introduced 2006 for world duty-free)
- Old Pulteney 23YO @ 46% (ex-sherry, introduced 2006 for world duty-free)

RAW MATERIALS: Soft process water and cooling water from the Loch of Hempriggs via the longest lade in Europe: 5.5 miles long, stone built by Telford to supply water to Pulteneytown. Maltings removed 1958; unpeated malt from independent maltsters.

PLANT: Cast iron semi-Lauter tun with a copper canopy (4.94 tonnes). Six cast iron washbacks lined with Corton steel. One wash still, with T-shaped lyne arm and the largest boil-ball in the industry (14,400 litres charge); one boil-pot spirit still – similar in shape to a 'smuggler's kettle' (13,200 litres charge). Both indirect fired by steam coils. Worm tubs.

MATURATION: Mainly bourbon and a small number of ex-sherry casks. All whisky bottled as a single is matured on site in seven dunnage warehouses (30,000 casks capacity).

STYLE: Fruity, oily (almond oil), malty, heavy, meaty – complex.

MATURE CHARACTER: Heavy as new-make, Pulteney becomes lighter and fresher as it matures. The nose is distinctly maritime, with oily notes, and light, fresh fruit. The taste is dry overall, and slightly salty, with traces of nuts. Medium - to light-bodied.

Rosebank Redeveloped

REGION
Lowland

ADDRESS
Camelon Road, Falkirk

OWNER
Diageo

CLOSED
1993

HISTORICAL NOTES: Rosebank was established within the maltings of the former Camelon Distillery (known to have been operating 1817–19) by local grocer James Rankine. The situation was ideal: on the bank of the Forth and Clyde Canal a mile from Falkirk, 'placed by the main road, on which there is a constant stream of traffic, and also fronting the canal, where boats and steamers are continually passing to and fro' (Barnard, 1885). Ironically it was the busy main road that caused Rosebank's ultimate demise.

Rankine began his operation in 1840 and enlarged the site five years later. By the 1860s the distillery was managed by his son, R.W. Rankine, and in 1864 he 'entirely rebuilt in modern form' (Barnard), using red brick. They had the canal on one side, the road on the other and were grouped around a courtyard. Next year he demolished the main Camelon Distillery buildings on the other side of the canal and built his maltings there, connecting them to the distillery by a swing bridge. Beyond this was Rosebank House, standing in three acres of gardens, the 'country residence' of Mr Rankine.

Together with Glenkinchie, Saint Magdalene, Grange and Clydesdale Distilleries, Rosebank formed S.M.D. in 1914, under the chairmanship of W.H. Ross, Managing Director of D.C.L., and joined the larger company in 1925.

In spite of its good reputation, the distillery was closed in 1993, largely owing to difficulties of access off the main road.

The main distillery buildings now house a Beefeater restaurant. Some of the warehouses have been demolished and redeveloped, and some have been converted. Part of the distilling equipment is stored on site (one of the stills was vandalised in December 2007 by copper thieves).

At the time of writing, it is rumoured that a new distillery may be built nearby by private enterprise, using the original stills and reviving the good name of Rosebank.

Rosebank had the highest reputation of any Lowland malt: in the 1890s there was 'an extraordinary demand for the make and many customers had to be content with an allocation of a smaller amount than they had ordered'.
Spiller

CURIOSITIES: The 1920s and 1930s were hard years for the whisky industry. Many distilleries closed. D.C.L. consolidated all their distilleries under the ownership of S.M.D. in 1930, and used the subsidiary to buy up and close down failing distilleries in order to control output and price. By 1935 S.M.D. comprised 51 malt whisky distilleries.

Like many Lowland malt distilleries, Rosebank favoured triple distillation.

EXPRESSIONS:
- Rosebank 12YO @ 43% (Flora & Fauna series)
- Rosebank 1979 19YO @ 60.2% (Rare Malts series, released 1998)
- Rosebank 1979 20YO @ 60.3% (Rare Malts series, released 1999)
- Rosebank 1981 20YO @ 62.3% (Rare Malts series, released 2002)
- Rosebank 1981 22YO @ 61.1% (Rare Malts series, released 2004)

Roseisle

REGION
Speyside
ADDRESS
Roseisle, Morayshire
PHONE
No
WEBSITE
No
OWNER
Diageo plc
VISITORS
No
CAPACITY
Unknown

HISTORICAL NOTES: In January 2007 Diageo announced their intention to build a 'super-distillery' near their maltings at Roseisle, to produce a range of whisky of varying styles for blending purposes.

Construction of the new distillery is well underway at the time of writing, and if all goes according to plan it will have opened in January 2009. It will have 14 stills, all the same shape and capacity; different styles of make (of broadly Speyside character) will be achieved by modifying the process. These were installed in late August 2008.

CURIOSITIES: When the maltings were built at Roseisle in 1979/80 it was planned to build a distillery alongside, but nothing like on this scale.

RAW MATERIALS: Malt from Roseisle. Water from springs on site.

PLANT: Two full-Lauter stainless steel mash tuns. Stainless steel washbacks. Seven plain wash stills (charge not yet decided), seven plain spirit stills (charge not yet decided). All indirect fired. All shell-and-tube condensers.

MATURATION: Mainly refill U.S. oak. Matured in Central Belt.

STYLE: Speyside.

Royal Brackla

REGION
Highland (East)

ADDRESS
Cawdor, Nairn, Highland

PHONE
01667 402002

WEBSITE
No

OWNER
John Dewar & Sons

VISITORS
By appointment

CAPACITY
3.7m L.P.A.

HISTORICAL NOTES: A map of Cawdor Estate from 1773 shows a 'malt brewhouse' on the site where Brackla Distillery was built in 1812. The founder was Captain William Fraser of Brackla, an irascible and outspoken gentleman, who inveighed against smuggling in the district before the Parliamentary Commission of 1821 ('I have not sold 100 gallons for consumption within 120 miles of my residence during the past year, though people drink nothing but whisky') and was repeatedly fined by H.M. Customs & Excise during the 1830s and 1840s for unknown offences!

After the royal warrant was granted, the distillery immediately became 'Royal' Brackla. Andrew Usher & Company, Edinburgh, were appointed agents in about 1844 and became partners in the business, so it is likely that some Brackla went into their blend Ushers O.V.G. after 1860. When the lease was regranted by Lord Cawdor in 1890 to Robert Fraser & Company, the partners were Andrew Usher II and his brother Sir John Usher. They rebuilt the distillery that year, and when Andrew Usher died in 1898, the firm was incorporated as the Brackla Distillery Company Ltd.

John Bisset & Company Ltd of Aberdeen bought the lease in 1926, converted it to a Feu Charter and sold the distillery to S.M.D. (D.C.L.'s production division) in 1943. A major refurbishment took place in 1964/65, when a second pair of stills were installed and all four converted to indirect firing by steam.

Royal Brackla was mothballed from 1985 to 1991, but resumed production that year and underwent a £2 million refurbishment in 1997 – just in time for it to be sold to Bacardi, along with John Dewar & Sons the following year.

CURIOSITIES: Cawdor Estate, the land upon which Brackla stands, was made legendary by Shakespeare in *Macbeth*, and the 'Thane of Cawdor' is still the current Earl of Cawdor. The play is set on the rolling coastal plain between Inverness and Forres (see *Glenburgie*).

James Augustus Grant, who accompanied Captain Speke on his last journey to discover the source of the Nile in 1860, wrote to his sister that after dinner they felt 'as comfortable as if we had our legs under your table drinking "Brackla"'.

Since he could not sell his whisky locally, Captain Fraser advertised in the *Aberdeen Chronicle* of 1828 that he had 'made an arrangement to have this *much admired spirit* sent up (to Aberdeen) by land, when a regular supply can be had weekly'.

Alfred Barnard (1887) mentions that 'the whisky is carted to the station six miles distant by a traction engine which brings back coals from Nairn'.

Brackla has among the longest fermentations of any distillery: an average of 80 hours, with short fermentations at 72 hours and long fermentations at 120 hours.

EXPRESSIONS:
The first bottling of Royal Brackla in recent years was in U.D.'s Flora & Fauna series (@ 10YO released in 1993). The 20YO Rare Malts bottling in 1998 at 59.8% won Best Whisky at the I.W.S.C. that year. Until recently the core range comprised a 10YO and a limited edition 25YO. Neither of these is currently bottled, but Dewar's have plans to repackage and bottle further expressions in 2009.

RAW MATERIALS: Floor maltings until 1966; unpeated malt from independent maltsters. Process water from Cawdor Burn and cooling water from a spring opened during World War II.

PLANT: Semi-Lauter stainless steel mash tun (12.5 tonnes per mash). Six Oregon pine and two stainless steel washbacks. Two plain wash stills (20,500 litres capacity, two plain spirit stills (23,000 litres). All indirect fired. All shell-and-tube condensers.

MATURATION: Five bonded warehouses, some dunnage, some racked (built 1975). Today all Dewar's own stock is tankered to Coatbridge and Glasgow for maturation in mainly refill American oak.

STYLE: Malty and fruity.

MATURE CHARACTER: Fresh, floral and grassy, with notes of cream and light coconut and a whiff of smoke. Smooth mouth feel, with vanilla cream; sweet taste to start, with malt, apples and pears, and sometimes spice. Medium-bodied.

Ro

Royal Lochnagar

REGION
Highland (East)
ADDRESS
Crathie, Ballater,
Aberdeenshire
PHONE
01339 742700
WEBSITE
www.malts.com
OWNER
Diageo plc
VISITORS
Visitor centre with display
area, a good shop (with
a range of Diageo's rarer
bottlings) and guided tours
CAPACITY
400,000 L.P.A.

HISTORICAL NOTES: Royal Lochnagar is Diageo's smallest distillery, and its showcase 'Malts Brand Home' used for V.I.P. visits and training, on account of its charm and picturesque location.

Deeside was long a hotbed of illicit distilling. After the 1823 Act, former illicit distillers took out licences and their erstwhile colleagues sometimes turned against them. Such was the case with James Robertson of Crathie, who built a distillery in Glen Feardan, north of the River Dee, and had it burned down. He then built a second distillery called Lochnagar, also on the north bank of the Dee in 1826. It too was burned. He built a third distillery, and again the entire premises were '. . . reduced to embers. Where or how the fire originated remains a mystery.' (*Aberdeen Journal*, 12 May 1841)

So it was a brave man who built New Lochnagar Distillery on the other side of the Dee in 1845, close to Balmoral Castle which was finished three years later for Queen Victoria and Prince Albert. This man was John Begg, whose name was later immortalised by the slogan for his blended whisky, 'Take a peg of John Begg'.

Knowing how interested Prince Albert was in 'things mechanical', Begg sent an invitation to Balmoral to come and inspect his 'works'. The Prince arrived next day, accompanied by the Queen and their three eldest children; they toured the distillery and he gave them all a dram. It must have been good stuff, for it was followed within days by the award of a Royal Warrant. Before long the distillery was calling itself Royal Lochnagar.

The distillery passed to John Begg's son and grandson, and then a family trust and, after 1902, a private limited company. During World War I the Directors approached D.C.L., which acquired the family's shares in 1916.

CURIOSITIES: Royal Lochnagar was Lord Macfarlane of Bearsden's favourite whisky. As Sir Norman Macfarlane, Chairman of U.D., he had initiated the first proprietary bottlings of the malt.

Lochnagar is a mountain that rises up behind the distillery and the Balmoral Estate. It was immortalised by Lord Byron: 'Oh, for the crags that are wild and majestic
The steep frowning glories of dark Lochna-gar.'

EXPRESSIONS:
Three bottlings were released in the Rare Malts series: 24YO from 1972 @ 55.7%, 23YO from 1972 @ 59.7% and 30YO from 1974 @ 56.2%. The core range comprises:
• Royal Lochnagar 12YO @ 40%
• Royal Lochnagar Selected Reserve @ 43% (a limited annual vatting of four specially chosen butts, two European and two American oak)

RAW MATERIALS: Process water from springs in the foothills of Lochnagar; cooling water from two reservoirs. Unpeated malt from Roseisle maltings.

PLANT: Open-topped cast iron rake-and-plough mash tun (5.4 tonnes per mash). Three Scottish larch washbacks (two of 37,000 litres; one of 18,000 litres). One plain wash still (6,300 litres charge), one plain spirit still (4,200 litres charge), both indirectly heated by steam. Worm tubs.

MATURATION: American oak hogsheads, European ex-sherry puncheons and butts (for single malt). One low racked bonded warehouse on site holding 1,300 casks, formerly a maltings. The remainder stored in Alloa.

STYLE: Light and grassy. Small stills and worm tubs should produce a heavy meaty malt, but the way they are operated (with air rests to cool the copper stills, and warm water in the worm tub) achieves this specification.

MATURE CHARACTER: Light toffee and planed hardwood on the nose, with some piney notes, boat varnish and linseed oil; dry overall. Sweet to short, then acidic, with an attractive lingering sandalwood aftertaste. Medium-bodied.

St Magdalene Redeveloped

REGION
Lowland

ADDRESS
Linlithgow, West Lothian

LAST OWNER
D.C.L./S.M.D.

CLOSED
1983

HISTORICAL NOTES: The first recorded licensee was Adam Dawson in 1797. He was a spokesman for the Lowland distillers and was succeeded by A. & J. Dawson in 1829.

The distillery stood beside the main road between Glasgow and Edinburgh, and its situation was greatly enhanced by the opening of the Union Canal between the two cities in 1822, and the arrival of the railway in 1842. It was a sizeable enterprise, with four stills (converted to indirect firing in 1971) and 19 warehouses, including one built of brick of 'enormous proportions' (Barnard).

A. & J. Dawson was incorporated in 1894, but was in difficulties by 1912, when a liquidator was appointed. A new company was formed later the same year with the same name, under the ownership of D.C.L., John Walker & Sons and J.A. Ramage Dawson.

In 1914 the Directors formed S.M.D. with four other Lowland distilleries (see *Rosebank*).

Saint Magdalene was one of the many casualties of world recession of 1983, when S.M.D. was obliged to close distilleries 'to bring the level of maturing stock into line with anticipated level of future sales'. The site has been redeveloped as residential flats.

CURIOSITIES: The name derives from the land near Linlithgow, known as Saint Magdalene's Cross, upon which the distillery was built in the late eighteenth century. It was once the site of a hospital of the same name and of an annual fair. The distillery was also known as Linlithgow.

Linlithgow was famous for its water. An old rhyme runs:

Linlithgow for wells,
Glasgow for bells,
Peebles for clashes and lees
And Falkirk for beans and peas

In the sixteenth century it was a centre of milling and malting, and in the eighteenth century for brewing and distilling. Saint Magdalene's water for cooling and for driving the water wheel came from the Union Canal; process water came from the town's supply, which originated in Loch Lomond.

The gigantic shell of Linlithgow Palace towers above Linlithgow Loch. A royal residence from the twelfth century, the existing ruin dates from 1425 to 1630. Mary, Queen of Scots was born here in 1542.

Colonel Ramage Dawson, who died in 1892, had 'extensive and valuable coffee plantations in Ceylon', an estate in Kinross-shire and the colonelcy of the Haddington Artillery, as well as owning the distillery.

EXPRESSIONS:

- Saint Magdalene 1970 23YO @ 58.43% (Rare Malts series, released 1994)
- Saint Magdalene 1971 23YO @ 59% (Rare Malts series, released 1995)
- Saint Magdalene 1979 19YO @ 60.8% (Rare Malts series, released 1998)
- Linlithgow 1973 30YO @ 59.6% (Special Releases, 2006)

Scapa

REGION
Highland (Island)

ADDRESS
St Ola, Kirkwall, Orkney

PHONE
01856 872071

WEBSITE
No

OWNER
Chivas Brothers

VISITORS
By appointment

CAPACITY
1.5m L.P.A.

HISTORICAL NOTES: The distillery stands beside the Lingro Burn and overlooks the spacious anchorage of Scapa Flow, where the German High Seas Fleet scuppered itself in 1919, and where a daring German submarine sank the aircraft carrier *Royal Oak* in 1939.

A local minister reported in 1701 that the parish held a large and ancient drinking cup, which had supposedly belonged to St Magnus (eleventh century) and 'full of some strong drink' was presented to Bishops of Orkney upon their arrival. 'If the Bishop drank it out, they highly praised him, and made themselves believe that they should have many good and fruitful years in his time'.

Scapa Distillery was built by John Townsend, a Glasgow blender, in 1885 and operated until 1919 when it was narrowly saved from total destruction by fire, thanks to sailors from the Grand Fleet, anchored in Scapa Flow, forming a chain of buckets from the sea. It then passed through various hands, until it was bought by Hiram Walker in 1954; they rebuilt it five years later, installing a Lomond-style wash still (see *Inverleven*, *Miltonduff*). It was again modernised in 1978, when the plates within the still were removed, so it now operates like a straight-sided traditional still. Again the distillery was mothballed in 1994, and from 1997 production was sporadic and done by staff from Highland Park Distillery nearby.

Ownership passed to Allied Distillers when they bought Hiram Walker in 1986/87, and in 2004 they surprised the industry by undertaking major refurbishment (at a cost of £2.1 million), launching the first proprietary bottling and establishing a fan club. Production was again halted in 2005 to allow completion of the refurbishment programme; later that year ownership passed to Pernod Ricard/Chivas Brothers, who resumed production in October 2005, 120 years after it opened.

CURIOSITIES: When Alfred Barnard visited Scapa in 1886 he found it to be 'one of the most complete little Distilleries in the Kingdom'.

The large water wheel, driven by the Lingro Burn, supplied power to the distillery.

Scapa has operated a Lomond wash still from 1959 to the present day. It is now the only distillery to have such a still (although adjusted). It is unusual among the island distilleries in specifying unpeated malt.

EXPRESSIONS:
Independent bottlings only until 2004 when Allied introduced a 14YO @ 40%.

• Scapa 14YO @ 40% (reintroduced in 2006)

RAW MATERIALS: Unpeated malt from Kilgours, Kirkcaldy; own floor maltings removed 1962. Cooling water from the Lingro Burn; process water from springs and the Coltland Burn.

PLANT: Stainless steel mash tun (3.76 tonnes per mash); six stainless steel washbacks. One remade Lomond-style wash still, now with no internal plates and a purifier (13,500 litres charge); one plain spirit still (9,000 litres charge). All indirect fired. Shell-and-tube condensers.

MATURATION: Mainly refill U.S. hogsheads, some first-fill.

STYLE: Heather pollen, honey and light spice.

MATURE CHARACTER: Scapa has a maritime character, with faint saltiness on the nose, together with floral/grassy notes and some scented wood. The taste is dryish and lightly spicy, with some vanilla and toffee notes. Medium-bodied.

Speyburn

REGION
Speyside

ADDRESS
Rothes, Moray

PHONE
01340 831213

WEBSITE
www.inverhouse.com

OWNER
Inver House Distillers

VISITORS
By appointment

CAPACITY
1.8m L.P.A.

HISTORICAL NOTES: Speyburn is a picturesque distillery tucked snugly into a steep wooded glen just outside Rothes. It was designed for John Hopkins & Company (owners of Tobermory Distillery) by the leading distillery architect, Charles Doig of Elgin, and built from stones quarried from an adjacent riverbed. It opened in 1897. Since the site was narrow, Doig also installed a 'Hennings pneumatic maltings' – the first drum maltings in any malt distillery – since it took up less ground-space. This operated until 1968. The wooden malt hoppers are still in use.

John Hopkins & Company joined D.C.L. in 1916 and Speyburn was licensed to the now forgotten Leith blenders, John Robertson & Sons. It was operated by S.M.D. from 1962; they converted the stills to indirect firing that year and rebuilt and re-equipped the mashhouse in 1974 (although not the stillhouse which remains as Doig designed it). Inver House Distillers bought Speyburn in 1991.

CURIOSITIES: Speyburn is little known in most markets, but it is in the top six bestselling malts in the U.S.A., and number one in Finland!

EXPRESSIONS:
U.D. bottled Speyburn as a 12YO in their Flora & Fauna series. Inver House now offer:
• Speyburn 10YO @ 40% (since 1992. Gold Medal, World Spirits Competition 2006)
• Speyburn 25YO Solera @ 58.5% (introduced 2005)

RAW MATERIALS: Own drum maltings until the 1967; now unpeated malt from independent maltsters. Soft process water from the Granty Burn, a tributary of the River Spey; cooling water from the Broad Burn.

PLANT: Traditional rake-and-plough mash tun (5.5 tonnes). Six Douglas fir washbacks. One plain wash still (12,500 litres charge); one plain spirit still (11,500 litres charge); both indirect fired by steam kettles since 1962. Worm tubs (with worms over 100m long).

Speyburn opened on the last day of 1897, the year of Queen Victoria's Golden Jubilee. The men worked all night in a violent snow storm and in a stillhouse that had no windows. Only one cask bore the historic date.

MATURATION: Mainly ex-bourbon casks, some European. 80% of spirit tankered and filled into cask at Airdrie; casks for bottling as a single matured on site in a two-floored warehouse, racked three high.

STYLE: Speyside: estery, floral, grassy, citric, but with a meaty note.

MATURE CHARACTER: A lightweight Speyside style: fresh and floral/fruity on the nose, with cereal notes. Predominantly sweet to taste, with green apples, pear drops and herbal-heathery notes. Light-bodied.

Speyside

REGION
Speyside

ADDRESS
Tromie Mills, Glentromie, Kingussie, Highland

PHONE
01540 661060

WEBSITE
www.speysidedistillery. co.uk

OWNER
Speyside Distillery Company Ltd

VISITORS
By appointment

CAPACITY
500,500 L.P.A.

HISTORICAL NOTES: After being demobilised from the Royal Navy (submarines), George Christie joined a former naval colleague as junior partner in the Glasgow firm of whisky brokers, W.R. Paterson & Company. Three years later (1949), they bought the whisky broker Alexander McGavin & Company (Glasgow) Ltd at auction from the Inland Revenue, in partnership with one Sandy Grant. George was appointed Managing Director, and in 1955 and 1964 bought out the other shareholders.

In 1955 he also founded the Speyside Distillery & Bonding Company, and next year bought Old Milton Estate, Glen Tromie, three miles from Kingussie. In particular he was interested in Tromie Mills, a barley mill dating back to the eighteenth century, which had been run for generations by a local family, and continued until 1965. When restoration of the building commenced in 1967, the mill and water wheel were retained, and are still in working order. The first spirit ran on 12 December 1990, while the formal opening of the distillery was celebrated with a lunch on 20 September 1991.

George Christie also founded Strathmore Distillery at Cambus, Alloa, in 1957 (see *North of Scotland* entry).

The company's HQ is in Rutherglen, Glasgow, where most of the make is matured, blended and bottled. George Christie sold his shares in Speyside Distilleries in 2000 to his son, Ricky, Ian Jerman and Sir James Ackroyd, who became Chairman of the company.

CURIOSITIES: Closer to the source of the Spey than any other distillery, on the bank of the Spey tributary, the River Tromie, and close to the village of Drumguish (pronounced 'Drumooish').

There was an earlier 'Speyside Distillery' in Kingussie. Founded in 1895 it ceased production in 1905 and was demolished in 1911. The present distillery appeared in the TV series *Monarch of the Glen* as Lagganmore Distillery.

The rebuilding of Speyside Distillery is the work of one man, the local dry-stane dyker, Alex Fairlie. It took him 20 years.

EXPRESSIONS:
As well as its single malts, Speyside produces around 20 blended whiskies and Glentromie blended malt. It also bottles single casks from other distilleries, selected by its (now retired) Master Blender, Robert Scott, under the Scott's Selection label (at cask strength) and Private Cellar (at 43%).

• Drumguish (no age statement, introduced 1993)
• The Speyside 12YO @ 40% (introduced 2003)
• The Speyside 15YO @ 40% (introduced 2007)

RAW MATERIALS: Soft process and cooling water from the River Tromie, via the former mill lade. Traditionally unpeated malt from independent maltsters, with small annual matches of heavily peated malt.

PLANT: Stainless steel 'Glen Spey' semi-Lauter tun with a stainless steel dome (four tonnes per mash, the last one built by Newmill Engineering, its inventor). Four stainless steel washbacks. One plain wash still (10,000 litres charge), one plain spirit still (6,000 litres charge). Indirect fired by steam kettles. Shell-and-tube condensers.

MATURATION: Mix of American barrels and remade hogsheads, with a small number of sherry casks. No bonded warehouses on site; matured in Rutherglen, Glasgow, where the bottling plant is located.

STYLE: Light, soft, sweet, vanilla, hint of liquorice.

MATURE CHARACTER: A light style of Speyside: predominantly cereal-like, with fresh apples and pears, and faint floral notes. The taste is sweet, with cereal and fruity notes. Light-bodied.

Springbank

REGION
Campbeltown

ADDRESS
Longrow, Campbeltown,
Argyll

PHONE
01586 552085

WEBSITE
www.springbankdistillers.
com

OWNER
Springbank Distillers
(J. & A. Mitchell)

VISITORS
By arrangement

CAPACITY
472,000 L.P.A.

HISTORICAL NOTES: Springbank is the only Scottish distillery, established in the nineteenth century, which is still in the ownership of its founding family.

In all likelihood it was originally called Longrow Street Distillery (too easily confused with Longrow Distillery next door , it soon became Springbank), and is said to have been founded in 1828 by one William Reid. He was related by marriage to the Mitchells, a well-known local family who had arrived in Kintyre from the Lowlands around 1600. Indeed, Archibald Mitchell may well have been distilling illegally on the site before Reid built his distillery; what is certain is that he soon ran into financial difficulties and ownership passed to his in-laws, John and William Mitchell, in 1837 (their brothers, Hugh and Archibald, had founded Riechlachan Distillery nearby, which operated from 1825 to 1934). By the following year they were selling whisky to John Walker of Kilmarnock at 8/8d (44p) per gallon.

The brothers quarrelled and in 1872 William left to join his other brothers at Riechlachan. John brought in his son Alexander as partner, the firm becoming J. & A. Mitchell, as it is today.

Springbank closed from 1926 to 1933, during the Great Depression, but was one of only three Campbeltown distilleries to survive the 1920s, when 17 distilleries closed in the town. The other survivors were Glen Scotia and Riechlachan, the latter closing in 1934. The present Managing Director, Mr Hedley Wright, is John Mitchell's great-great grandson.

In 2004, Hedley Wright opened Glengyle Distillery, down the road from Springbank, which had been founded originally in 1872 by his great-great uncle (see entry). Springbank currently makes around 150,000 litres of spirit per annum, and has no plans to increase this, owing to the fact that for periods of the year the staff devote themselves to malting and to distilling at Glengyle (see entry). Indeed, in July 2008, it was announced that for the next two years the distillery would be operating at reduced capacity, while new warehousing is being built.

Springbank is the most traditional distillery in Scotland. It is also the only distillery, established in the nineteenth century, still in the ownership of its founding family.

CURIOSITIES: As well as distilling, John Mitchell was 'a rare judge of sheep and Highland cattle ... tenant at one time of no fewer than seven farms', according to his obituary. He died in 1892, aged 91.

The *Daily Mail* of 16 June 1974 reported that an hotelier in Galashiels was displaying a bottle of 50YO Springbank to customers at 10p a viewing: 'He paid £29 for it – the wholesale value of the whisky ... It's a sobering thought when he tells you what it would cost for a dram – if the liquid gold was up for sale (which it isn't). Without so much as a blush, he puts a price tag of £2 on a fifth (of a gill) measure.' How times have changed: a 50YO Springbank (probably from the same batch of 36 bottles) fetched £3,800 at auction in 2001!

Springbank malts all its barley (a proportion of which is grown locally) in its own floor maltings, using locally cut peat. Its mash tun is rake-and plough; it has three stills, and employs a complex near-triple distillation; its wash still is direct fired by oil, and fitted with rummagers, as well as being indirect fired by steam; it has a worm tub on one spirit still. It bottles on site. The whole place has an antique air, with not a computer to be seen.

J. & A. Mitchell bought the well-established independent bottler, Cadenhead's (originally of Aberdeen) in 1969. Around the same time, the site of Longrow Distillery (1824–96), adjacent to Springbank, was acquired. One of its warehouses is still used, and another houses Springbank's bottling plant; the site of the original stillhouse is now a car park. In 1973, the first bottling of Longrow was made from heavily peated malt in Springbank's own stills, and this was joined in 1997 by the first release of Hazelburn, triple distilled from unpeated malt. Hazelburn itself was another Campbeltown distillery, which closed in 1925.

In 2007 Springbank introduced a whisky school for enthusiasts who want to learn about production – from malting to blending and bottling. The course lasts five days and is limited to six people per week.

EXPRESSIONS:

Many proprietary bottlings have appeared in recent years, including a number of limited edition 'vintages' (Springbank 21YO, 25YO and 32YO; Longrow 1989, 1990, 1991, 1992, 1993, 1994, 1995, mostly at 10YO), and since 2002 a series of Wood Expressions (finished in ex-port, sherry, rum, Tokaji and Barolo casks). The core expressions are:

- Springbank 10YO @ 46%
- Springbank 10YO @ 57% (100° proof)
- Springbank 15YO @ 46%
- Longrow 10YO @ 46%
- Longrow 10YO @ 57% (100° proof)
- Longrow 14YO @ 46% (sherry matured)
- Hazelburn 8YO @ 46%

RAW MATERIALS: Soft water from Crosshills Loch. Own floor maltings; Springbank malt dried for six hours over peat (cut from near Campbeltown Airport) and then for 18–24 hours over hot air. Longrow malt is dried over peat for around 27 hours, then hot air. Hazelburn malt has no peating.

PLANT: Cast iron open-topped traditional mash tun (3.64 tonnes per mash). Six Scandinavian boatskin larch washbacks. One plain wash still (11,000 litres charge) direct fired by oil burners and indirect fired by internal steam coils (unique in Scotland). Rummager. Two plain spirit stills, indirect fired (7,500–8,000 litres charge). Worm tub on first spirit still; condensers on wash and second spirit stills.

Longrow is double distilled; Hazelburn triple distilled; Springbank 2.5 times distilled. 80% of the low wines from the wash still charges the first spirit still in the usual way, and the distillate goes to the feints receiver, where it mixes with the foreshots and feints from the third still. 20% goes straight to the low wines and feints charger of the third still, where it is mixed with the distillate from the feints receiver. This is then distilled in the third still, with feints and foreshots going to the feints receiver.

MATURATION: Mainly first-fill ex-bourbon barrels, followed by first-fill ex-sherry; around 20% refill casks; also Madeira, port and Demerara Rum casks. Six bonded warehouses on site; four traditional dunnage, two racked seven high. The entire make is matured on site.

STYLE: Springbank: light peatiness, oily, sweet and heavy. Longrow: heavy, sweet and distinctly peaty. Hazelburn: light, sweet, with hay and malt notes.

MATURE CHARACTER: Springbank needs long aging, and takes it superlatively well. At 10–15yo it only has 'potential': hints of strawberries and cherries and bananas on the nose, with distinct smokiness. A creamy mouth feel, with some butterscotch and mint, some sweet malt, a light smokiness. Medium-bodied, becoming fuller with age.

Strathclyde

ADDRESS
Moffat Street, Glasgow
PHONE
01329 724347
OWNER
Chivas Brothers
CAPACITY
39m L.P.A.

1927 was not the most auspicious year to open a distillery, a time of industrial depression in the U.K. and Prohibition in the U.S.A.; nevertheless, Seager Evans had confidence in the future.

HISTORICAL NOTES: Strathclyde Grain Spirit Distillery was built in 1927 by Seager Evans, the long established (1805) firm of London gin distillers, in order to secure supplies of spirit for rectification. It stands on the south bank of the River Clyde in Glasgow, and draws its water from Loch Katrine in the Trossachs.

The move towards Scotch whisky production was boosted by the acquisition of the wine and spirits merchant, W.H. Chaplin & Company, in 1936, which had bought the well-known brand name Long John from the successors to Long John Macdonald of Ben Nevis Distillery in 1911. Next year Seager Evans bought Glenugie Distillery in Peterhead.

In 1956 Seager Evans was bought by the American distillers Schenley Industries Inc. of New York State, and this provided a welcome injection of capital at a time when blended Scotch was taking off worldwide. Ownership of the Scottish distilleries was transferred to Strathclyde & Long John Distilleries Ltd, which soon became simply Long John Distillers, and after 1970 Long John International. In 1975, this was sold to Whitbread & Company Ltd., the brewers, whose spirits interests were bought by Allied-Lyons plc in January 1990 for £454 million.

Strathclyde was rebuilt between 1973 and 1978, with two columns for grain whisky production and five for neutral spirit. Having closed their Dumbarton Distillery in 2002, Allied spent more than £7 million increasing Strathclyde's capacity from 32 to 39 million litres per annum. When Allied was broken up in 2005, Strathclyde Distillery went to Chivas Brothers.

CURIOSITIES: In 1956/57 a new malt distillery, named Kinclaith, was built within Strathclyde Distillery to provide fillings for Long John. After Long John International was sold to Whitbread, Kinclaith was dismantled in 1976/77 to make way for an enlarged Strathclyde.

Never bottled as a single by its owners.

RAW MATERIALS: Wheat from independent merchants.

PLANT: Two column stills for grain whisky; five for neutral spirit.

MATURATION: Filled into butts, hogsheads and barrels, and matured on site.

STYLE: Light and sweet, slightly creamy with bubblegum notes.

Strathisla

REGION
Speyside
ADDRESS
Keith, Moray
PHONE
01542 783044
WEBSITE
www.maltwhisky
distilleries.com
OWNER
Chivas Brothers
VISITORS
Visitor centre
CAPACITY
2.4m L.P.A.

HISTORICAL NOTES: The distillery was founded in 1786 by a group of local worthies, to convert their surplus grains into cash – similar moves were taking place all over Scotland at the time. Originally the distillery was named Milltown, which became Milton after 1825 (although the make was called 'Strathisla'), and in 1830 it came into the hands of William Longmore, banker and grain merchant. In due course it passed to his son-in-law, J. Geddes Brown, who incorporated the business as William Longmore & Company Ltd. Most of the shares were subscribed by local people.

It is interesting to note that Sir Robert Burnett & Company of London (the gin makers) were bottling 'Longmore's Strathisla' as a single in the 1880s, in 'immense quantities' (*Moray & Nairn Express*, 1885): 'Wherever one travels one finds that those who know what good whisky is speak in the most glowing and appreciative terms of the produce of Milton Distillery at Keith.'

Longmore & Company owned Milton until 1950, when it was sequestrated and bought for £71,000 by James Barclay, who immediately sold to the Seagram Company. Thenceforward the distillery was named Strathisla, after its product.

At the time Longmore & Company was wound up, Milton was controlled by a shady London financier named Jay Pommeroy, who had siphoned off large stocks of mature whisky and 'disposed of them in a manner which was calculated not to attract any taxation liability', according to the judgement in the Court of Session, that is, he sold them on the black market for huge profit, there being a chronic shortage of mature whisky at the time.

Seagram's immediately expanded production and installed two new stem-heated stills alongside the coal-fired pair in 1965, as well as building extensive warehousing nearby. Seagram's whisky interests were acquired by Pernod Ricard in 2001, and Strathisla is managed by their subsidiary, Chivas Brothers.

Like many others, Strathisla had a distillery cat to keep rodents under control. The present one arrived in 1993 as a stowaway in a cargo of casks from Kentucky, starving and drunk from the fumes of the barrels. She was accordingly named 'Dizzy'!

CURIOSITIES: In January 1876, *The Banffshire Journal* reported a fire at Milton Distillery, which consumed the byre next to the threshing mill: 'out of 66 cows in the byre, 30 perished in the fire, at a loss of £700; along with 500 quarters of barley, an excellent threshing machine and a steam engine ... The damage was estimated at £3,800.' Three years later there was an explosion in the malt mill, a common peril caused by 'a small piece of stone coming in contact with the cylinder [of the mill] and originating a spark which set fire to the fine, powdery and very explosive [dust from the mill]'.

A conspicuous feature of the distillery is the water wheel, installed in 1881 to provide power, and used until 1965 to drive the rummagers in the wash stills.

Milton/Strathisla has the highest pagoda roofs of any Scottish distillery (although they do not look like it, since the distillery is small), and, unusually, they were not designed by Charles Doig (the inventor of the pagoda roof and doyenne of distillery building) but by another distillery architect, John Alcock.

James Barclay (1886–1963) was one of the most colourful characters in the whisky industry during the post-war decades. He started as a clerk at Benrinnes Distillery in 1902, then worked for Peter Mackie at White Horse. With a partner, he bought George Ballantine & Son in 1919, and J. & G. Stodart (blenders) in 1922, and immediately started to arrange distribution in the U.S.A. – which at the time was 'dry'. In Canada, he became friendly with Harry Hatch, the owner of Hiram Walker, Gooderham & Worts, the largest distiller in Canada, and sold Ballantine's to him in 1935. Next year he bought Miltonduff and Glenburgie Distilleries on behalf of Hiram Walker, and joined the Board of Hiram Walker (Scotland) Ltd. Somewhat mysteriously, he resigned in 1937 and even more mysteriously transferred his allegiance to Walker's main rival, Seagram, paving the way for their entry to the Scotch whisky industry by the purchase of Chivas Brothers, of Aberdeen, and then of Milton/Strathisla.

Strathisla is the oldest working distillery in the Highlands, and is one of the most attractive in Scotland, tastefully restored in 1995 and a listed building.

EXPRESSIONS:

Most bottlings (and there are some very old and fine ones) come from Gordon & Macphail.
- Strathisla 12YO @ 43% (reintroduced 2002)
- Strathisla 1991 15YO @ 55.4% (ex-bourbon cask, released 2004)

RAW MATERIALS: Floor maltings until 1961; now unpeated malt from Paul's, Buckie. Production water from Fons Bulliens Well, which, it is believed, was used by monks for brewing beer in the thirteenth century.

PLANT: Stainless steel, traditional rake-and-plough mash tun, with a copper dome (5.12 tonnes). Ten Oregon pine washbacks. Two boil-pot wash stills (12,500 litres charge); two boil-ball spirit stills (7,000 litres charge). Direct fired until 1990s, now all indirect fired. Shell-and-tube condensers.

MATURATION: Mainly refill U.S. hogsheads, some first-fill.

STYLE: Sweet, fruity and estery.

MATURE CHARACTER: Strathisla is a rich malt at its best, with deep fruity scents, including apricots and plums, sweet malt, sandalwood and even a whiff of smoke. It has a pleasant, full texture in the mouth and a sweet, sherried taste, becoming tannic/dry towards the end. Medium-long finish. Medium-bodied.

Strathmill

REGION
Speyside
ADDRESS
Keith, Moray
PHONE
01542 882295/883000
WEBSITE
www.malts.com
OWNER
Diageo plc
VISITORS
No
CAPACITY
1.8m L.P.A.

HISTORICAL NOTES: Strathmill began life in 1891 as Glenisla-Glenlivet, within a converted flour mill, itself built in 1823 and called Strathisla Mills. Its name was changed four years later when it was bought by the London gin distillers, W. & A. Gilbey (who already owned Glenspey Distillery and would later buy Knockando Distillery).

In 1962 Gilbey's merged with United Wine Traders (including Justerini & Brooks) to form International Distillers & Vintners (I.D.V.); six years later Strathmill was expanded to four stills, and purifiers were added to increase reflux and lighten the spirit. I.D.V. was bought by the brewer Watney Mann in 1972, and both were immediately absorbed by the Grand Metropolitan Hotel Group. Grand Metropolitan and Guinness merged to form Diageo in 1997.

CURIOSITIES: It was from here that the first whisky tanker was used to carry spirit to blenders. The tanker was named *Whisky Galore*, which probably dates it to the 1950s.

'[Until 1905] Gilbey's refused to admit that anything but pure malt could be called "Scotch whisky", but it was gradually appreciated that malt whisky was too heavy for a southern climate.' (*Merchants of Wine*, Alec Waugh)

EXPRESSIONS:
Except for the two butts (25YOs) which were bottled in 1992 to celebrate the distillery's centenary, there are no official bottlings apart from:
• Strathmill 12YO @ 43% (Flora & Fauna series, introduced 2001)

RAW MATERIALS: Process water drawn from a spring on site; cooling water from the Isla Burn. Non-peated malt from Burghead in Elgin.

PLANT: Stainless steel Lauter tun with a peaked canopy (nine tonnes per mash); six stainless steel washbacks. Two boil-ball wash stills (11,000 litres charge) and two boil-ball spirit stills (6,700 litres) with purifiers. Shell-and-tube condensers.

MATURATION: Sherry butts and refill hogsheads; six warehouses on site.

STYLE: Light, grassy, malty.

MATURE CHARACTER: A light Speyside style, designed for blending (principally J. & B.). The nose is sweet and estery, with floral and fresh-fruity notes (reminiscent of tangerine, oranges and sweet apples). The taste is also sweet, with fruity notes. Medium- to light-bodied.

Talisker

REGION
Island (Skye)

ADDRESS
Carbost, Isle of Skye

PHONE
01478 614300

WEBSITE
www.malts.com

OWNER
Diageo plc

VISITORS
Visitor centre and shop

CAPACITY
1.9m L.P.A.

HISTORICAL NOTES: Founded in 1830 by Hugh and Kenneth MacAskill, tacksmen (substantial tenant farmers), who had acquired the lease of Talisker House (where Johnson and Boswell stayed in 1764) and its associated estate from Macleod of Macleod.

Importing barley and coal and exporting whisky, all by sea, was costly. The MacAskills sold to the North of Scotland Bank in 1848, and two subsequent licensees went bankrupt before the distillery was bought by Roderick Kemp in 1876 (see *Macallan*). With his partner, Alexander Grigor Allan (see *Dailuaine*), the distillery was extended in 1900 and the pier and cottages built. It came under the control of the Big Three and D.C.L. in 1916, and was absorbed by the latter in 1925.

Until the stillhouse was rebuilt in 1961/62, following a devastating fire, Talisker was triple-distilled. Today's distilling regime achieves the same goal by increasing reflux in the spirit stills (see below). Floor maltings closed in 1972. The visitor centre opened in 1988.

CURIOSITIES: On its way to the worm tub, the spirit stills' lye pipes describe an inverted 'U', just before which is a purifier (a return pipe to the still). This greatly increases the amount of reflux – a past manager estimated that 90% of the vapour that reached the U-bend was returned and redistilled.

A unique characteristic of Talisker is the peppery, even chilli-peppery 'catch' as you swallow. Nobody knows where it comes from.

EXPRESSIONS:

Talisker is one of only a handful of malts bottled as singles in the early twentieth century. Until it was selected as a Classic Malt in 1988 it was bottled at 8YO, thereafter at 10YO. An oddity of the make is that it is traditionally bottled at slightly higher than standard strength. Very few independent bottlings have been done, since the malt is extensively used in the Johnnie Walker blends.

Robert Louis Stevenson famously remarked in 1887: 'The King o' drinks as I conceive it – Talisker, Islay or Glenlivet.'

- Talisker 10YO @ 45.8%
- Talisker Distillers Edition (finished in Amoroso sherry-wood @ 45.8%)
- Talisker 20YO (distilled 1982, bottled 2003 @ 58.8%, limited and numbered bottles)
- Talisker 25YO (distilled 1979, bottled 2004 @ 56.7%, limited and numbered bottles)
- Talisker 28YO (distilled 1977, bottled 2003 @ 52.3%, limited to 300 bottles)

RAW MATERIALS: Medium-peated malt (18–25ppm phenols) from Glen Ord Maltings (7–8 in final spirit). Production water from a burn rising on Cnoc nan Speireag (Hawkhill) behind the distillery; process water from Carbost Burn.

PLANT: Semi-Lauter mash tun (eight tonnes); six wooden washbacks. Two boil-ball wash stills (14,000 litres charge), with a horseshoe-shaped U-bend on the lye pipe before it enters the worms tub, and a purifier pipe, leading to greater reflux; three plain spirit stills (11,300 litres charge). Indirect fired by steam coils and pans. Worm tubs.

MATURATION: Mainly refill U.S. hogsheads; a small amount of refill European wood. 4,500 casks on site; remainder filled and matured in Central Scotland.

STYLE: Smoky and spicy, with maritime notes and high pungency. Its keynote flavour (for me) is chilli-pepper in the back of the throat.

MATURE CHARACTER: Talisker is always bottled at slightly higher strength than other whiskies, which enhances its pungency. It is elemental and maritime. Beaches, seaweed, salt spray, with spice, dried fruits and distant bonfires. The taste is sweeter than expected, with rich fruits, fragrant smoke and chilli pepper. Full-bodied.

Tamdhu

REGION
Speyside
ADDRESS
Knockando, Aberlour,
Moray
PHONE
01340 870221/ 87220
WEBSITE
www.edringtongroup.com
OWNER
The Edrington Group Ltd
VISITORS
Trade and V.I.P.s only
CAPACITY
4m L.P.A.

In the early 1980s, labels of Tamdhu 10YO bore the legend: 'Now calmed in deep pools to reflect softly on the day; soon to well the tumbling torrents of the Spey'

HISTORICAL NOTES: In 1896 three distilleries were planned for Knockando parish: Tamdhu, Knockando and Imperial. The moving force behind Tamdhu was William Grant, a Director of Highland Distilleries and agent for the Caledonian Bank in Elgin. The place he chose beside the Knockando Burn was well-supplied with pure water from springs, and according to local tradition had been used by illicit distillers in days gone by. As important, it was adjacent to the Strathspey railway. He soon raised the funds required to build the distillery (£19,200) from fifteen whisky brokers and blenders, and appointed Charles Doig to design it.

According to Alfred Barnard, who visited two years later, it was one of the 'most modern of distilleries'. A road was constructed to connect with the main road, there was a siding off the railway line and houses were built for the workforce and Excise officers; 20 men were recruited, mostly being paid £1 per week (the cooper was the highest paid at £1.35 per week). The distillery went into production in mid July 1897.

Production climbed until 1903, then fell back, until it was halved between 1906 and 1910. The distillery closed 1911/12, reopened 1913 and continued to prosper until 1925. With the onset of the Great Depression, it close again in 1928, and remained so until 1948. In 1950 Saladin maltings replaced the earlier floor maltings. These remain to this day: Tamdhu is the only distillery still using Saladin boxes, and one of only three distilleries which malts 100% of its requirement on site. It also supplies other distilleries owned by Edrington. The distillery was doubled in size (to four stills) in 1972, and two more stills were added in 1975.

CURIOSITIES: In the early months of production, the spirit was found not to have the 'body' of other Glenlivet-style makes. The Manager believed that the spring water was to blame and experimented with water drawn from the Knockando Burn, which, he

Anticipating increased traffic on the Strathspey railway, its owner, the Great North of Scotland Railway Company, built a station at Tamdhu, called Dalbeallie. In 1976 this became the distillery's visitor centre.

reported, made for a 'thicker and better spirit'. He also began to use locally grown barley (most of the barley used in the early months of production was 'foreign'). Some of the partners, however, preferred the spring water make.

EXPRESSIONS:
Tamdhu was first launched as a single in 1976 (at 8YO); this became 10YO in 1979.
The only available proprietary bottling today bears no age statement.

RAW MATERIALS: Soft water from bore-holes on site and a spring beneath the distillery. Saladin box maltings since 1950, producing lightly peated malt, from locally sourced peat.

PLANT: Semi-Lauter mash tun (11 tonnes per mash). Nine Oregon pine washbacks. Three plain wash stills (10,500 litres charge), three plain spirit stills (13,000 litres charge); all stills indirect fired by steam. Shell-and-tube condensers.

MATURATION: Ex-sherry, ex-bourbon, refill hogsheads and butts.

STYLE: Fresh honeyed apple, with a light smokiness. Good depth.

MATURE CHARACTER: Tamdhu is a 'well-mannered' malt, well-made and displaying all the virtues of Speyside. The nose is sweet and estery, with fresh fruits (including Ogen melon), nail varnish remover and a hint of smoke. The mouth feel is voluptuous, the taste sweet and fruity, with a trace of peat. Medium-bodied.

Tamnavulin

REGION
Speyside
ADDRESS
Ballindalloch, Moray
PHONE
01479 818031
WEBSITE
www.whyteandmackay.
co.uk
OWNER
Whyte & Mackay Ltd
VISITORS
No
CAPACITY
4m L.P.A.

A 1982 advertisement for Tamnavulin proclaimed: 'Fewer than one in 500 will pick up the Gaelic this year' with the strapline, 'Say "Tamnavulin" and let the malt speak for itself.'

HISTORICAL NOTES: Tamnavulin was built by the Tamnavulin-Glenlivet Distillery Company, a subsidiary of Invergordon Distillers Ltd, in 1965/66. At the time it was one of only two distilleries in Glenlivet (the other being The Glenlivet; in 1973/74 they were joined by Braeval, originally named Braes of Glenlivet). It was equipped with six stills, reflecting the demand for Scotch at that time.

It is utilitarian in design, although it enjoys an attractive situation in a steep glen carved by the River Livet. In the mid 1980s the old carding mill that gives its name to the place was converted into a visitor centre, but this is currently closed.

Whyte & Mackay bought Invergordon in 1993 and mothballed the distillery two years later. In January 2007 the company started a major refurbishment, which was completed in August the same year, by which time Whyte & Mackay had been bought by United Breweries of India (May 2007). It is now in full production, the malt being almost entirely used for blending.

CURIOSITIES: 'Mhuilinn' (pronounced 'voolin') is the Gaelic for 'mill'; 'Tamnavulin' is 'the mill on the hill'.

EXPRESSIONS:
A number of limited edition Stillman's Drams have appeared, aged from 21 to 30 years. The core expression is:
• Tamnavulin 12YO @ 40% and 43%

RAW MATERIALS: Unpeated malt from independent maltsters. Process water from springs in the Easterton surrounding hills; cooling water from the River Livet or Allt a' Choire.

PLANT: Stainless steel full-Lauter mash tun (10.52 tonnes per mash); four stainless, four mild steel washbacks. Three plain wash stills (18,000 litres charge); three plain spirit stills (15,000 litres charge). All indirect fired. Shell-and-tube condensers.

MATURATION: Mix of ex-sherry, ex-bourbon and refill hogsheads. Matured on site in racked warehouses.

STYLE: Light, sweet, slightly peppery and grassy.

MATURE CHARACTER: The label on the 12YO states 'Naturally Light' and this sums it up. The nose is fresh and herbal, with dried parsley, green vegetables, lemongrass, even a hint of camphor. The latter comes through in the mouth feel, which is cooling, even minty, with lemon meringue and camomile tea in the taste. Light-bodied.

Teaninich

REGION
Highland (North)
ADDRESS
Alness, Ross and Cromarty
PHONE
01349 882461/885001
WEBSITE
www.malts.com
OWNER
Diageo plc
VISITORS
By appointment
CAPACITY
2.8m L.P.A.

'Beautifully situated on the margin of the sea . . . the only distillery north of Inverness that is lighted by electricity . . . besides which it possesses telephonic communication.'
Alfred Barnard, 1887

HISTORICAL NOTES: The district around Alness, where stands Teaninich (pronounced 'Chee-an-in-ick'), is Munro country. It was known as Ferindonald, from the Gaelic 'Fearainne Domnuill' or Donald's Land – a reference to the founder of the clan, who received lands here from Malcolm II (1005–34) for help against Norse invaders. 'Teaninich' comes from 'Taigh an Aonaich' meaning 'the house on the hill'.

Captain Hugh Munro owned the Teaninich estate and built the distillery here in 1817 with the encouragement of the local lairds who were determined to stamp out the widespread illicit distilling in the county and wanted to provide farmers with an alternative legal outlet for their barley crop. This was only partially successful: three of the four legal distilleries founded in Ross-shire at this time failed.

He was succeeded by General John Munro, who was much abroad in India and leased the site to Robert Pattison (1850), then John McGilchrist Ross (1869). General Munro was an exemplary landlord. During the 'Hungry Forties', he not only supported his poor tenants with money, but 'administers to their relief by daily personal visits, by supplying them with medicines, distributing among them meals and other provisions, and by providing them with fuel during the rigour of the winter season'. (*New Statistical Account*, 1845)

Ross gave up the tenancy in 1895 and was succeeded by Munro & Cameron, whisky brokers and spirit merchants in Elgin. They extended and refurbished Teaninich in 1899, and in 1904 Innes Cameron became sole proprietor. He died in 1932, and the following year his trustees sold to S.M.D. (D.C.L.). It was closed from 1939 to 1946, as a result of wartime restrictions on barley supply, but otherwise has been in continuous production throughout its long life (except for 1985–1990).

The stillhouse was refitted in 1962 and a second pair of stills added – a pair of 'very small stills' had been removed in 1946 – and all four were converted to internal heating by steam. In 1970 a brand new stillhouse was built alongside, with six stills – this was a common S.M.D. practice at the time (see *Linkwood/Glendullan, Brora/Clynelish, Glenlossie/Mannochmore*). Unlike the others it was simply named 'A. Side'; the milling, mashing and fermentation part of the original distillery ('B. Side') was rebuilt three years later, and a dark-grains plant built on site in 1975. At this time, Teaninich was the largest of S.M.D.'s distilleries, with a capacity of 6m L.P.A. The two sides were operated separately, and their makes vatted together prior to maturation. B. Side was mothballed in 1984 and decommissioned in 1999.

CURIOSITIES: Captain Hugh Munro was known as 'the blind captain', having lost his sight owing to an injury during the Napoleonic War, aged 24.

Innes Cameron had substantial interests in Benrinnes, Linkwood and Tamdhu Distilleries and became Chairman of the Malt Distillers Association.

Teaninich has a unique Asnong hammer mill to grind its malt, rather than the more usual roller mill. It also employs a unique mash conversion vessel, where a vortex stirs the mash like a watery porridge. The 'porridge' then goes to a Meura filter press where it is squeezed between 24 cloth plates, and the wort collected. A second water is then added, through the filter; the remaining liquid, called 'weak worts', becomes the first water of the next batch. The filter plates are then separated to allow the draff to be collected. Each pressing takes two hours, and it takes three pressings to fill one washback. This technique is used in the brewing industry, but not by whisky distillers. It was installed at Teaninich in 2000.

EXPRESSIONS:

Three bottlings were released in Diageo's Rare Malts series:
• Teaninich 1972 23YO @ 64.9% (Rare Malts series, released 1995)
• Teaninich 1972 27YO @ 64.2% (Rare Malts series, released 1999)
• Teaninich 1973 23YO @ 57.1% (Rare Malts series, released 1996)

RAW MATERIALS: Process and cooling water from the Dairywell Spring. Unpeated malt from Glen Ord Maltings.

PLANT: Stainless steel mash conversion vessel in place of a mash tun (four tonnes per mash – a very small mash; three mashings to fill one washback). Eight larch washbacks. Three boil-ball wash stills (16,500 litres charge); three boil-ball spirit stills (15,600 litres charge); all indirect fired by steam pans and coils. Shell-and-tube condensers.

MATURATION: Mainly refill ex-bourbon hogsheads, some ex-sherry butts. New make tankered to Menstrie for cask filling and maturation.

STYLE: Grassy, oily.

MATURE CHARACTER: Teaninich is a robust malt, in the North Highland style. The nose is sweet and slightly waxy, with dandelion, green leaves, green apples and gooseberry notes. The mouth feel is smooth and mouth-filling, and the taste lightly sweet with citric hints and a thread of smoke. Medium-bodied.

Tobermory

To

REGION
Highland (Island)

ADDRESS
Tobermory, Isle of Mull,
Argyll

PHONE
01688 302645

WEBSITE
www.burnstewart
distilleries.com

OWNER
Burn Stewart Distillers

VISITORS
Visitor centre and shop

CAPACITY
850,000 L.P.A.

HISTORICAL NOTES: Tobermory Distillery has had a chequered history. Like Pulteney, the village itself was planned in the 1780s to be a 'fishing station' by the landlord, the fifth Duke of Argyll, with the encouragement of the British Fisheries Society. The work was organised by 'Mr Stevenson of Oban' (see Oban Distillery) and the Duke's chamberlain, but the plan was criticised by another Stevenson, Robert, the great lighthouse builder and father of Robert Louis, and one way or another Tobermory never became a serious fishing port.

The distillery may have been founded during this period – 1795 or 1798 – by John Sinclair Esq., 'merchant' and proprietor of Lochaline in Morvern, although he did not receive a charter to the land until 1823, and there is no sign of a distillery on the site in William Daniell's engraving of Tobermory in 1813. Barnard says, with unusual brevity, that 'the distillery was established in 1823'. It was originally named 'Ledaig'.

Sinclair seems to have been the licensee until 1837, then there is a gap until 1878, then a couple of owners, the last of whom was sequestrated in 1887, soon after which Tobermory Distillery was acquired by John Hopkins & Company, who went on to buy Speyburn Distillery in 1897, and joined D.C.L. in 1916.

S.M.D. mothballed Tobermory in 1930 (it was subsequently used as a canteen and a power station), before selling it in 1972 to Ledaig Distillery (Tobermory) Ltd, a partnership between Pedro Domecq and a Liverpool shipping company. Ledaig Distillery went into production in 1972, but by 1975 the new owner was in receivership and four years later it was sold to the Kirkleavington Property Company, of Cleckheaton in Yorkshire, which converted some of the distillery buildings into flats in 1982, and rented others for cheese storage. Production was resumed in 1989, then Tobermory Distillery was sold to Burn Stewart Distillers for £600,000 (plus £200,000 for stock) in 1993.

The distillery's situation on the sheltered shore at the mouth of the fast-flowing Tobermory River met all supply requirements: water, barley, fuel, not to mention the shipping of casks of whisky.

CURIOSITIES: Tobermory, the brand, has been used for blended Scotch, The Malt Scotch (a blended malt) and single malt whisky. The malt whisky distilled from 1972 to 1974 was bottled as Ledaig (and is highly sought after). Since Burn Stewart took over the brand names have been rationalised: Tobermory is an unpeated malt and Ledaig heavily peated.

EXPRESSIONS:
- Tobermory 10YO @ 40%
- Tobermory 1972 32YO @ 50.1% (Oloroso sherry cask, bottled 2005)
- Tobermory 15YO @ 43% (limited edition, released 2008)
- Ledaig Original @ 40%
- Ledaig 10YO @ 40%
- Ledaig Sherry Finish @ 40%

RAW MATERIALS: Soft peaty water from Gearr a'Bkimm lochan above the distillery. Unpeated malt from Greencore and heavily peated malt (35ppm phenols) from Port Ellen maltings.

PLANT: Cast iron rake-and-plough mash tun with a copper canopy (five tonnes per mash); four Oregon pine washbacks with no switchers. Two boil-ball wash stills (18,000 litres charge). Two boil-ball spirit stills (14,500 litres charge). Indirect fired. Shell-and-tube condensers.

MATURATION: Primarily first-fill and refill bourbon casks, with some ex-sherry casks. Small number of casks on site; rest matured at Deanston Distillery.

STYLE: Malty and smoky.

MATURE CHARACTER: Historically, Tobermory has been variable. The 'Standard' 10YO is somewhat maritime and somewhat industrial (in the faint, oily smokiness); cereal notes abound, with light fruitiness. The mouth feel is soft and the taste dryish, with nuts and apple brandy, and a hint of smoke. Light-bodied.

Tomatin

REGION
Highland (Central)

ADDRESS
Tomatin, Inverness-shire

PHONE
01808 511234

WEBSITE
www.tomatin.com

OWNER
Tomatin Distillery Company
(Marubeni Europe plc)

VISITORS
Visitor centre and gift shop

CAPACITY
5m L.P.A.

HISTORICAL NOTES: Tomatin means 'the hillock of the juniper' (in Gaelic 'tom - aiteann '), and at over 1,000 feet this is no mean hillock! The first distillery here, just off the A9 some ten miles south of Inverness, was built in 1897 by a group of local businessmen trading as the Tomatin Spey District Distillery Company Ltd. They went into liquidation in 1906, but the distillery was reopened by the New Tomatin Distillers Company Ltd in 1909.

The distillery was extended from two stills to four in 1956; two more were added in 1958, four in 1961, one in 1961 and a staggering further twelve stills in 1974, as well as a dark-grains plant. With 23 stills, Tomatin now had the greatest capacity of any malt whisky distillery – 12m L.P.A. per annum – although it has never operated to capacity, and 11 of the original stills were dismantled, more than halving capacity.

Tomatin Distillers plc in 2002 went into liquidation in 1986 and the distillery was sold to Takara Shuzo Company and Okura & Company of Japan, both long-standing customers of the distillery. This was the first time a Japanese company had entered the Scotch whisky industry. Marubeni replaced Okura around 2000, and the consortium was joined by the Japanese distributors Kokubu in 2006.

CURIOSITIES: The hamlet of Tomatin stands on an old cattle drovers' road, and there was an illicit still here, beside the 'Old Laird's House' where the drovers would fill their flasks.

Tomatin was the first whisky distillery to introduce the Lauter mash tun from the German brewing industry in 1974, when the distillery's capacity was doubled. Prior to this all mash tuns were traditional infusion vessels with rake-and-plough (rack-and-pinion) stirring gear. The virtue of the Lauter tun is that its rotating arms are equipped with 'knives' which gently lift the malt bed to allow the worts to drain, rather than agitating the entire bed with rakes that revolve as well as rotate. This makes for clearer worts, especially if the mash tun is a full-Lauter,

The old established brand of blended Scotch, The Antiquary, is owned by Tomatin and bottled at 12 and 21 years. It was created by John and William Hardie, whose partnership was said to have been founded in 1857, which makes it one of the earliest blends.

where the knives can be raised and lowered as well as rotating.

EXPRESSIONS:
Usually classified as a Speyside, Tomatin describes itself on its label as Single Highland Malt. Vintages from 1973 and 1962 were released in 2005 and 2006, and from 1967, 1975, 1980 and 1990 (as well as a 30YO and a 40YO) in 2007. Further vintages are released each year.
The core range is:
- Tomatin 12YO @ 40% (which succeeded the 10YO in 2004)
- Tomatin 18YO @ 40% (introduced 2006)
- Tomatin 25YO @ 40% (limited release, introduced 2005)
- Tomatin 30YO @ 49.3% (1,500 bottles only, introduced 2008)
- Tomatin 40YO @ 42.9% (1,614 bottles only, introduced 2008)

RAW MATERIALS: Water from Allt-na-Frithe, 'the free burn'. Floor maltings until 1973. Unpeated and peated malt (2–5ppm phenols) from Simpson's and Greencore.

PLANT: One stainless steel Lauter tun (eight tonnes per mash) – also an old traditional tun in place. Twelve stainless steel washbacks (and six disused ones of cast iron). Six boil-ball wash stills (16,800 litres charge; six boil-ball spirit stills (16,800 litres charge); all indirect fired. Shell-and-tube condensers.

MATURATION: Mainly refill hogsheads; also sherry hogs, bourbon barrels and a small amount of new hogs from Speyside Cooperage. Finish in Spanish ex-sherry for about nine months to a year.

STYLE: Light, fresh, grassy, some vanilla.

MATURE CHARACTER: The nose is sweet, malty and aromatic with vegetal notes. The taste is sweet to start, with cereal flavours supported by caramelised fruits (orange especially) and assorted nuts. A very faint smokiness. Medium-bodied.

Tomintoul

REGION
Speyside
ADDRESS
Tomintoul, Moray
PHONE
01807 590274
WEBSITE
www.tomintouldistillery.
co.uk
OWNER
Angus Dundee Distillers plc
VISITORS
By appointment
CAPACITY
3.3m L.P.A.

HISTORICAL NOTES: The functional-looking distillery was built in 1964/65 by two firms of whisky brokers and blenders in Glasgow (Hay Macleod Ltd and W. & S. Strong Ltd), who sold to L.O.N.H.R.O. in 1973. The latter bought Whyte & Mackay the same year, and ownership was transferred. Capacity doubled in 1974 (to four stills). W. & M. (now owned by Jim Beam) sold the distillery to the London-based blenders Angus Dundee Ltd in 2000.

CURIOSITIES: Established 50 years, Angus Dundee is a blending and bottling company owned and managed by three generations of the Hillman family. The acquisition of Tomintoul was the company's first venture into distilling. Glencadam was acquired in 2003.

Always a sweet and typical Speyside style, Angus Dundee immediately began to experiment with peated malt. The first fruit of this is the young and pungent Old Ballantruan, named after the distillery's water source.

EXPRESSIONS:
First bottled as a single in 1974. Since Angus Dundee acquired the distillery they have released:
• Tomintoul 10YO @ 40% (in 2002)
• Tomintoul 16YO @ 40% (in 2003)
• Tomintoul 27YO @ 40% (in 2004)
• Old Ballantruan N/A (no age) @ 50% (in 2005, a peaty malt distilled in 2001)
• Tomintoul 1976 23YO decanter (bottled 2000)
• Tomintoul 12YO @ 40% (from ex-Oloroso wood, limited edition released 2007)

RAW MATERIALS: Water from Ballantruan Spring. Malt from independent maltsters, usually unpeated.

PLANT: Semi-Lauter mash tun (11.6 tonnes). Six stainless steel washbacks. Two boil-ball wash stills (15,000 litres charge); two boil-ball spirit stills (9,000 litres charge). All indirect fired by steam. Shell-and-tube condensers, one a multi-pass to create hot water for the evaporator.

Tomintoul (pronounced 'Tomintowel') is familiar to U.K. radio listeners for usually being the first village to be cut off by snow!

MATURATION: Mainly refill hogsheads; some first-fill and some Oloroso sherry butts. Six high racked warehouses on site (holding 114,000 casks in total). Many other sites used.

STYLE: Light, fragrant, floral, fruity. Speyside, now also with a peaty variant.

MATURE CHARACTER: The bottle describes Tomintoul as 'The Gentle Dram'. The style is light and delicate; the nose grassy, perfumed, lemony; the taste sweet, with breakfast cereal and nuts and a shortish finish. Light-bodied.

Tormore

REGION
Speyside

ADDRESS
Advie, Grantown-on-Spey,
Moray

PHONE
01807 510244

WEBSITE
www.tormore.com

OWNER
Chivas Brothers

VISITORS
By appointment

CAPACITY
3.7m L.P.A.

HISTORICAL NOTES: Tormore was one of several distilleries built to satisfy the post-World War II thirst for whisky, and the first to be raised from scratch on a greenfield site. It was built between 1958 and 1960 by Schenley International, U.S. agents for Dewar's, which had bought Seager Evans in 1956 (owner of Long John) and the Black Bottle blend in 1959.

The design for the distillery was commissioned from Sir Albert Richardson, past President of the Royal Academy. A contemporary described it as 'a masterpiece of distillery architecture' and whisky writer Michael Jackson compared it to 'a spa offering a mountain-water cure'!

In 1972 capacity was doubled (to eight stills), and three years later Schenley sold out to Whitbread. Whitbread's spirits division was in turn acquired by Allied Lyons in 1989, and Allied bought by Pernod Ricard/Chivas Brothers in 2005.

CURIOSITIES: As late as 1983, Tormore was being labelled and promoted as The Tormore-Glenlivet: the Glenlivet appellation was still deemed to be a guarantee of quality, although most of the 28 distilleries which once adopted the suffix had by then dropped it.

The neat lawns in front of the main building are decorated with bushes clipped into a topiary of still-shapes. All but three of the smart white houses that surround the distillery, which were built for distillery workers, are now owned privately.

The conspicious distillery clock is programmed to play four different tunes per hour. Broken for many years, it was restored to life in 2007.

EXPRESSIONS:
Tormore was being promoted in North America by the early 1980s, and in 1991 Allied introduced its Caledonian Malts range (Miltonduff, Glendronach, Laphroaig and Tormore – the latter later replaced by Scapa). Previous proprietary bottlings were at 5, 10 and 15 years. Currently the official bottling is:
• Tormore 12 years old @ 40% (introduced 2004)

'Nothing but the land endures, and from its heart springs forth The Tormore'
Early 1980s promotional booklet

RAW MATERIALS: Unpeated malt from independent maltsters. Soft water from Achvockie Burn.

PLANT: Full-Lauter mash tun (10.4 tonnes); eight stainless steel washbacks. Four plain wash stills (11,000 litres charge); four plain spirit stills (7,500 litres charge). All fitted with purifiers. All indirect fired (steam heated by oil). Shell-and-tube condensers.

MATURATION: Mainly refill U.S. hogsheads; some first-fill.

STYLE: Sweet, fruity and estery.

MATURE CHARACTER: Tormore's label describes it as 'The Pearl of Strathspey'; reflecting the whisky's 'brilliant appearance and honouring the freshwater pearl mussels flourishing in the pure clean waters of the River Spey'.

A firm Speyside character with a malty, nutty (almonds, coconuts) nose. A pleasant, smooth texture and a sweet, honeyed taste, drying in the relatively short finish. Medium-bodied.

Tu

Tullibardine

REGION
Highland (South)

ADDRESS
Blackford, by Auchterarder, Perthshire

PHONE
01764 682252

WEBSITE
www.tullibardine.com

OWNER
Tullibardine Distillery Ltd

VISITORS
Visitor centre, restaurant and sizable retail park

CAPACITY
2.7m L.P.A.

HISTORICAL NOTES: The distillery was designed and built by William Delmé-Evans in 1949 (the first 'stand alone' distillery – that is, not within another distillery – to be built since 1900, presaging the boom of the 1950s and 1960s). He went on to design Jura and Glenallachie distilleries.

It was sold to Brodie Hepburn (whisky blenders in Glasgow) in 1953, and passed to Invergordon in 1971 (expanded to four stills in 1973/4), then to Whyte & Mackay when they bought Invergordon in 1993 (who mothballed it the next year).

In 2003 a consortium of whisky men bought the distillery and resumed production, having appointed the highly experienced John Black as Manager, and devised a cunning scheme to develop part of the site as an up-market retail centre – Tullibardine stands beside the main road from Glasgow to the Highlands (the A9).

CURIOSITIES: Reviving the distillery was only possible if the adjacent ground could be turned into a retail park. The consortium took an option to buy, dependent upon obtaining planning permission and finding a key tenant (which turned out to be Baxter's of Speyside). Once this had been achieved, and other tenants found, the whole retail site was sold to Kenmore, a leading property developer. This raised the money to start production. Current running costs are around £100,000 per month.

Scotland's most famous hotel, Gleneagles, is a neighbour. The first 'country club' hotel in the U.K., it was completed in 1924 and retains an old-fashioned charm, for all its state-of-the-art luxury, including the best restaurant in Scotland and comprehensive sporting facilities (including four golf courses).

EXPRESSIONS:
Small amounts of Tullibardine were bottled at 10YO by Invergordon and its successor, but never promoted. The new owner has released a number of single cask bottlings each year, at natural strength, including casks from 1964, 1965, 1966,

Blackford, where Tullibardine Distillery is located, has been famous for its water for hundreds of years. The local brewery produced an ale for the coronation of King James IV in 1488, and today the famous Highland Spring water is bottled there.

1968 and 1975. The core range comprises:
- Tullibardine 1993 @ 40% (since 2004)
- Tullibardine 1992 @ 46% (non chill-filtered, predominantly first-fill ex-bourbon casks)
- Tullibardine 1988 @ 46% (non chill-filtered, predominantly ex-sherry casks)
Also a wood-finished range @ 46%, mainly from 1993: currently port-wood, Marsala-wood, sherry-wood, Moscatel-wood, Sauternes-wood, rum-wood.
- John Black 10YO blended malt @ 46% (peated style, introduced 2008)
- John Black 8YO blended malt @ 46% (honeyed style, introduced 2008)

RAW MATERIALS: Soft water from the Danny Burn, with its source in the Ochil Hills, where the brewery water came from. Unpeated malt from Greencore Maltings, Carnoustie.

PLANT: Stainless steel full-Lauter mash tun with a peaked canopy (six tonnes), nine stainless steel washbacks. Two plain wash stills (15,000 litres charge) and two lamp-glass spirit stills (11,000 litres charge). All indirect fired. Shell-and-tube condensers.

MATURATION: Predominantly ex-bourbon barrels, with some Oloroso sherry and Pedro Ximinez hogsheads and butts. Racked warehouse on site.

STYLE: Sweet, fruity and malty.

MATURE CHARACTER: Tullibardine is remarkably consistent in its make. The key flavour is malt, balanced by a zesty fruitiness. The nose is all of this, and some peach and melon notes. The taste is sweet to start, then drying, with biscuits and light caramel in the middle. Medium-bodied.

Facts and Figures

DUNCAN TAYLOR

UNIQUE WHISKIES OF DISTINCTION

Who Owns Whom?

Including a brief account of recent changes in ownership. (Earlier histories appear under individual entries.)

BEAM GLOBAL SPIRITS & WINE (FORTUNE BRANDS)

Beam Global is the latest incarnation of the owners of Jim Beam (the world's bestselling bourbon), itself owned since 1969 by the holding company, American Brands (now Fortune Brands). Jim Beam bought Whyte & Mackay in 1990, changed its name to J.B.B. (Greater Europe) in 1996 and sold to a management buy-out in 2001, when the name changed again to Kyndal Spirits.

Fortune Brands re-entered the Scotch whisky industry with the surprise purchase of William Teacher & Sons and its associated distilleries when Allied Domecq was broken up in 2005 (see Chivas Brothers below).

Malt distilleries: Ardmore, Laphroaig

BEN NEVIS DISTILLERY LTD (NIKKA, ASAHI BREWERIES)

Malt distilleries: Ben Nevis

BENRIACH DISTILLERS LTD

Malt distilleries: BenRiach, Glendronach

BLADNOCH DISTILLERY LTD

Malt distilleries: Bladnoch

BRUICHLADDICH DISTILLERY LTD

Malt distilleries: Bruichladdich, Port Charlotte (proposed)

BURN STEWART DISTILLERS PLC (C.L. WORLD BRANDS)

Burn Stewart was acquired in 2002 by Trinidad-based C.L. World Brands, owners of Angostura Bitters, Hine Cognac and Rhum Rum.

Malt distilleries: Deanston, Tobermory, Bunnahabhain

CHIVAS BROTHERS LTD (PERNOD RICARD)

Owned by Pernod Ricard since 2001, Chivas Brothers had been owned by the Canadian distilling giant Seagram since 1949. Seagram bought Strathisla Distillery the next year and built Glen Keith in 1957, Braeval in 1973 and Allt-a-Bhainne in 1975. In 1978, The Seagram Company acquired The Glenlivet Distillers (owning The Glenlivet, Glen Grant, Caperdonich, Longmorn and BenRiach Distilleries), but decided to divest itself of its massive interest in alcoholic beverages in 2001, when its assets were divided between Pernod Ricard and Diageo.

In 2005, Pernod Ricard went on to acquire the majority of Allied Domecq's distilleries (Glenburgie, Glentauchers, Imperial, Miltonduff, Tormore, Scapa) and its leading blended whisky, Ballantine's, selling Glen Grant to satisfy the Monopolies and Mergers Commission.

Until these developments, Pernod Ricard had been a small player in the Scotch whisky industry, through its subsidiary Campbell Distillers (owning Aberlour, Glenallachie and Edradour Distilleries – the latter later sold). Now it is the second largest distiller in the world.

Grain distilleries: Strathclyde

Malt distilleries: Aberlour, Allt-a-Bhainne, Braeval, Caperdonich, Glenburgie, Glenallachie, Glen Keith, The Glenlivet, Glentauchers, Imperial, Miltonduff, Longmorn, Tormore, Scapa, Strathisla

JOHN DEWAR & SONS LTD (BACARDI PLC)

Bacardi, the family-owned rum distiller, entered the Scotch whisky industry when it bought William Lawson Distillers Ltd and Macduff Distillery in 1992.

When Grand Metropolitan (Independent Distillers & Vintners) merged with Guinness (United Distillers) in 1997, the Monopolies and Mergers Commission insisted that they divest themselves of a major brand. As a result, John Dewar & Sons, together with five distilleries, was sold to Bacardi.

Malt distilleries: Aberfeldy, Aultmore, Craigellachie, Macduff, Royal Brackla

ANGUS DUNDEE LTD

Malt distilleries: Glencadam, Tomintoul

DIAGEO PLC

Diageo was formed as a holding company in 1998, following the merger of Grand Metropolitan and Guinness the previous year, with United Distillers & Vintners (U.D.V.) as its alcoholic beverages subsidiary, combining the previous operational divisions, United Distillers (U.D.) and International Distillers & Vintners (I.D.V.). The name 'Diageo' comes from 'dia' (Latin for 'day') and 'geo' (Greek for 'world'), suggesting that the company's brands are sold everyday, all over the world. In 2000, the corporate structure was simplified, so that U.D.V. was replaced by Diageo as the trading entity, and in 2002 U.D.V. ceased to exist.

United Distillers came about in 1987, following the acquisition by Guinness of the leading Scotch whisky company, The Distillers Company Limited (D.C.L.).

Grain distilleries: Cameronbridge, Port Dundas, 50% of North British

Malt distilleries: Auchroisk, Benrinnes, Blair Athol, Caol Isla, Cardow, Clynelish, Cragganmore, Dailuaine, Dalwhinnie, Dufftown, Glendullan, Glen Elgin, Glenkinchie, Glenlossie, Glen Ord, Glen Spey, Inchgower, Knockando, Lagavulin, Linkwood, Mannochmore, Mortlach, Oban, Roseisle (proposed), Royal Lochnagar, Strathmill, Talisker, Teaninich

THE EDRINGTON GROUP LTD

Another name change! Edrington was formerly called Highland Distilleries (established 1887) – this became a public limited company in 1982, then withdrew from public listing in 1998, when the name was altered to Highland Distillers Ltd. The company had always been closely associated with Robertson & Baxter (Glasgow whisky brokers and blenders, established 1861). In 1944, ownership of R.&B. (and the complex relationship with Highland) passed to the three grand-daughters of the founder. To avoid punitive death duties and secure the independence of the firm, in 1961 the sisters transferred all their capital to a holding company, Edrington Ltd (named after a family farm in Berwickshire), then gifted the shares they received in exchange to a charitable trust, The Robertson Trust – now one of Scotland's leading charitable institutions. Edrington Ltd became The Edrington Group in 1999, when it took over Highland Distillers Ltd.

Grain distilleries: 50% of North British

Malt distilleries: Glenrothes, Glenturret, Highland Park, 70% of The Macallan, Tamdhu

THE GLENGLASSAUGH DISTILLERY COMPANY LTD (THE SCAENT GROUP)

Malt distilleries: Glenglassaugh

THE GLENMORANGIE COMPANY (LOUIS VUITTON MOËT HENNESSY)

Glenmorangie Distillery was gradually acquired by its largest customer, Macdonald & Muir, blenders in Leith (established 1893) between 1918 and 1930. By the late 1990s M. & M. had adopted the name of their acquisition, and Glenmorangie had become a public company.

This was bought by the French luxury goods company, Louis Vuitton Moët Hennessy (L.V.M.H.) in 2004, and taken out of public ownership.

Malt distilleries: Ardbeg, Glenmorangie, Glen Moray

GORDON & MACPHAIL
Malt distilleries: Benromach

J. & G. GRANT
Malt distilleries: Glenfarclas

WILLIAM GRANT & SONS LTD
Grain distilleries: Girvan
Malt distilleries: Ailsa Bay, Balvenie, Kininvie, Glenfiddich

HUNTLY DISTILLERY COMPANY LTD
Malt distilleries: Huntly (proposed)

INVER HOUSE DISTILLERS LTD (INTERBEV)
Inver House was founded in 1964 as a subsidiary of the American company Publicker Industries, and was bought out by its Directors in 1988. In 2001 Inver House Distillers Ltd was bought by Pacific Spirits, a subsidiary of ThaiBev plc, Southeast Asia's largest alcoholic beverage company, and integrated into that company's international division, International Beverage Holdings Ltd (InterBev) in 2006.

Malt distilleries: Balblair, Balmenach, Knockdhu, Pulteney, Speyburn

ISLE OF ARRAN DISTILLERS LTD
Malt distilleries: Isle of Arran

KILCHOMAN DISTILLERY COMPANY LTD
Malt distilleries: Kilchoman

LOCH LOMOND DISTILLERY LTD
Grain distilleries: Loch Lomond
Malt distilleries: Glen Scotia, Loch Lomond

IAN MACLEOD & COMPANY LTD
Malt distilleries: Glengoyne

J. & A. MITCHELL
Malt distilleries: Springbank, Glengyle

MORRISON BOWMORE DISTILLERS LTD (SUNTORY)
Malt distilleries: Auchentoshan, Bowmore, Glen Garioch

SPEYSIDE DISTILLERY LTD
Malt distilleries: Speyside

TOMATIN DISTILLERY COMPANY LTD (TAKARA & OKURA)

Malt distilleries: Tomatin

TULLIBARDINE DISTILLERY COMPANY LTD

Malt distilleries: Tullibardine

WHYTE & MACKAY LTD (UNITED BREWERIES GROUP)

In 1881, James Whyte and Charles Mackay bought the wine and spirits company they had been working for, Allan & Poynter of Glasgow (established 1843). One of the conditions of sale was a change of name. The company was acquired by Sir Hugh Fraser's S.U.I.T.S. group in 1971, which was acquired by L.O.N.H.R.O. ten years later. W. & M. was sold to Brent Walker in 1988, then, in 1990, to American Brands (which became Fortune Brands – see Beam Global above). In 2001, Vivien Immerman led a management buy-out, backed by a German bank; four years later he bought out the bank, and in 2007 sold the company to the United Spirits Division of the United Breweries Group, the largest brewer and distiller in India.

Grain distilleries: Invergordon

Malt distilleries: Dalmore, Fettercairn, Isle of Jura, Tamnavulin

Top Ten Single Malts 2007

Glenfiddich 927,000
The Glenlivet 613,000
The Macallan 570,000
Glenmorangie 330,000
Glen Grant 312,175
Cardhu 251,000
Aberlour 200,000
Laphroaig 175,000
Balvenie 173,000
Bowmore 130,000

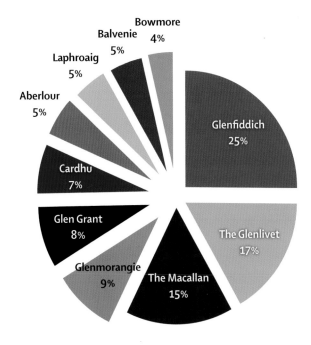

Source: *The Scotch Whisky Industry Review 2008* by Alan Gray, Sutherlands, Edinburgh

World Consumption of Bottled Malt Whisky 2000–2007

2000 15,470,000 (litres of pure alcohol)
2001 14,550,000
2002 16,030,000
2003 16,950,000
2004 18,960,000
2005 20,500,000
2006 24,480,000
2007 23,170,000

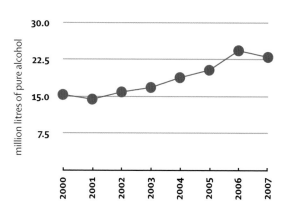

Source: *The Scotch Whisky Industry Review 2008* by Alan Gray, Sutherlands, Edinburgh

Major Consumers of
Bottled Malt Whisky 2007

France 48,000,000 (litres of pure alcohol)

U.S.A. 34,000,000

Spain 33,000,000

U.K. 29,000,000

Singapore 13,000,000

South Africa 12,000,000

Venezuela 12,000,000

South Korea 11,000,000

Thailand 11,000,000

Germany 11,000,000

Germany
5%

Thailand
5%

South Korea
5%

Venezuela
6%

South Africa
6%

Singapore
6%

France
22%

USA
16%

Spain
15%

UK
14%

Source: *The Scotch Whisky Industry Review 2008* by Alan Gray, Sutherlands, Edinburgh

Leading Independent Bottlers

The 18 companies listed below are probably the best known of the independents. All are based in the U.K. I have not listed those which are principally distillers and blenders (like Ian Macleod & Company and Angus Dundee & Company).

This article first appeared in 'The Malt Whisky Yearbook 2008' (MagDig Media). As well as a thumbnail sketch of each company, Ingvar Ronde, the editor of the publication, asked me to enquire of some of the leading firms how they viewed the future for independent bottlers.

ADELPHI DISTILLERY

The Adelphi Distillery stood in the Gorbals district of Glasgow, on the site of what is now the Glasgow mosque. It was one of the largest whisky distilleries in Scotland, with both pot and patent stills. It ceased production in 1902, although the warehouses continued to be used until the 1960s.

The name was revived in 1992 by the great-grandson of the last owner, Jamie Walker, who had served an apprenticeship with Inver House Distillers and who established his company as an independent bottler of single cask single malts. He sold to two lairds from Argyllshire, who recruited Alex Bruce from the wine trade (formerly Justerini & Brooks) to act as Marketing Director. The company bottles around 50 casks a year.

'Yes, buying casks at their optimum maturity is becoming harder, especially when we are only selecting the top 5–10% of those on offer.

However, by cementing good supply relationships, and implementing a flexible approach to labelling, wood management, and future diversification, we firmly believe we can continue to offer an exceptional range of single cask bottlings to our customers and, at the same time, promote the quality and vast spectrum of Scotch Whisky as a whole. We are, if you like, an ambassador for the industry, a role that the independent bottler both is able, and can be proud, to perform.'

Alex Bruce, Marketing Director

BERRY BROTHERS & RUDD

The company traces its origins to 1698, and its venerable shop occupies the same site, although it was rebuilt in 1734. Like many whisky companies, the firm began as general grocers. By the 1820s it was listing wines and spirits, and storing its own casks, and during the latter half of the nineteenth century, the firm concentrated increasingly on this side of the business, allowing the grocery side to dwindle.

Berry Brothers' entry into the wider world of whisky came in 1923, with the introduction of Cutty Sark. Arising out of this, the firm also acquired the exclusive right to the Glenrothes brand name, although the distillery continued to be owned by Highland (now Edrington). Berry Brothers continued to offer its own malts, but only to private customers until 2002, when it was resolved to lay down more casks and expand the Berry's Own Selection range. Doug McIvor was appointed Spirits Manager: his and the company's guiding policy is simple: 'We only bottle what we enjoy drinking ourselves.'

Currently Berry Brothers offer between 25 and 30 expressions.

'We've been bottling whisky for over a hundred years and we hope still to be offering our customers a diverse selection of single malts a hundred years from now.'
Doug McIvor, Spirits Manager

BLACKADDER INTERNATIONAL

Blackadder was established in 1995 by John Lamond and Robin Tucek (authors of the much reprinted *The Malt Whisky File*, 1995). Robin now runs the business from Sweden, where he lives. He bottles around 100 casks of malt whisky a year in his Raw Cask, Aberdeen Distillers, Clydesdale Original and Caledonian Connections ranges. None of his whiskies is chill-filtered or coloured; many are bottled at cask strength. They are sold through specialist shops and bars in Europe, Japan and North America.

WILLIAM CADENHEAD & COMPANY

Established in Aberdeen in 1842, Cadenhead's is Scotland's oldest firm of independent bottlers. William Cadenhead, brother-in-law of the founder, who took over the business in 1858, was himself a well-known poet. The business remained in his family until 1972, when it was bought by J. & A. Mitchell, owners of Springbank and Glengyle Distilleries. It is now based in Campbeltown, with shops in Edinburgh's Old Town and in Covent Garden, London. Bottlings are at both standard and natural strength; the whisky is non chill-filtered and un-tinted. Cadenhead's offers a range of Scotch malts and also bottles non-Scotch whiskies, rums, cognacs and gins.

COMPASS BOX WHISKY COMPANY

Compass Box was founded in 2000 by former Diageo Marketing Director (Premium Malts), John Glaser. His goal is summed up by the firm's website description: 'Creators of hand-crafted, small batch Scotch whiskies in distinctive and original styles.'

Winner of *Whisky Magazine*'s Innovator of the Year award so many times it is embarrassing, passionate and idiosyncratic, Compass Box offers a beautifully crafted and packaged range of blended malts (mostly using only two malts), single grains, blended whiskies and an orange-infused whisky. The company also has an excellent website at www.compassboxwhisky.com.

'First, the company's essence is to explore new flavours and create new whiskies, so we are more flexible than traditional independent bottlers of single malts. Second, we don't purvey single malts by name, and I think this will make it easier for us to obtain quality whisky as producers become more concerned with guarding their trademarks.'
John Glaser, Managing Director

DEWAR RATTRAY

Founded by Andrew Dewar and William Rattray in 1868, A. Dewar Rattray began trading as an importer of French wines, Italian spirits and olive oil. By the end of the century, the firm was representing a number of well-known Highland malt distilleries – most notably Stronachie.

In 2004, the company was revived by Tim Morrison, previously of Morrison Bowmore Distillers and fourth generation descendent of Andrew Dewar, with a view to bottling single cask malts from different regions in Scotland.

GORDON & MACPHAIL

Established by James Gordon and John Alexander MacPhail in 1895, in the same Elgin premises it occupies today. James Gordon had already completed an apprenticeship in selecting and blending teas, wine and whisky, and from the outset he was responsible for buying casks from neighbouring distilleries. Within a year, he was joined by John Urquhart.

G. & M. have been filling their own casks since 1900, and in 1956, when John Urquhart's son, George, became Senior Partner, he took the unprecedented step of launching a range of single malts under the Connoisseurs' Choice label. Within a few years he was offering these malts for sale in Italy and France – a pioneering step.

Just as he had joined his father, so George was joined by his own children – Ian, David, Michael and Rosemary. By 1991 the firm had a staff of over 100 and new administrative offices were built adjacent to their bonded warehouses on Boroughbriggs Road, Elgin. In 1993 George realised a lifetime's ambition: to own a distillery. He bought Benromach, spent five years refurbishing and returned it to production in 1998.

George Urquhart died in 2002, but the company he developed from a small local business to global status remains a family concern, under the capable management of his children and grand-children.

G. & M. list over 300 own bottlings (mainly at 40%, some at 43%, some at cask strength) and hold a stock of over 800 whiskies (including blends) in their shop.

'Our relationship with distilleries goes back over 100 years, and since we fill our own casks, we can ensure quality, and don't have to buy from brokers. As well as young stock, we hold stocks of mature whisky going back to the 1930s – enough to look after our needs for the foreseeable future!'
Ian Chapman, **Marketing Director**

HART BROTHERS

A family business established in the 1980s by Alistair Hart (a former blender with Whyte & Mackay) and his brother Donald, who have now been joined by their sons Jonathan and Andrew. The firm specialises in single cask single malt bottling, and their selection guideline is simple: the whisky must please Alistair Hart.

INVERARITY VAULTS

Established by Hamish Martin in 1994, with the assistance of his father Ronnie Martin, former Director of Production with United Distillers, Inverarity bottles its own malts (from Speyside at 10 and 14YO – the latter won a gold medal at the I.W.S.C. 1999 – and Islay at 10YO). The company also has its own blend (created by Ronnie Martin), offers a wide selection of directly imported wines and has the U.K. agency for Champagne Ruinart.

DOUGLAS LAING & COMPANY LTD

Founded in 1948 and managed by the sons of the founder, Fred and Stewart Laing, the company offers a range of single malts and blended whiskies and trades internationally.

Fred and Stewart are familiar friendly faces at whisky fairs around the world. In the 25 years that they have controlled the family firm, they have greatly expanded the business, notably into single cask bottlings from their large stock of casks, built up over the past 50 years. Their reliable Old Malt Cask range was introduced in 1998 – bottled without chill-filtration or tinting, usually at 50% – and now lists around 100 malts. A super deluxe range, Old & Rare, was later introduced, with single casks of exceptional quality being bottled at cask strength and presented in fancy wooden chests.

'Remember, we come from a blending background, specialising in super-premium blends for Far East markets. We came into the single malt category when that market dipped in the late 1990s, to accommodate stock surpluses. We still have a large reserve of mature stock – much of it built up by our ongoing fillings programmes – enough to support our blending and single malt requirements, with stock left over for exchanges.'
Fred Laing, Managing Director

JAMES MACARTHUR & COMPANY LTD

Founded in 1982 'with the aim of selecting whiskies from Scottish Distilleries which were not well-known or had ceased to operate and bottling them at cask strength', according to their website. Sounds familiar, but 1982 was relatively early to have such ambitions. The company currently lists 30 single cask, cask strength malts.

MURRAY MCDAVID

Mark Reynier, Gordon Wright and Simon Coughlin established Murray McDavid (the name comes from two of Mark's grandparents) in 1995. The firm offers a narrow, highly selective range, with around 25 expressions at any one time. Unlike most independents, their bottlings are vattings of four or five casks (same distillery, same age, at 46%, without chill-filtration or tinting and all bottled on Islay and reduced with Islay water), in order to achieve both consistency and complexity. Divided into three categories: the Mission Range (unusual aged stock), the Celtic Heartlands range (old stock from the 1960s) and the Murray McDavid range. The latter employs a unique A.C.E. (Additional Cask Evolution) programme, which Mark Reynier describes as 'an exploration of the attributes of French oak combined with American oak'.

Joined by James McEwan, Mark Reynier bought Bruichladdich Distillery in 2000.

*'I foresee a split amongst independent bottlers into the
few who can still offer old mature whisky of high quality,
those who will be obliged to offer younger whiskies (some
of which may well be of inferior quality) and those who
experiment and offer interesting new flavours, derived
from the wood. While we will continue to offer first-rate
old- and medium-aged single bottlings, we are exploring
the latter. As ever, we have a number of ideas in the pipe-
line ... Watch this space!'*

Mark Reynier, Managing Director

SCOTCH MALT WHISKY SOCIETY

The Scotch Malt Whisky Society is a club, established
in 1983, and makes its single cask bottlings available
to its members at full-strength, without chill-filtration
or tinting. It has its base in Leith, Edinburgh, in the
oldest commercial building in Scotland, the ancient
Vaults, with branch clubhouses at Queen Street,
Edinburgh, and in Hatton Garden, London, and
franchised branches in Australia, Austria, France, Italy,
Japan, Netherlands, Belgium, Luxembourg, Sweden,
Switzerland and the U.S.A. The Society was taken over
by Glenmorangie in 2003, on the recommendation
of its Board of Directors, in order to secure supplies
of mature malt whisky, but remains a separate entity.
Currently it bottles 150–200 casks per annum.

*'Because we are part of the Glenmorangie Company, the
Scotch Malt Whisky Society continues to be in a good
position to secure a wide variety of interesting malts in
the years to come.'*

Kai Ivalo, Director

SCOTT'S SELECTION

The eponymous Robert Scott worked in distilleries for
50 years, finishing as Manager of Bladnoch and then
Speyside Distilleries. On his retirement in 2001, he was
persuaded by George Christie, Chairman of Speyside, to
put his huge experience of evaluating whisky to good
use by selecting and bottling (at cask strength, without

chill-filtration or tinting) a range of single casks. The casks are selected by him and the current Speyside Manager, Andrew Shand, and marketed by Speyside in 30-odd countries. Currently the list includes around 30 single malts, single grains and one single blend (1964) from Lochside Distillery.

Recently, Speyside also introduced a Private Cellar range to Sweden (currently around 20 expressions, bottled at 43%, chill-filtered and tinted, to accommodate the complexities of the state monopoly regulations).

SIGNATORY VINTAGE SCOTCH WHISKY COMPANY

Based in Leith, the Port of Edinburgh, and founded in 1998 by Andrew and Brian Symington, Signatory lists some 50 single malts from operating, mothballed and closed distilleries, which they bottle themselves at natural strength and at 43%. Andrew Symington bought Edradour Distillery from Pernod Ricard in 2002.

'*The tree will be severely shaken, and a lot of dead wood will drop out. I realised this some years ago and invested heavily in mature whisky. As a result we have considerable stocks to use ourselves or swap with producers – certainly enough to cover ourselves for the next decade.*'
Andrew Symington, Managing Director

DUNCAN TAYLOR & COMPANY

Duncan Taylor & Company began as whisky brokers and blenders in Glasgow in 1938, with a focus on exporting their own blended whiskies to the U.S.A. They have been filling their own casks and laying down whiskies since the 1960s, and when Euan Shand bought the company and its stocks in 2001, he acquired 'one of the largest privately held collections of rare Scotch whisky casks in the world'. Operations were moved to Huntly, Aberdeenshire, where the company also bottles its whiskies. The range includes Rarest of the Rare (single cask, cask strength whiskies of great age from demolished distilleries), Duncan Taylor Collection (single cask, cask strength malts and grains aged 17–42 years), N.C.2 (mainly single casks, 12–17 years, non chill-filtered at 46%), Battlehill (younger malts at 43%), Lonach (vattings of two casks from same distillery at same age (usually over 30 years to bring them up to a natural strength of over 40%), Big Smoke (Islay whiskies at 40% and 60%). The company has won three out of eight *Whisky Magazine* Independent Bottler of the Year Awards.

Duncan Taylor obtained planning permission to build a new distillery in Huntly in May 2007.

'Sure, if the producers refuse to sell us new fillings, it will be difficult to operate as an independent bottler. Having said this, we have bought a lot of mature whisky over the past few years, and we have maturing stock sufficient to last many years.'
Euan Shand, Managing Director

THE VINTAGE MALT WHISKY COMPANY

An independent family company established in 1992 by Brian Crook, formerly Export Sales Manager with Morrison Bowmore, Vintage Malt offers a small range of single malts under its own names – Finlaggan, Tantallan, Glenalmond etc. – and some under the distillery's own name in the Cooper's Choice Range.

WILSON & MORGAN LTD

One of the few non-Scottish independent bottlers of single cask malt Scotch, Wilson & Morgan was founded in 1992 by Fabio Rossi, whose family firm (wine and olive oil merchants in Venice and later Treviso) had been involved with importing Scotch since the 1960s. The foundations of his stock were laid in the early 1990s, when he toured Scotland for the first time, laying down casks, following his own guidelines for selection: trust your palate and your instinct. Many of his single casks malts offered in his Barrel Selection range are wine-finished; they are bottled at 46% and cask strength, without chill-filtration or tinting.

THE WHISKY DISTILLERIES

OF THE

UNITED KINGDOM

THE MANUFACTURE
OF
WHISKY AND PLAIN SPIRIT.

J M Nettleton

Sources and Acknowledgements

PUBLICATIONS

The first person to write in detail about the distilleries of Scotland was Alfred Barnard in *The Whisky Distilleries of the United Kingdom* (Harpers, 1887). His book was reprinted by David & Charles in 1969 and 1987 (the latter with an introduction by Professor Michael Moss), and by Birlinn Ltd, Edinburgh, in 2003 (with an introduction by Richard Joynson). This substantial, engaging book is the bible of 'distillery baggers'.

In 1987, the centenary of Barnard's magisterial publication and a time when the whisky industry was in some difficulties, the original publisher commissioned a contemporary version from Philip Morrice (author of the useful *Schweppes Guide to Scotch*): *The Whisky Distilleries of Scotland and Ireland* (Harpers, 1987). Before this appeared Brian Spiller, the Distillers Company archivist, had written short and scholarly accounts of that company's 50 distilleries, published as individual pamphlets (*D.C.L. Distillery History Series*, 1981–83).

Among more recent publications, I was glad to have Misako Udo's *The Scottish Whisky Distilleries* (Black & White Publishing, Edinburgh, 2006) to hand, and the invaluable *Malt Whisky Yearbook 2008* (edited by Invar Ronde, Magdig Media, Shrewsbury, 2007). Gordon & Macphail's *Distillery Profiles* in their periodical *Scotch Whisky News* were useful, as was Ulf Buxrud's *Rare Malts* (Quiller Press, London, 2006) in relation to Diageo's distilleries.

Many monographs about individual distilleries have been published over the years, usually by the distillery's owner. Some are now long out of print; some are more about marketing than history, but some are excellent – I would single out for special praise *The Legend of Laphroaig* by Hans Offringa and Marcel van Gils (Still Publishing, Netherlands, 2007) and *The Island Whisky Trail* by Neil Wilson (NWP, Glasgow, 2003).

By and large, information from the Internet was shallow and unreliable.

In regard to historical overviews, *The Making of Scotch Whisky* by Michael S. Moss (mentioned above) and John Hume (James & James, Edinburgh, 1981) is always on my desk, as is H. Charles Craig's seminal *The Scotch Whisky Industry Record* (Index Publishing, Dumbarton, 1994). I have to admit to consulting my own *Scotch Whisky: A Liquid History* (Cassell, London, 2003) from time to time as well. I owe a special debt to Dr Nicholas Morgan, scholar and sceptic, for many hours of conversation and access to Diageo's extensive archive.

For information about production and maturation I am more indebted to individuals than books, and would particularly like to thank Dr Jim Swan, Dr Douglas Murray, Dr Jim Beveridge, Dr Bill Lumsden, Neil Cochrane, Andrew Ford, Paul Lockyer and Philip Murray. The leading current text on the subject is *Whisky: Technology, Production and Marketing* (edited by Inge Russell, Academic Press, London, 2003). *The Science and Technology of Whiskies* (edited by J.R. Piggott, R. Sharp and R.E.B. Duncan, Longman, Harlow, 1989) is an interesting milestone between Inge Russell's book and J.A. Nettleton's *The Manufacture of Whisky and Plain Spirit* (Aberdeen, 1913), which was long the bible for distillers. Nettleton was to production what Barnard was to whisky tourism, which brings us full circle.

PEOPLE

As always, friends in the whisky industry have been generous with their time and information, and I am immensely grateful to them. I would particularly like to acknowledge those who checked my text and supplied me with information: Alasdair Anderson (Tamdhu); Russell Anderson (Highland Park); Raymond Armstrong (Bladnoch); Iain Baxter (Inver House); Michael Beamish (Tullibardine); Marcel Bol (Whisky Import Nederland); Johan van Boxmeer (The Old Pipe, St Oedenrode); Carol Brown (Edrington Group); Graham Brown (Tobermory); Steven Burnett (Macduff); Neil Cameron

(Glenturret); Douglas Campbell (Tomatin); John
Campbell (Laphroaig); Graham Coull (Glen Moray);
David Cox (Macallan); Ronnie Cox (Glenrothes); Jason
Craig (Highland Park); Katherine Crisp (Burn Stewart);
Francis Cuthbert (Daftmill); Bob Dalgarno (Macallan);
David Doig (Fettercairn and Tamnavulin); Gavin
Durnin (Loch Lomond); Douglas Fitchett (Glencadam);
Callum Fraser (Deanston); Tom Garioch (Tomintoul);
Hector Gatt (Glen Scotia); Peter Gordon (Wm Grant
& Sons); Donald Graham (Royal Brackla); Micky
Heads (Ardbeg); Robbie Hughes (Glengoyne); David
Hume (Wm Grant & Sons); Jan Kok (Whisky Import
Nederland); Lothar Lange (Whisky-Raritäten); Alastair
Longwell (Ardmore); Bill Lumsden (Glenmorangie);
Graham Macwilliam (Edrington Group); Des
McCagherty (Edradour); Alan McConnochie
(BenRiach); Jim McCowan (Cameronbridge);
John McLennan (Bunnahabhain); Ian McWilliam
(Glenfarclas); Ian Mackie (Whyte & Mackay); Stephen
Marshall (John Dewar & Sons); Euan Mitchell (Isle
of Arran); Alastair Murphy (North British); Marcin
Miller (Glenrothes); Stephanie Mingam (Chivas
Brothers); Douglas Murray (Diageo); Karen Murray
(Auchentoshan); Stuart Nickerson (Glenglassaugh);
Pauline Ogilvy (Glenmorangie); John Peterson (Loch
Lomond); Stuart Pirie (Scapa); Robert Ransome
(Glenfarclas); Mark Reynier (Bruichladdich); Stuart
Robertson (Springbank); Colin Ross (Ben Nevis); Jacqui
Seargeant (Bacardi); Graham Sewell (Cameronbridge);
Andrew Shand (Speyside); Euan Shand (Huntly); Greg
Stables (Glen Grant); David Stewart (Wm Grant &
Sons); Andrew Symington (Edradour); Alexander
Tweedie (Macallan); Billy Walker (BenRiach); Karen
Walker (Inver House); Anthony Wills (Kilchoman); Alan
Winchester (Chivas Brothers); Vanessa Wright (Chivas
Brothers); Bob Wylie (Morrison Bowmore)

Many thanks to Jo Hanley for the photographs. A
special thank you to Jeni Cumming, my research
assistant. And a huge debt to my editor, Alison Rae.

Charles MacLean

M.A., LL.B., W.S., F.S.A. (Scot)

Charles MacLean is a writer whose special subject is Scotch whisky, about which he has published ten books to date, including the standard work on whisky brands, *Scotch Whisky* (Mitchell Beazley, 1993) and the leading book on its subject, *Malt Whisky* (Mitchell Beazley, 1997; translated into French, German, Swiss, Danish, Italian, Dutch, Polish, Russian and Portuguese), both of which were shortlisted for Glenfiddich Awards. (In addition to whisky, he has published eight further books, mainly on Scottish social history.)

Whisky: A Liquid History was published by Cassell in September 2003 and won 'Wine & Spirits Book of the Year' in the James Beard Awards 2005 and 'Best Drinks Book' in the International Food Media Awards 2005, the most prestigious American gastronomic prize. *MacLean's Whisky Miscellany* (Little Books, 2004, revised 2006 and republished as *Whisky Tales* 2006), followed. In 2007 he was Editor in Chief of the global *Eyewitness Companion to Whisky* (Dorling Kindersley, 2008).

He was founding editor of *Whisky Magazine* and of the Russian magazine *Whisky*, is whisky correspondent for *Scottish Field* and regularly contributes articles to magazines in Britain, The Netherlands, the U.S.A. and Canada. He is the host of a TV channel (accessed via the internet) dedicated to the world of whisky, www.singlemalt.tv.

He was trained in 'the sensory evaluation of potable spirits' by the Scotch Whisky Research Institute in 1992 and has presented numerous tastings and talks in the U.K. and abroad for whisky companies, corporations, universities and clubs, and on radio and TV. He is a member of the Judging Panel (Spirits) of the International Wines & Spirits Competition.

He acts as a consultant to the whisky industry on a variety of matters, and over the past 25 years has written promotional materials for all the leading companies and brands. He was elected a Keeper of the Quaich, the industry's highest accolade, in 1992 for 'his services to Scotch over many years'.

He holds degrees in Art History (St Andrews) and Law (Dundee), is a Writer to Her Majesty's Signet, a Fellow of the Society of Antiquaries of Scotland, a Visiting Lecturer to the Smithsonian Institution, Washington, an Honorary Fellow of Massey College, University of Toronto and of Champlain College, University of Trent, a Councillor of the Clan Maclean and a member of the Society of Authors. He lives near Edinburgh with his wife and three sons.